ROUTLEDGE LIBRAL
RUSSIAN AND SOVIE'

CW00741921

Volume 1

25 YEARS OF SOVIET RUSSIAN LITERATURE (1918–1943)

25 YEARS OF SOVIET RUSSIAN LITERATURE (1918–1943)

GLEB STRUVE

Routledge
Taylor & Francis Group

LONDON AND NEW YORK

This edition first published in 2021
by Routledge
2 Park Square, Milton Park, Abingdon, Oxon OX14 4RN

and by Routledge
52 Vanderbilt Avenue, New York, NY 10017

Routledge is an imprint of the Taylor & Francis Group, an informa business

First published as Soviet Russian Literature in 1935 by George Routledge & Sons, Ltd.
This new and enlarged Edition first published in 1944 by George Routledge & Sons, Ltd.

British Library Cataloguing in Publication Data
A catalogue record for this book is available from the British Library

ISBN: 978-0-367-68495-2 (Set)
ISBN: 978-1-003-15462-4 (Set) (ebk)
ISBN: 978-0-367-72391-0 (Volume 1) (hbk)
ISBN: 978-0-367-72393-4 (Volume 1) (pbk)
ISBN: 978-1-003-15461-7 (Volume 1) (ebk)

Publisher's Note
The publisher has gone to great lengths to ensure the quality of this reprint but points out that some imperfections in the original copies may be apparent.

Disclaimer
The publisher has made every effort to trace copyright holders and would welcome correspondence from those they have been unable to trace.

25 Years of Soviet Russian Literature (1918-1943)

New and enlarged edition of
SOVIET RUSSIAN LITERATURE

By

Gleb Struve

Lecturer in Russian Literature, School of Slavonic and East European Studies, University of London

London
George Routledge & Sons, Ltd.
Broadway House : 68-74 Carter Lane, E.C.

SOVIET RUSSIAN LITERATURE, *first published* 1935
New and Enlarged Edition, 25 YEARS OF SOVIET RUSSIAN LITERATURE,
first published January 1944
reprinted January 1946

Printed in Great Britain by LOWE and BRYDONE LTD.,
London. N.W. 10

Contents

		PAGE
PREFACE TO THE NEW EDITION		vii
INTRODUCTION		xi

CHAPTER

I. PRE-REVOLUTIONARY WRITERS AFTER 1924 . . . 1

   1. Literature and the Revolution 1
   2. Bely 3
   3. Gorky 5
   4. A. N. Tolstoy 8
   5. Ehrenburg 11
   6. Veresaev 13
   7. Prishvin and Sergeyev-Tsensky 15
   8. Zamyatin 17

II. TWO REVOLUTIONARY ROMANTICS 23

   1. Babel 23
   2. Vsevolod Ivanov 27

III. THE REVIVAL OF THE NOVEL 32

   1. The Serapion Brothers 32
   2. Fedin 33
   3. Leonov 42
   4. Kaverin 49
   5. Slonimsky and Savich 55
   6. Lavrenev, Malyshkin, and Lebedenko . . . 57

IV. WRITERS OF EVERYDAY LIFE 60

   1. Chroniclers of the Revolution 60
   2. Seyfullina 61
   3. Romanov 63
   4. Lidin 65
   5. Kataev 67
   6. Zoshchenko 69
   7. Ilf and Petrov 76
   8. Levin and some others 77

V. THE PROLETARIAN WRITERS 79

   1. From the "Proletkult" to the Five-Year Plan and
      After 79
   2. Gladkov 88
   3. Panferov 91
   4. Libedinsky 93
   5. Fadeyev 95

Contents

CHAPTER   PAGE

V. THE PROLETARIAN WRITERS—*continued*

    6. Sholokhov 98
    7. Malashkin and others 100

VI. YURY OLESHA AND HIS "ENVY". 103

VII. LITERATURE OF THE FIVE-YEAR PLAN 114

VIII. "COUNTER-REVOLUTIONARY" TENDENCIES IN SOVIET
    LITERATURE 127

    1. The "neo-bourgeois" and "kulak" spirit in
        Literature 127
    2. Zamyatin's *We* 130
    3. Pilnyak's *Mahogany* 138
    4. Budantsev's *Sufferings of Mind* 142
    5. Bulgakov 145

IX. THE HISTORICAL NOVEL 153

X. THE POETS 165

    1. Decline of Poetry 165
    2. Mayakovsky and Esenin 165
    3. Pasternak 169
    4. Tikhonov 172
    5. Selvinsky and Constructivism 174
    6. Bagritsky 175
    7. Aseyev 176
    8. Bezymensky and Other Proletarian Poets . . 178
    9. The Poets' Prose: Mandelstam, Pasternak, Tikhonov 181

XI. THE DRAMA 186

XII. LITERARY CRITICISM AND LITERARY THEORIES . . 201

    1. Formalism 201
    2. Sociological Method 215

XIII. GOVERNMENT POLICY IN MATTERS OF LITERATURE . 220

    1. From 1918 to the Five-Year Plan . . . 220
    2. The "Reform" of 1932 and After . . . 229

XIV. LATEST DEVELOPMENTS: SOCIALIST REALISM.—NATION-
    ALISM *versus* "WESTERNISM" AND "CLASSICISM"
    versus "MODERNISM". 238

EPILOGUE: 1935-1943 253
BIBLIOGRAPHY 321
SUPPLEMENTARY BIBLIOGRAPHY 333
INDEX 342

Preface to the New Edition

MY book on Soviet Russian Literature was written in 1934. It was at the time the first, and still remains, I believe, the only comprehensive survey, in any language, of post-revolutionary Russian literature. It had, on the whole, a good reception, and most of the critics spoke of my "dispassionateness" and "objectivity". The chief accusation levelled against me (based apparently not so much on the book itself as on a certain "foreknowledge") was my "lack of sympathy" with my "subject", by which was obviously meant my lack of sympathy with the present political régime in Russia. As I was writing about Russian literature, and not about the Soviet Union in general, I refused to take this accusation seriously. To counter it, one may well ask whether in order to write impartially about German literature under the Nazis it is essential to be in sympathy with Hitler and what he stands for. Let alone the fact that certain aspects of the Soviet régime and outlook have, in the course of time, undergone such radical changes that those who were in sympathy with it at a certain given moment had to find themselves, if they were men of fixed principles, in violent opposition to it, while with others it must have worked the other way round. The accusation does not really deserve answering.

The book is now being reprinted as it was written, with the addition of an "Epilogue" covering the period from 1935 to 1943.

There is nothing I wish to retract from my earlier judgments, though I admit that one can easily err in an estimate of a literature so much in the melting pot as is literature in Russia since the Revolution. I would have liked to make certain alterations in the arrangement of my book and to correct my style—the book originally was written in great haste, being born in the main of my lectures in the University of London—and I must apologize to my new readers for my slipshod writing here and there.

The Epilogue, which brings the story up to date, is of necessity brief and scrappy. For some time, and especially during the first two years of the Anglo-German war, very few books and literary publications found their way through to this country; when they come now, it is with great delay, and it has therefore not been very easy to follow the new developments in detail. Whenever possible I have tried to base my judgments, as before, on first-hand knowledge of the original works. I had therefore to give up the idea of discussing all the works of individual authors in full, and to confine myself to the main trends of development and to a few representative works. I am quite aware of inevitable gaps and possible errors in my account, and can only hope to be able to fill those gaps on some future occasion.

I have touched but briefly on the subject of literature and the war. From the welter of works dealing with the present war—many of them sketches and stories of transient value—only a few have reached this country. It is not easy to select among the numerous war works those which are of distinct literary value. It is hardly to be expected in any case that a work of outstanding and permanent value will be produced while the war is on. A certain perspective is needed for a full-scale treatment of a national upheaval of such magnitude. The first Patriotic War of 1812 (the present war is officially known in Russia as " the Second Patriotic War ") did not produce

any contemporary masterpiece. Zagoskin's *Roslavlev*—
the best-known of the novels produced by a writer who
lived through it—was not written till 1832 and was but
a feeble echo of the event. Had Pushkin lived longer he
might have tried his hand at the subject. As it is, it was
left to the genius of Tolstoy, who was not born till sixteen
years later, to immortalize the period, at a distance of
some fifty years, in his great epic. Whether there is at
present among the Soviet novelists an author capable of
tackling the task, is difficult to say. Three possible names
would suggest themselves : Alexey Tolstoy, Sergeyev-
Tsensky and Sholokhov. None of them is, however, of
Tolstoy's rank, and all, if they were to tackle a contemporary *War and Peace*, would lack the detachment with
which Tolstoy approached his theme.

The Russian Revolution has lived through its twenty-
five years. So has the post-revolutionary Russian literature. To show its changing scene during this quarter of a
century has been one of the objects of this book. Whatever may be my " bias ", I hope I have succeeded in
doing so. With a literature abounding in works written—
to use a phrase of Ilya Ehrenburg—" for the one second ",
it is not easy to pass final judgments, to assess the enduring,
permanent value of a literary work. Some of my readers
may be struck by the apparent paucity of such enduring
works. This is inevitable. Literature of the Revolution
has produced many works of human and documentary
interest, but hardly a single great work of art. Perhaps
the Revolution has been too insistent a background for
literature. What Soviet literature reflects, is this ever-
present background or the bright but fragmentary flashes.
It has failed so far to encompass, in fearless detachment,
the whole of the Revolution. It has also been too much
governed by external impulses. It is certainly the poorer
for the absence of a certain type of works—works of deep

human significance such as are represented in modern English literature by E. M. Forster's *Howards End*, by Charles Morgan's *The Voyage*, by the best of Virginia Woolf's books. Nor has the war yet produced works of lasting literary value. What the future holds in store for Russian literature is not for me to surmise. It depends, after all, on what lies in store for Russia after her many and terrible ordeals crowned by the horrors of the present war. It is an ordeal by fire, and every true Russian hopes to see his country emerge from it purified, freer, and happier.

HOUNSLOW-BARNET,
  April 1943.

P.S.—An additional bibliography of some English books bearing on literature and art in the Soviet Union, and of principal translations of Soviet works, published since 1935, will be found at the end of the volume. It does not claim to be complete. No translations published in the U.S.A. have been included : there seem to be quite many of them.

Introduction

THE first question which arises when one approaches the problem of present-day Russian literature is: Whether there is such a thing as Soviet literature,[1] or whether the Russian literature of to-day, even if we take only the literature inside Russia, ought to be regarded as merely a phase—a very special one, determined by peculiar, extra-literary conditions—in the general evolution of Russian literature? Should the answer be that there is such a thing as Soviet literature, as distinct from Russian literature, another question arises, namely: Where are its origins to be sought, what are its chronological limits? Can all post-revolutionary literature confined to the geographical limits of the U.S.S.R. be regarded as Soviet literature? Does the history of Soviet literature coincide in time with that of the Soviet régime in Russia?

Let us assume for a moment that there is such a thing as Soviet literature. Even then it is obvious that it can by no means be identified with the whole of post-revolutionary Russian literature. There is a definite continuity between pre-revolutionary and post-revolutionary literature. The Russian revolution, which set out to renovate the whole fabric of society, to create new social and æsthetic values, did not and could not produce, suddenly and out of nothing, a literature of its own. To begin with, it was forced to rely upon the existing

[1] I speak here, as elsewhere in my book, of Soviet *Russian* literature, that is of literature in the Russian language. There is in the Soviet Union such a thing as national minorities' literatures—of late their development has been particularly encouraged; but they represent a thing apart, of which I am not competent to judge and write. When Soviet literature is spoken of as embracing these, it means, of course, something totally different from what I mean here.

literary forms and groups. But the history of literature in Russia since the Revolution is, in one of its important and vital aspects, a history of the determined and conscious efforts on the part of the Communist Government to create a specific Soviet literature according to a pre-conceived plan. And therein lies at least a partial answer to the second part of the question formulated above.

The methods and the policy resorted to by the Communist Government of Russia in trying to achieve that aim varied in course of time, but the aim was always there. Just as in other fields of life, the Communists now exercised a stronger pressure in matters of literature, now felt themselves obliged to retreat and make concessions. In dealing, therefore, with literature in Soviet Russia one cannot set aside the purely political issues nor can one discuss it apart from the Government's policy in literary matters. Throughout its history we see a constant interaction between the political forces acting from above and trying to control it and to impose on it their " plan ", just as in other domains of life, and the purely literary tendencies, now struggling against that control now endeavouring to adapt themselves to it.

In Prince D. S. Mirsky's two-volume history of Russian literature (*A History of Russian Literature* and *Contemporary Russian Literature*), the English reader interested in things Russian has had an excellent survey of the literature of Russia from its origins up to 1924. It covers thus also the first five or six years of the post-revolutionary period, of the so-called Soviet literature. The purpose of the present book is to serve as a sequel to D. S. Mirsky's book on contemporary Russian literature, to bring it up to date, to give a picture of the development of literature inside Soviet Russia during the years after 1924. For the sake of greater unity of presentation, Russian literature outside Russia, the so-called *émigré* literature, is not comprised within the scope of my work, though it has to be granted that without this a picture of present-day Russian literature must needs remain incomplete. The thread is picked up where it was left off by Prince Mirsky. Though a certain amount of overlapping is inevitable, the fact that the early period of post-revolutionary literature which he treats, more or less summarily, in his second volume, may be regarded as a transitional period, makes my task easier.

Two principal stages can be distinguished in that transitional period. The first, lasting from 1917 to 1921 and coinciding politically with the period of the so-called War Communism, may be described as a period of disintegration of the existing literary forms and traditions and dislocation of the contending literary schools. This process had really begun some time before the Revolution, even before the War.

In pre-revolutionary Russian literature of the twentieth century there were two principal movements or schools : the Realists and the Symbolists. The former were a survival of the great age of the Russian realistic and psychological novel, which as a literary genre had gradually degenerated, to take a new lease of life, in a different form, in the subtle and peculiar art of Chekhov's short stories, from which, in one way or other, nearly all the twentieth century Realism proceeded. But of the two the Symbolist movement was, in the literary evolution of Russia during that period, by far the more important and vital. By 1910 it had certainly become the dominant element and it comprised nearly everything that was talented and alive in modern Russian literature. It had renovated its spirit, raised the standard of poetical technique, opened new vistas before literature and freed it from the fetters of social and political tendentiousness and from the narrow tenets of naturalism. The period from 1900 to 1910 or 1912 is rightly described as the period of Symbolism. The important thing about Russian Symbolism is that it was something more than a mere literary school, that it implied a reversal, not only of the literary technique, but of the whole æsthetic and spiritual outlook; it coincided with the rise of individualism and religious idealism; it brought about a general revaluation of the traditional values of the Russian intelligentsia. Therein lay perhaps its own undoing. Symbolism as a literary movement died towards 1912, one might almost say of exhaustion—chiefly because it wanted to be something else in addition to being a literary school, because it aspired, according to one of its most gifted and outstanding protagonists, Andrey Bely, to become a religion. There was a tendency, towards the close of the Symbolist period, within the Symbolist school itself, to greater Realism, a tendency to bring poetry nearer to life. It was manifested in the latest phase in the work of Alexander Blok, the greatest of all the Symbolists and for that matter of all the modern Russian poets. Moreover, two schools sprang up as a reaction against the misty philosophical and religious trend in Symbolism. One of them was really born of Symbolism and embodied many of its poetical and technical achievements. It was called Acmeism and, as far as labels are of any use, it may be conveniently described as Neo-Classicism. Its principal exponents were the poets Gumilev, Akhmatova and Osip Mandelstam. One of its catchwords proclaimed by the poet Kuzmin in an early controversy with the Symbolists, was "beautiful clarity". It tried to clothe words, as a medium of poetry, with a new flesh—the Symbolists had tended to disembody them; it asserted the supremacy of the concrete logical element in verbal craft as opposed to the hidden, associative, musical element on which the Symbolists laid such stress. Though romantic in some of its manifestations it strove on the whole towards greater Realism and simplicity.

The other movement that declared war on Symbolism and helped towards its ultimate disintegration was Futurism. Russian Futurism was a peculiar growth even though in its origins it had something in common with the Italian Futurism of Marinetti. It was not a homogeneous movement, it lacked a positive programme. It was essentially negative. Whether it would have enjoyed that momentary triumph, which it did actually enjoy, had there been no political revolution, is a debatable point. As it was, two factors contributed towards its alliance with the new revolutionary power of Russia. The first of these was the fact that when the Revolution broke out the Bolsheviks had no force in literature on which they could rely (except a few individual writers, like Bryusov and some others, who immediately took sides with them) and had therefore to look for help to the extreme Left school in literature, which happened to be Futurism. The second was the personal ascendancy of Vladimir Mayakovsky in the Futurist camp. Mayakovsky was the most gifted and powerful of their poets at the time, and having no real sympathy with some of the abstract theoretical tenets of Futurism or with their experiments in "trans-sense" poetry, he was well aware of the possibilities which the need of the new revolutionary Government in literary and artistic propaganda offered to the advancement of art for the masses and this was his own conception of what should be art. It was he who vulgarized and popularized Futurism, turning it into a suitable weapon of revolutionary propaganda. Throughout the initial period of the Communist Revolution, Futurism was closely linked up with propagandist art and virtually dominated the literary life in Soviet Russia. It was a kind of literary monopoly. As in the preceding period, poetry continued to predominate over all other literary forms. This was partly due to the abnormal conditions of life then prevailing in Russia. Printing was made difficult, and the number of books published dwindled enormously. Literature continued to subsist in its oral variety—the place of publications was taken by oral recitals in the numerous poets' cafés in Moscow, virtually monopolized by the Futurists and their literary allies. It was the so-called " café period " of Russian literature.

Thus, during those first years the Soviet Government made use of the Futurists as the only available literary group which could serve its propaganda purposes and which by its very nature had access to the masses. But the Bolsheviks were all the time fully aware of the temporary and unstable character of this alliance; they realized the ultimate divergence between their own and the Futurists' aims. Even at that early stage they set themselves the task of creating a real class art at the service of the proletarian dictatorship. For this purpose, parallel with encouraging the Futurists, they set up the so-called " Proletkults " or studios of proletarian culture, where non-Communist specialists, chiefly poets of the older generation, were engaged in training young and promising writers from the working class. The experiment which went on for some years proved a failure. This failure was admitted and embodied in the resolutions of the Russian Communist Party. From now on it was necessary to proceed along some new lines in the creation of a literature which would befit the new order of society. This became the main concern of the Russian revolutionary Government in the domain of literature. One of the objects of the present book is to try and show to what extent this task has been achieved and through what vicissitudes of policy it has been pursued.

INTRODUCTION

The first stage in that transitional period in the history of Russian literature, characterized by the monopoly of Futurism, the exclusive predominance of poetry and the unsuccessful attempts at fostering artificially the proletarian literature, ended in 1921. An end was put to it, on one hand, by the termination of the Civil War, and on the other by the introduction of the New Economic Policy. The latter brought to life private publishing companies, enlivened the literary and bookselling activities in general, and helped to create a relatively greater freedom of artistic work. At the same time, the Civil War being over, a number of young writers who had been fighting in the Red Army, returned to normal and peaceful life, while the Civil War itself supplied a vast and rich material which had to be digested and embodied in literary works. The next period in Soviet Russian literature, which lasted approximately from 1921 to 1924, can therefore be described as the period of Civil War literature. More generally one can say that from this moment on, the Revolution became, and still remains, the principal theme of Soviet Russian literature. The new revolutionary prose which sprang up during this period was out to describe the Revolution and to grasp its meaning. But in the first place to describe, to put on record, to preserve for the posterity what had been and was going on. In keeping with the general character of the first period of the Revolution, the interest of the young Soviet prose writers was primarily centred on its elemental and romantic aspect. Civil War, the guerrilla warfare on the outskirts of Russia, the famine of 1921, peregrinations and adventures all over the wide expanse of Russia—such were the main themes of this first revolutionary prose. Its form, its manner, its style were in keeping with this theme. The young Soviet writers, who were out to put hurriedly on record their rich stock of experience, did not care for long and elaborate novels, for large canvases. The form of a short story, an anecdote, told in a hurry, without any deep psychological probing, without any detailed analysis, but often in a lyrically strained tone, was predominant. In the case of longer works, such as some of the novels of Pilnyak, Nikitin, Malyshkin and others, these had no unity of plot, the narrative being conducted simultaneously on numerous planes and constructed according to the laws of a musical theme with variations. From the formal point of view these works were greatly influenced by two prose writers of the age of Symbolism, namely Andrey Bely and Alexey Remizov. To Bely can be traced back their musical construction; the constant shifting of the planes with recurring *leitmotivs*, often symbolical; the feverish, unnatural, hyperbolic diction. Through Bely all these writers go back to Gogol, more than to any other of the older Russian writers. Remizov's influence is felt in their predilection for the anecdote, for ornamental speech, for the exact rendering of the peculiarities of local and individual intonations. And through Remizov this young Russian literature was looking back to Leskov. Thus, somewhat unexpectedly, Gogol and Leskov became the most powerful and living factors of influence in the shaping of post-revolutionary Russian literature.

The cruel experience of the Civil War taught these young Russian writers to face indifferently and fearlessly the most horrible sights, and to tell, in a cool and detached manner, of terrible and ghastly things. Some pages of Pilnyak or Vsevolod Ivanov, who are the typical writers of this " dynamic " or " ornamental " prose period and of whom more in the subsequent chapters of my book, have no match in outspokenness, cynicism and cruelty. Such is, for instance, Ivanov's story called *Hollow Arabia*, where he tells in a detached, matter-of-fact way, of the starving peasants driven to cannibalism somewhere in the East of Russia. One of the characteristics of nearly all the imaginative literature of this period is that, despite its stark Realism, its obvious tendency not to mince words and to depict reality as it was, there is in it a distinct touch of unreality. So fantastic, and often gruesomely fantastic, had life become in those days, such unexpected adventures did it hold in store, that the borderline between the real and the unreal seemed to be deleted, and that in setting out to be thoroughly realistic the most fantastic effects were achieved : life was, indeed, " stranger than fiction."

It was only gradually that out of this welter of ornamental and dynamic prose there emerged, towards 1924, definite literary genres—first, the short pointed *nouvelle* of Babel, and then the novel as revived by Fedin, Leonov and Kaverin. Since then the novel remains the dominant literary genre in Soviet Russian literature.

The account of the last ten years of Soviet literature that follows is not strictly chronological. Nor is it exhaustive. The output of these ten years has been quantitatively so enormous that a mere enumeration of names and titles would make a whole book. My object was rather to show the main trends of development of Soviet literature and to characterize its main facts. To make the picture more complete and objective, I have illustrated my account with quotations from Soviet works, especially in the case of lesser known writers and less familiar aspects. If there are any gaps or " disproportions ", they are due to the difficulty of procuring Soviet literature in London : in this respect I have been working under very unfavourable conditions.

I owe a debt of gratitude to Sir Bernard Pares for his encouragement in my work as Lecturer in the School of Slavonic and European Studies, this book having been

partly an outcome of my lectures; to Mr. Hamish Miles
for having kindly consented to go through the proofs
and made some valuable suggestions; to M. Valentin
Glasberg, of Paris, who supplied me with some fresh
data for the French part of the bibliography; and to
Miss Olga Babitsyna for the help she gave me in the
actual preparation of this book for the press.

P.S.—My book was already written when Mr. Max
Eastman's *Artists in Uniform: A Study of Literature and
Bureaucratism* (George Allen & Unwin Ltd.) appeared.
Rather scrappy in parts, it contains, however, some
valuable material. But being openly controversial itself,
it has given rise to a new controversy about the problem
of the writer's freedom in Soviet Russia. There can be,
I think, no two opinions on this question: the artist,
and the writer above all, is not free in the Soviet Union.
He is not quite free in the choice of his subjects, he is not
free in their treatment. At various periods the degree
of his freedom varied—how and to what extent, my book,
I hope, will show. For those, however, who might be
inclined to reproach me for not having dwelt sufficiently
on that aspect of the problem to which Mr. Eastman's
book is devoted, I would like to point out that I approached
the subject from a different angle: I was writing an
objective history (inasmuch as one can do so with regard
to what is contemporary) of the last ten years of Soviet
Russian literature, and I wanted to show, not what
literature in Soviet Russia was *unable* to accomplish
because of being stifled and " bureaucratized " (which it,
no doubt, is), but rather what it *has* achieved *in spite
of* all the efforts at bureaucratization.

HOUNSLOW,
     10th February 1935.

SOVIET RUSSIAN LITERATURE

CHAPTER I

PRE-REVOLUTIONARY WRITERS AFTER 1924 [1]

1. *Literature and the Revolution*

AFTER the Revolution the older writers with a few exceptions lapsed into silence. One of the leading Soviet critics, writing of this period, says that the majority of the pre-revolutionary Russian literature took an openly hostile attitude to the newly established revolutionary government and hoped for its speedy downfall. Many of the best-known writers of the older generation soon left Soviet Russia and after the defeat of the White Armies emigrated abroad : Bunin, Kuprin, Artsybashev, later on Merezhkovsky, Remizov,S hmelev, and Boris Zaytsev of the novelists ; and Balmont, Mme Hippius, and later on Khodasevich, Marina Tsvetaeva, and Georgy Ivanov, of the poets. Of those who remained in Russia only a few joined the Bolsheviks from the very beginning : Gorky and Serafimovich among the novelists, and Bryusov and the Futurists among the poets. The two greatest poets of the age of Symbolism, Blok and Bely, accepted and sang the Revolution in its elemental national-messianic aspect : Blok in his *Twelve* (one of the most remarkable poetic works of the revolutionary period) and *The Scythians*; and Bely in his *Christ Is Risen*, a very feeble piece of

---

[1] For an account of the earlier work of these writers see D. S. Mirsky's *Contemporary Russian Literature.*

I

rhetoric. But Blok died in 1921, completely disillusioned by the Revolution and having renounced the idea of his *Twelve*, after which he had created nothing of any importance. Bely, after a period of temporary semi-emigration, returned in 1923 to Russia where he remained until his death in January 1934. Of his work after 1924 I will speak below. Of the other leading pre-revolutionary poets Nikolay Gumilev published after the Revolution some of his best and most mature verse, but he was shot in 1921 for taking part in an anti-Soviet organization. He, just as Anna Akhmatova, Fedor Sologub and Osip Mandelstam, felt quite out of touch with the Revolution. Sologub's post-revolutionary output, until his death in 1928, was very small and he once more returned to pure lyrical poetry. Anna Akhmatova published only one book in 1921, containing some of her best and profoundest lyric and since then her name has almost completely disappeared from Russian literature. Osip Mandelstam who published in 1922 his wonderful *Tristia*, collected in 1928 his earlier poems together with the new ones which were not numerous, but this collection had a very cool reception from the Soviet critics : Mandelstam's lack of harmony with the spirit of the times, especially in the period of the revolutionary reconstruction, was quite obvious. His attention was as usual concentrated on " eternal " or historiosophical themes treated and presented in a striking and very personal way. (*For Mandelstam's prose see Chapter X.*)

But some of the older writers, Gorky and Veresaev of the old Realist school, Prishvin, Sergeyev-Tsensky, Zamyatin of the Neo-Realists, continued to write and publish in Russia after the Revolution. They were joined by Alexey Tolstoy and Ilya Ehrenburg, of whom the former had spent the first years of the Revolution with the White Armies and in emigration, and returned

to Russia in 1923, and the latter, after having several
times changed his views and allegiance, has now more
or less settled down in Paris where he had lived before
the Revolution and where he feels most at home in the
atmosphere of the Montparnasse cafés, paying now and
then short visits to Moscow where he is received like a
distinguished foreigner.

2. *Bely*

Andrey Bely (1880–1934) was, after 1928, the only
personal link between the post-revolutionary (Soviet)
literature and the great age of Symbolism. All other
Symbolists had either died (Blok, Bryusov, Sologub) or
left Russia (Balmont, Hippius, Vyacheslav Ivanov). A
revolutionary by temperament, Bely accepted the Revolution from the very beginning. But like Blok and some
other poets he accepted it at first as he saw it, not as it
was ; not on the social and political plane, but on the
religious and cultural, as a national upheaval which would
enable Russia to fulfil her mission in the world. In Bely's
eyes this mission was coloured with anthroposophic ideas—
he was a disciple of Dr. Rudolf Steiner. But his acceptance
of the Revolution did not receive any adequate poetic
expression—its only outcome was a rather poor poem
Christ Is Risen. Later on, especially after his return in
1923 from Berlin where he had spent a little over a year
and gone through one of the most painful personal
crises in his life which nearly brought him to a lunatic
asylum, Bely tried to establish a closer touch with the
Revolution. But his attitude to it lacked consistency. In
its practical political aspect the Communist Revolution
was alien to his nature, he could not feel congenial to it.
Whatever his spiritual and intellectual vagaries may have
been, his outlook on the world was fundamentally religious

3

and idealistic, and he could not feel in sympathy with the materialistic doctrine of Marxism. All his professions to the contrary sounded far-fetched and insincere. His best achievements were in the pre-revolutionary past. In the history of Russian literature he will be remembered above all for his two novels (*Petersburg* and *The Silver Dove*) ; for his best lyrical poems in *The Urn* and *Ashes* ; and for his *Symbolism*. The only post-revolutionary poetical work of Bely which is on the level with his early verse is his poem *The First Meeting*, where he restores to us the atmosphere of his youth and that of the intellectual *élite* of Moscow in the early years of our century. His novels written after 1924—*The Moscow Crank, Moscow Exposed*, and *Masks*—form parts of a vast whole in which some of Bely's earlier personages make their reappearance. They reveal Bely's usual qualities, and especially his masterful handling of a complicated plot, which here has a touch of a melodramatic film. But on the whole they are inferior to his early novels. His shortcomings (the monotonousness of his rhythmical prose ; the abstractness of his psychological presentation ; the tiresomeness of his verbal inventions) are more apparent in them than before. At the same time they do not open new vistas as did *Kotik Letaev*, which, even if a failure, was a brilliant failure, and an anticipation of some of James Joyce's most daring experiments. During the last years of his life Bely was working at his *Memoirs*, parts of which had appeared before under different titles. Their third volume, entitled *The Beginning of the Century*, appeared just before his death (he died on 7th January 1934). They are interesting as everything which Bely wrote, but in the course of writing them he changed his original plan : from an autobiography they became rather a history of his time. Yet for a historian Bély was not objective enough, and the element of personal grudge is

4

strongly felt in them. At the same time one feels a tendency, obviously dictated by political considerations, to read a new meaning, in the light of subsequent happenings, not only into the events of the past, but even into the author's inward experience. Nevertheless Bely's *Memoirs* remain a valuable and interesting document of a brilliant epoch in the history of Russian literature, written by one of its most versatile representatives in whose soul a genius and a fool co-existed.

Bely's place in modern Russian literature is very great not only on account of his personal contribution to it, but also because of the influence which his formal innovations had exercised on young Russian writers ; the ornamental prose writers of the first years of the Revolution, and especially Pilnyak, owed him very much. But none of his disciples have produced anything equal to their master's best work, and in the long run Bely's tradition in the Russian prose did not prove enduring— even in the ornamental prose the influence of Leskov's and Remizov's *skaz* manner was more fruitful and lasting. And in the recent developments towards Realism there is a definite tendency to discard all " Belyisms ". Bely's efforts to harness himself to the cart of the Revolution were therefore rather pathetic. Whatever may lie in store for the Russian literature, Bely will never be regarded as a typical figure of its " Soviet " period : his place, including his post-revolutionary work, is in the age of Symbolism.

3. *Gorky*

More than ever since the Revolution, Maxim Gorky has come by now to be regarded as the doyen and " leader " of Soviet Russian literature. If some years ago it was quite correct to say that " his work is profoundly unlike all the work of the younger generation—first of all, for his complete lack of interest in style, and, secondly, for his very unmodern interest in human psychology '' (Mirsky)—the position is not quite the same now. Not that Gorky has changed and come nearer to the young Russian literature, but the post-revolutionary Russian literature has of late been moving, or trying to move, in the direction which brings it nearer to Gorky's art —to his Realism relieved by revolutionary Romanticism. Sholokhov, Fadeyev, even Leonov and Fedin, are nearer to Gorky than were Pilnyak and the '' ornamentalists '', or Kaverin and Olesha. It is not accidental that the latest tendency towards '' Socialist Realism '' (see Chapter XIV) is being encouraged and sponsored by Gorky. Gorky's position in Soviet literature has been very high ever since his unequivocal adherence to the Communist régime. A *persona grata* with the Soviet Government, a kind of its official representative in the European world of letters where he had to act as *advocatus diaboli*, Gorky was looked upon by the younger generation of Russian writers, who made their appearance in 1918-22, as an elder friend and protector (writers like Babel and Ivanov profess to owe him their literary career), but never as a literary master. Things are quite different now. With Socialist Realism as the literary slogan of the day, Gorky is naturally looked upon as a master from whom the young writers must learn both their method and their attitude. To write '' like Gorky '' is a sign of literary excellence.

I do not propose to discuss here Gorky's place in Russian literature. In D. S. Mirsky's book [1] the reader will find a fair and adequate estimate of the different periods and different aspects of Gorky's work. It remains to be seen what his output has been since 1924. Apart from some short stories he has published a couple of

[1] *Contemporary Russian Literature*, pp. 106-120.

plays and two regular novels: *Artamonov's Business* (1925; translated into English as *Decadence*), and *The Life of Klim Samgin* (three volumes of this monumental work have been translated and published in English separately under different titles: *Bystander*, *The Magnet*, and *Other Fires*). The former was the first real novel Gorky wrote after 1911, after *Matvey Kozhemyakin*. It showed that he was by no means a spent force. It was better than any of his middle-period work and reminded one of the best passages of *Foma Gordeev*. There was in it even more firmness, concentration and solidity—which many of Gorky's novels lacked—in addition to his usual gift of keen observation. It is a story of a self-made bourgeois family in its three generations. All the characters: the old Artamonov, the founder of the family's prosperity, a strong, self-willed man; his sons and grandsons in whom there are already signs of imminent decay; their wives and other episodic figures are portrayed very vividly. As usual with Gorky the story combines great vigour and vitality with a keen vision of the gloomy, sombre side of life, not only in its outward manifestations, but also in the inner workings of human nature. In spite of the lifelikeness and variety of its characters, of whom Gorky shows not only their darker sides, there hangs about the whole story that atmosphere of gloom which is so characteristic of Gorky's view of old Russia, and one of the features of his Realism. It is felt also in his *Life of Klim Samgin*, a vast epic of forty years of Russian life, where the main attention is centred on the revolutionary *milieu* and its activity. This long-drawn novel lacks, however, the power and concentration of its predecessor.

Gorky's attitude to the Russia of the past is summed up well in the following words of Klim Samgin: " Everything is possible. Everything is possible in this mad country where men are desperately inventing themselves, and where all life is a bad invention."

In some of his recent stories Gorky has been trying to shift the focus of his Realism, to replace its usual " minus " sign by the " plus " sign in speaking of the Soviet realities.

4. A. N. Tolstoy

Count Alexey N. Tolstoy became a Soviet writer in 1922 when, in connection with the so-called *Change-of-Landmarks* movement, he, until then an *émigré*, returned to Russia. Since then he has gradually come to occupy a very prominent place in present-day Russian literature, being one of the few novelists of the older generation who live there.

Tolstoy is a writer of great natural gifts and force, a born Realist. He is at his best when he describes real life, especially the life he knows, his work is then full of vitality and verve and his characters brimful with life. But nearly all his post-revolutionary work suffers precisely because he has been unable to find a congenial theme. He seems to have been on the look-out for it ever since his return to Russia, and has tried his hand at several genres. Fundamentally a man of the past, a cross between a country gentleman and a literary bohemian, he evidently felt lost in the turmoil of revolutionary life. He did not want to draw his subject from the past and he was not sufficiently familiar with the new actuality to make it a source of inspiration. Hence his tendency, manifested in the first years of the Revolution, to escape into the realm of fantasy, to combine fantastic plots with revolutionary ideas. In *Aelita* (1922) he has given a combination of a Utopian romance in the manner of H. G. Wells with a typical Russian realistic psychological novel seasoned with strong revolutionary element. The fantastic plot is centred round the arrival on Mars of a Soviet expedition and an attempt to start there a social revolution. Upon this fantastical social theme are superimposed two favourite themes of Tolstoy: the theme of love that is stronger than death and than any sense of revolutionary duty, personified in the Russian engineer Los and the beautiful Martian woman Aelita; and the theme of elemental revolt embodied in the person of Gusev, the best-drawn and most lifelike character in the story. He is a Red Army soldier who places himself at the head of the Martian proletariat, but who, as the Communist critics have pointed out, is himself neither proletarian nor Communist. Gusev's revolutionism has a strong nationalistic colouring and when he comes to Mars his first thought is to proclaim its annexation to Soviet Russia. In spirit he is a typical anarchist, and it is this anarchistic and nationalistic tendency in the Revolution, as well as its aspect of elemental revolt, that makes Tolstoy sympathize with it. His affinity with this side of the Revolution finds also an expression in the story called *A Manuscript Found Under a Bed*, where an old degenerating squire, who hates the Revolution, cannot help admiring its purely Russian elemental dimensions.

Tolstoy has once more explored the fantastic element in his play *The Revolt of Machines* where life in its elemental instinctive manifestations is made to triumph over the principle of mechanical rationalization; and in the novel *Engineer Garin's Hyperboloid*. Garin is a type of a strong ruler, a superman, who engages in a struggle against the whole world and dreams of ruling it on the principle of caste division: the upper caste, the best, will govern and create; others will perform the procreating functions; still others, devoid of all superfluous passions and ideas, will become a kind of robots; and the rest will be exterminated.

9

Seven Days in which the World was Robbed is a fantastic satire, not particularly illuminating as such, but giving scope to Tolstoy's skilful handling of absurd situations—it is full of gay lightness.

A totally different genre is represented by *The Way Through Hell* which was begun by Tolstoy when he was still an *émigré*, but completed in Russia. It is a vast picture of the Russian pre-revolutionary society, just before and during the War and in the first year of the Revolution, especially of the intelligentsia. It is drawn in very sombre colours, showing the disintegration and the purposelessness of that life. It has some very good realistic pictures and episodes and some well-drawn characters, but it is spoilt by Tolstoy's tendency to give more than a picture of life, to philosophize about history and to give a historical summary of Russian life before and during the War.

In *Blue Cities* Tolstoy chose a contemporary Soviet theme—the everlasting theme of the conflict of two forces that are at grips in post-revolutionary Russia : the force of rational organization and that of elemental instinctive life, sometimes in its lowest animal manifestations. In the end it is life that triumphs. This is always the case with Tolstoy ; any other solution would be contrary to his nature.

In *Vasily Suchkov* Tolstoy has painted everyday Soviet life of the post-Nep period, conveying that mood of disillusionment which in those days was so widespread.

Tolstoy's contribution to the Five-Year Plan literature was not of much account ; his novel *The Black Gold* is a badly constructed melodrama on the subject of foreign and Russian *émigré* intrigues round Soviet oil. His search for a congenial theme remained fruitless, and by nature he was incapable of writing anything good to order. Such a congenial theme came, however, from an unexpected quarter and enabled Tolstoy to come into his own in *Peter the First*, a big historical novel at which he has been working for the last four years and of which two volumes have so far appeared. Here his natural gifts, his sense of life, his faculty of drawing lifelike characters and—last but not least—his excellent racy Russian, were given full play. More will be said about this novel in Chapter IX.

5. *Ehrenburg*

Ilya Ehrenburg (b. 1891) who, like Alexey Tolstoy, rallied to the Soviets after 1921, is one of the most prolific Soviet writers. Since *The Extraordinary Adventures of Julio Jurenito* he has published over ten novels and collections of stories, not to speak of plays, books of essays, travel impressions, etc. Ehrenburg's talent and skill are undeniable, but most of his novels are not good literature ; the ease and rapidity with which he produces them inevitably affect their quality : they are a mixture of fiction and journalism, and in some of them the element of journalism predominates. Ehrenburg knows how to handle his plot, how to make it thrilling and attractive, he has wit, his satire is often caustic and pointed, he knows how to make shallow thoughts look deep and significant, but the psychology of his characters is usually crude and made to fit in with preconceived abstract schemes. He loves sharp contrasts and ignores all finer shades. His characters are either paragons of abstract virtues (such are his ideal ascetic Communists like Kurbov in *The Life and Undoing of Nikolay Kurbov*—despite his temporary " downfall "), or embodiments of all that is worst in human nature, like some of his bourgeois and capitalist scoundrels. Some of his novels are more like political pamphlets in the form of thrillers, *e.g.* : *Trust D.E.* (1923) which gives the imaginary picture of the downfall of

Europe and the triumph of the soulless capitalist civilization of America; or 10 *H.P.* Ehrenburg is one of the few Russian writers who knows his Europe well, albeit superficially (he sees it almost entirely from the comfortable vantage-point of an *habitué* of the Montparnasse cafés), and can write novels about European life and politics, thus supplying a need, which is badly felt in Soviet Russia, for exotic sensationalism. One of his latest novels *Moscow Does Not Believe in Tears* (1932) is a somewhat melodramatic story about the life of the Russian *émigrés* in Paris. There are no gross distortions in it, but only a small corner of that life is shown—Ehrenburg's range is never wide. One of Ehrenburg's best and most human novels, where the element of thrilling sensationalism is relegated to the background, is *In Protochny Lane* (1927; translated into English as *In a Moscow Street*) of which the action is set mainly in Moscow. Both the pictures of everyday life and the psychology of the characters are here on a much higher level than in most of his other novels. Ehrenburg's latest novel, *The Second Day* (a reference to the Book of Genesis), deals with the Soviet actuality and the problems of Socialist construction and the evolution of a new type of man. There is, however, in it the usual touch of scepticism—Ehrenburg is by nature incapable of any enthusiasm; a deeply-rooted cynicism is after all his fundamental and most permanent quality. He is one of those men who have lost faith in everything. He speaks himself of that loss of faith quite frankly in his most personal, autobiographical and memoir-like novel *The Summer of* 1925, which at the time of its appearance was denounced by the Communist critics as an expression of the widespread post-Nep mood of depression and disillusionment, though with Ehrenburg it had really nothing to do with Nep or the " weekdays " of the Revolution—

it was an expression of his innermost nature. It is this cynicism, this loss of faith, that accounts for his changes of opinion. With all this, Ehrenburg remains a writer in whose works there is always to be found something interesting, although sometimes the grains of gold are very difficult to separate from the dross in which they are embedded.

6. Veresaev

Vikenty Veresaev (real name Smidowicz; b. 1867) is one of the old-school Realists. His novels, whether pre-revolutionary or post-revolutionary, have not much intrinsic value, but he is a scrupulous and observant witness of the social and psychological processes of his time, and his testimony always has a definite documentary value. This applies above all to two of his post-revolutionary novels: *In a Blind-Alley* (1924; translated into English under the title *The Deadlock*) and *The Sisters* (1933). In the former he draws an interesting picture of the mental and psychological state in which the Russian democratic and Socialist intelligentsia found itself when it had to face the Revolution and especially the problem of its terroristic excesses. Himself a Socialist and on the whole sympathizing with the main ideas of the October Revolution, Veresaev has succeeded in making his novel an impartial and penetrating picture of the mental state of the intelligentsia in the first years of the Revolution. He shows us both the young and the old, both those who accept and those who protest against the Revolution, and does it with great psychological insight, even though without any particular brilliance. His picture is by no means comprehensive, but it is throughout conscientious and impartial and this makes his novel worth reading. The figure of Katya, a typical young girl of the intelligentsia, morally pure and intellectually

honest, frank and straightforward in her democratic nega-
tion of the Revolution in its Bolshevik forms, stands out
as a memorable creation. Veresaev portrays life as it is,
without making concessions to any officially imposed
dogmas.

The same, and perhaps to a still greater extent, applies
to Veresaev's recent novel *The Sisters*, which gives a
similarly scrupulous and lifelike picture of the life and
mentality of the Young Communist League (*Komsomòl*)
in the persons and through the eyes of two sisters, two
young girls who come from a bourgeois family but join
the Young Communist League. The novel is partly
written in the form of their joint diary with alternate
entries by each sister. The sisters are different in
character and in outlook : Lelka, much more sober and
matter-of-fact in her whole-hearted acceptance of Communism ; Ninka spoilt by romantic individualism, by a
strong propensity to introspection and critical analysis.
While Lelka goes to work in a factory (the life and work
of a big rubber-shoe factory near Moscow, drawn *sur
le vif* with all its lighter and darker sides and with the
peculiar atmosphere of the Young Communist League,
occupies an important place in the novel) and plunges
into the party activities there, Ninka passes through a
crisis of individualism, of doubts and hesitations. The
two sisters meet finally in the country where both are
engaged in party work during the period of land collectivization. The author shows Ninka, who in her work
obeys only her own intuition and common sense, as
ultimately triumphing over her sister, who, in her narrow-
minded and blind adherence to party instructions, finds
herself behind the times when Stalin springs upon them
his famous article *Giddiness from Success*, denouncing the
excesses of collectivization and decreeing a change of
policy.

Veresaev's novel on its appearance made a great sensation; it was talked about a great deal, and on the whole warmly welcomed by the Soviet critics. But gradually the latter came to realize that the picture of the inner life and workings of the Young Communist League was in many respects far from flattering, whereas the climax of the novel seemed to suggest that the right path for the party worker lay in ignoring party instructions and following his or her intuition—Ninka in her work had actually forestalled comrade Stalin. Since then a veil of oblivion seems to have been drawn over Veresaev's novel and in the recent discussions on Socialist Realism it has not even been mentioned.

Like Leonov, Veresaev sharpens up his political and social antagonisms by intercrossing them with family conflicts: apart from the contrast between Lelka and Ninka he shows us both sisters in opposition to their mother who is an open enemy of the Soviet régime, a slightly comical but lifelike character.

7. *Prishvin and Sergeyev-Tsensky*

Mikhail Prishvin (b. 1873), whose early writings were rather half-journalistic, half-ethnographic sketches than fiction in the proper sense, but who also revealed himself before the Revolution as one of the best painters of animals and wild nature in Russian literature (*In the Land of Unscared Birds, Hunting for Happiness*, etc.), began publishing after the Revolution his first novel which he himself described as his first real " story of a man." Its first part appeared in 1924 under the title *Kurymushka*—it is the story of the hero's early childhood written with a fine perception of the inner workings of a child's mind. The first volume of the whole work conceived as a vast chronicle with an ever-growing political element (the hero, Misha Alpatov, first introduced to the reader as Kurymushka, becomes in his youth an ardent Marxist) appeared in book-form in 1927 under the title *Kashchey's Chain*. Kashchey is an evil personage of Russian folk-lore, and in the author's idea "Kashchey's chain" symbolizes the fetters of moral and social prejudices from which man must free himself. In his manner Prishvin owes not a little to Remizov.[1] The early chapters of the novel, dealing with the romantic inner world of Kurymushka's childhood and describing the peculiar atmosphere of a land-owning merchant family, remain its best. There are also some very good things in the part which describes the years spent by Misha Alpatov at school in a remote Siberian town whither his uncle takes him after he is sent down from another school. Prishvin, who has travelled extensively all over Russia, is very good at bringing out the local exotic oddities of its various parts. There is also in everything that Prishvin writes, not only in his animal and nature stories, that quality of virile healthy optimism which marks him off from some of the dominant tendencies in Russian literature, from Dostoevsky and Chekhov just as well as from Remizov and Gorky. This does not imply, however, that Prishvin shuns the seamy side of life : in *Kashchey's Chain* this seamy side is shown both in its moral and social aspects, but with Prishvin it never engenders morbid depression.

An author who before the Revolution stood half-way between the Realists and the Symbolists and of whom personally very little seems to be known, is Sergey Sergeyev-Tsensky (b. 1876). His principal post-revolutionary work is a long novel, *Valya*, the first part of which, called *Transfiguration*, appeared in 1923 in Simferopol and was reprinted in 1927. Sergeyev-Tsensky, whose early work was characterized, in the words of D. S. Mirsky, by

[1] See Mirsky, *Contemporary Russian Literature*, pp. 295-96.

16

" exaggerated exuberance and elaboration of style," evolved as time went by a much more sober and quiet manner, and in *Valya* there is no such elaborate exuberance. But he has retained his preference for odd, uncommon people, and the characters of the novel represent a queer collection. In the centre of *Transfiguration* stands an architect whose life is focused on the memories of his late unfaithful wife, who occasionally appears to him. A lame schoolboy who in some strange fit of dreaminess threw himself under a carriage and is now engaged in writing a work which is to prove the pathological nature of God ; an old doting colonel and his gaunt, blind wife, with an irresistible passion for cards ; their daughter, a former actress, who as a young girl left her parental house to go on a pilgrimage and led afterwards a life full of adventures, and whose mysterious femininity now exercises a spell over the architect and some other male personages of the novel— such are some of the principal characters. The first part ends dramatically : the architect kills in a station dining-room his late wife's lover who also turns out to be the former lover of the colonel's daughter. The action of *Transfiguration* is set before the war in the Crimea, the landscape of which is evoked with great power. All the collisions of the novel are on the purely individual plane, but the author's preface suggests that in its further development the novel was to have a much wider scope and significance ; unfortunately I have been unable to obtain its sequel.

8. *Zamyatin*

Evgeny Zamyatin (b. 1884) is a naval engineer by his original profession. He was educated at the Polytechnic Institute in Petrograd, graduating in 1908 from the Shipbuilding Faculty. During his student years he took

an active part in the revolutionary movement as member
of the Social-Democratic party. As he put it himself in
an autobiographical note written a few years ago, "I
was then a Bolshevik, now I am not." In 1906 he was
arrested and put in prison, and it is one of the jokes of
destiny that seventeen years later, in 1922, under the
Soviet régime, he had to spend some time in the same
prison, in a cell opening into the same corridor.

Zamyatin's first story was published in 1902, but he
did not take seriously to writing until much later. 1911
saw the publication of his *Tales of Country Life*, strongly
influenced by Gogol and Remizov and picturing the
meanness and squalor of life in a small provincial town.
His next work, *At the World's End*, about the life of an
out-of-the-way Russian garrison in the Far East, led to
the confiscation of the review in which it was published.
For four years Zamyatin wrote nothing. The years
1916–17 he spent in England supervising the construction
of Russian ice-breakers. Two stories—*The Islanders* and
The Man-Hunter—were the outcome of that stay in
England. In both, English life is treated in terms of a
biting satire. In 1918 Zamyatin returned to Russia and
during the first years of the Revolution took an active
part in the literary life of Petrograd, lecturing on literature,
on technical problems of prose writing, serving on various
editorial and theatrical committees, guiding young writers
in their first steps in literature. His influence was
particularly strong with the Serapion Brothers. Zamyatin's
own output in those years was not very great. Some of
his best and most characteristic stories were, however,
written during this period—*The Cave, Mamay, The North*.
In 1922 he wrote his satirical tales (*Fairy-Tales for Grown-
up Children*) which remind one partly of Saltykov-
Shchedrin and partly—in manner—of Leskov. In 1923
he took to the theatre and wrote a play, *The Fires of*

St. Dominic, which, under an historical disguise—its action is set in the time of the Spanish inquisition—was supposed to contain a bitter invective of the Soviet Government, of the Cheka and its methods. This was followed by two other dramatic works: *The Society of Honorary Bell-Ringers*, a variation on the theme of *Islanders*, and *The Flea*, a dramatic adaptation of Leskov's famous story, a piece of great farcical verve in the style of the Italian Commedia dell' Arte. Both have been staged with great success in Russia. In 1928 he wrote a tragedy in verse called *Attila* (the subject attracts him and he has for some time been engaged on a novel about Attila), but it has neither been published nor performed. One of his recent plays has been forbidden by the Soviet censorship. In the last years play-writing has been Zamyatin's chief occupation. He says himself that " if once in your life you have seen a theatre audience moved by your play, you will never forget it, especially if this happened to be in our days in Russia where it is not an ordinary public, but the people before whom the doors of the theatre have just opened and who receive their impressions in a vivid and fresh way."

Zamyatin's only long novel, *We*, was written in 1922–24. It was forbidden by the Soviet censorship and has never been published in Russia (see further in Chapter VIII). *We* is so far Zamyatin's only attempt at a great novel with an entertaining and complicated plot, more or less rooted in European traditions. His early stories go back to the Russian traditions. To Gogol and Leskov rather than to Turgenev, Tolstoy or Dostoevsky. In his short autobiographical note Zamyatin says that his childhood was spent almost without companions, their place being taken by books: " I still remember—he says—the thrill which Dostoevsky's *Netochka Nezvanova* and Turgenev's *First Love* gave me. These were the

elders and they terrified me ; Gogol was a friend."
From Gogol, Zamyatin gets his interest in depicting the
meaner and baser sides of human nature—all his earlier
stories of Russian provincial life bear an imprint of
meanness and vulgarity. It is also meanness, coated with
a thin veneer of hypocritical respectability, that he chose
to see and satirize in English life. From Gogol and
Leskov, Zamyatin has also inherited his predilection for
verbal effects, for stylistic elaborateness, for ornamentalism
of speech. Zamyatin's early manner may be described as
Realism with a touch of the grotesque. Later on he
developed a style of his own, a peculiar blend of Realism
with Symbolism and Imaginism which Prince Mirsky has
aptly compared to Cubism in painting. Zamyatin himself
describes his manner as Neo-Realism. In a recent interview with a French journalist he said :

"What is Realism in general ? If you examine your
hand through a microscope you will see a grotesque
picture : trees, ravines, stones—instead of hairs, pores,
grains and dust. Is this Realism ? To my mind it is
more genuine Realism than the primitive one. And to
pursue the comparison, while Neo-Realism uses a
microscope to look at the world, Symbolism used a
telescope and pre-revolutionary Realism an ordinary
looking-glass. This naturally determines all the images,
the whole formal structure."

Zamyatin's Neo-Realism certainly tends to Imaginism.
Some of his best stories (*The Cave, Mamay*) have for
their kernel a complex of metaphorical images round
which they grow. It is, however, wrong to think that
there is nothing in Zamyatin beyond these verbal effects,
this love of ornamentalism. Both *The Cave* and *Mamay*
convey to perfection the atmosphere of the terrible years
of War Communism and have a genuinely tragic accent.
There is also a tragic human accent in a very short story,

almost a poem in prose, about a Red Army soldier who rejoices at having killed a class enemy and whose heart is suddenly seized by sentimental pity at the sight of a frozen sparrow. Zamyatin's images often reflect the mathematical turn of his mind. He has a peculiar liking for geometrical images—his characters are symbolized by geometrical figures. Squareness is the principal characteristic of Baryba in *Tales of Country Life*. It is also the main attribute of one of the characters in *Islanders*. In *We* the two heroines are geometrically contrasted : one is plump and round (and her letter is " O ") ; the other is thin and angular (and her letter is " I "). Like Gogol, Zamyatin characterizes his personages chiefly by their outward appearance, in which he grotesquely emphasizes some particular feature ; his method is that of a cartoon artist ; thus in *Land Surveyor*, a pathetically humorous story with a sad ending, the image of the hero drawn with a few strokes of the pen—a huge head on fly's legs—is impressed upon the reader like a caricature. There is a marked difference in the construction of Zamyatin's longer and shorter stories. If, in his shorter stories, the story itself can be compared to a concentric outgrowth of a central image, of a " mother-metaphor," his longer stories resemble Cubist pictures ; they seem to consist of a number of broken pieces forming a peculiar pattern. In one of his critical articles (he is an acute and penetrating critic) Zamyatin champions the method of broken narrative conducted simultaneously on several planes, a method frequently applied in modern literature. It has been most thoroughly applied by Zamyatin in *The Story About What Matters Most*, in which the Revolution is regarded *sub specie aeternitatis* and which has been denounced by the Communist critics as fundamentally anti-revolutionary. But even in those of his stories which are written in a seemingly continuous manner one gets this impression of brokenness. An exception is *The Flood* (1926), a tragic story of love, jealousy and murder, written with more directness and simplicity and less ornamentalism than is usual with Zamyatin, and free from any satirical or political element, purely human in its interest, more intensely psychological, perhaps, than any of Zamyatin's work.

In 1931 Zamyatin left Soviet Russia and is now living in France. By nature he is a heretic, an eternal rebel against the established order of things, with a strong leaning to primitivism. Our time seems to him to offer a parallel to the age of Attila. He sees it as an age of great wars and social cataclysms. " To-morrow "—he says—" as then, we shall perhaps witness the downfall of a very great but too old civilization. . . ."

In the very first years of the Revolution Zamyatin expressed his opinion that Communist Russia would not produce a real literature. " Real literature," he said, "can exist only where it is produced, not by painstaking and well-intentioned officials, but by madmen, hermits, heretics, dreamers, rebels and sceptics." To this class of men Zamyatin himself belongs : it is very characteristic that he was a Bolshevik before the Russian Revolution and ceased to be one when Bolshevism became the official doctrine in power.

CHAPTER II

1. *Babel*

HALF-WAY between the transitional period and the revival of the realistic psychological novel stands a writer, who in 1924 was almost at once recognized as one of the most talented and original among the younger Soviet writers. His name is Isaac Babel. Born in Odessa in 1894, he grew up in the typical atmosphere of a Jewish bourgeois family where Jewish traditions were very strong. Educated in one of the secondary schools in Odessa, at the age of fifteen he conceived a passionate liking for the French language and literature. French writers were his first literary masters, and his early youthful stories were written in French. This mingling of the traditional Jewish atmosphere, and the study of the Talmud and of the Hebrew language, with the Latin precision and clarity of the French and their literature, to which was later added the influence of the Russian Revolution seen in its most elemental, romantic and cruel aspects, resulted in a strange product full of contrasts and paradoxes.

Babel's literary career began in 1916, when Gorky, who was then editing the review *Letopis*, published his first two stories. They were full of intense eroticism and even led to judicial proceedings against Babel. The stories which Babel wrote after that, however, were turned down by Gorky, who thought them very bad. For seven years Babel disappeared from literature and engaged in active life. He took part in the Civil War and in the war against Poland, serving with Budenny's Red Cavalry, afterwards occupying different posts in Soviet administration, and working as a journalist in Tiflis and elsewhere.

As he says himself in his autobiographical note, "It was only in 1923 that I learned to express my thoughts clearly and not at too great length, and then I took to writing again." In 1923–24 he published a number of short stories which formed two volumes and in 1926 appeared his famous *Red Cavalry*, stories based on his experience with Budenny's army in Poland. In 1927 it was followed by *Jewish Tales* and two longer auto-biographical stories, *The Story of My Dovecote* and *The First Love*. Since then he has been writing other short stories and plays and is now engaged on a big novel.

It has been pointed out that.Babel was the first in Soviet literature to revive a definite literary genre, that of a pointed short *nouvelle*, modelled to a certain extent on those of Maupassant. (Maupassant and Flaubert, together with Gogol and Gorky, have often been spoken of as Babel's chief literary masters.) His stories with their clear and distinct outlines and stylistic concentration came as something new after the welter of shapeless, loose productions of the " dynamic prose " writers. Yet Babel himself had much in common with those dynamic prose writers and differed as much as they did from the realistic and psychological novelists who were about to make their appearance. He had the same predilection for "*skaz*", for ornamentalism, for the exotic revolutionary subjects, the same aversion from psychologism. But at the same time he had a feeling for form and his manner differed from the *skaz* manner of the dynamic prose writers in that it was not a mere reproduction of the actual intonations, but a combination of different and often contrasting elements, in which the principle of stylistic organization was predominant. In Babel's stories of the Revolution and the Civil War, as well as in his *Jewish Tales*, everything is held together by style; without it, as the organizing and formative factor, they would crumble to pieces.

Babel's attitude to life is purely sensuous and æsthetic. He is attracted by the bright, picturesque, unusual things in life. His Jewish stories, in which he conveys with great mastery the peculiarities of both the life and the speech of the Jews of Odessa, are pervaded with the same exoticism. Instead of the traditional petty bourgeois Jewish *milieu*, Babel shows us something quite out of the ordinary—the world of the Jewish gangsters and bandits seen as something romantically and exotically pathetic. In the Revolution too, Babel's attention is drawn to its exotic and romantic aspects, to the unusual and paradoxical. All his stories about the life of the Red Cavalry are full of this Romanticism. Babel, who has a very keen vision and a great sense of line and colour, is especially sensitive to the cruelty and excessiveness of life, both in its physiological and psychological manifestations. He shows the carnal side of the Civil War, its physiology. He dwells with particular delight on the scenes of plunders, riots, executions, of senseless, instinctive cruelty. It is the animal instinct of destruction that he shows above all in the Civil War, and this is why his Red Cavalry provoked a protest from Budenny himself, who denounced it as a one-sided and distorted picture. Babel's stories of the Red Cavalry are not realistic snapshots of its everyday life, they are full of hyperbolism, of romantic exaggerations, of a peculiar pathos, where the cruel and the heroic merge into each other. The erotic element, treated also romantically and hyperbolically, in spite of its apparent naturalism, is very strong in Babel;

he likes crude and outspoken physiological details, often revolting in their nakedness. His favourite method is that of contrast and paradox. Nearly all his stories are based on contrasts, both psychological and stylistic. Throughout the *Red Cavalry* there runs a contrast between the cruelty, elemental blindness and crude sensuousness of that which he describes and its perception through the spectacles of a typical educated Jew, short-sighted, physically weak and psychologically out of harmony with his surroundings, and in addition burdened with a sceptical attitude to the world. Parallel to this there is always a contrast between Babel's poetical landscapes, reminiscent of Gogol's hyperbolical descriptions (and sometimes, by his choice of coloured epithets, of the Imaginist poetry), and the crude physiological naturalism of some of his scenes. Babel's Romanticism, full of pathos though it is, is tempered, or, one might almost say, poisoned, by his characteristically Jewish irony. Babel often sets off the unusualness of his " romantic " situations by introducing small matter-of-fact details :

> " Just before my windows a few Cossacks were executing for espionage an old Jew with silvery beard. The old man was screaming and trying to tear loose. Then Kudrya, of the machine-gun detachment, took his head and hid it under his arm. The Jew hushed and spread his legs. Kudrya took out a dagger with his left hand and carefully butchered the old man without bespattering himself."

Babel is by no means a painter of everyday life, a writer of " *byt* ", whether of the Red Army or of the Odessa Jewry ; nor is he a psychological novelist. With him everyday life has become a romantic decoration, and his characters are as romantically conventional. There is a strong leaning towards theatricality in him, towards crude and sudden effects. But—once more—Babel is primarily a consummate stylist. Whatever material he takes for his story he deforms it stylistically, subordinates it to his stylistic designs. In this Babel approaches Flaubert, though in his composition he has little in common with the great French writer. In his autobiographical stories, *The Story of My Dovecote* and *The First Love*, Babel seems to adopt a somewhat different manner. They are less ornamental, stylistically simpler and reveal a tendency towards psychological investigation, which was completely absent in Babel's earlier stories where the characters were shown to us purely outwardly and with the aid of stylistic devices, so to speak. Babel's rapidly attained popularity and reputation suffered a certain setback during the period of the Five-Year Plan literature, when his romantic irony and individualism naturally proved to be out of place. Since then Babel has not published anything of importance, and it remains to be seen in what direction his talent will develop.

2. *Vsevolod Ivanov*

Another revolutionary Romantic, who has some points in common with Babel but differs from him in many others, is Vsevolod Ivanov. Unlike Babel, he is a Russian of the Russians and hails from Siberia, where he was born in 1895. Like many other writers of the Revolution, Ivanov has had an adventurous life and tried many and varied professions, including those of a clown in a circus, a compositor, etc. Like Babel he wrote his first story in 1916 and sent it to Gorky, who advised him, however, to learn and read more before he took to writing. During the Revolution he took part in the Civil War, especially in the guerrilla warfare in Siberia and Central Asia, and became one of its poets. His first book of stories published in 1921 dealt with the Civil War. He was a typical representative of the dynamic prose current in Russian literature and belonged to the Serapion Brothers' group, one of his Siberian stories appearing in their almanac. His best-known works of this early period were *Armoured Train No. 14–69* (a story of the Civil War, later dramatized and successfully staged by the Moscow Art Theatre), *Coloured Winds* and *Skyblue Sands.* The two latter are novels in name, but hardly real novels in form: they are too shapeless and loose for that, without any clearly outlined plot, very typical of the " dynamic " fiction of the period, full of ornamentalism and of local colouring. One of Ivanov's chief characteristics is his lyrical pantheism, his sense of nature and of man's fusion with it. There is a touch of romantic primitivism in it. Ivanov likes to dwell on subconscious emotions, on the meaninglessness and aimlessness of life and of human behaviour, of which the motive forces are often obscure and inexplicable. There is behind it a tragic note, a fundamental pessimism, which goes, however, together with the writer's relish in life. Like Babel, Ivanov has a predilection for sharp and unexpected dramatic situations and naturalistic descriptions, romantically reflected. Life for Ivanov is always cruel and senseless, and man, a toy in the hands of dark and blind passions. "A man's soul is like a bear's: it cannot find its own pathway," is Ivanov's animal formula of the aimlessness of human behaviour. In 1923 Ivanov published a short novel *The Return of Buddha* which constituted a new development in his work: it was less ornamental, less " local ", and had a plot of adventures. After that Ivanov tried his hand at a political proletarian novel (*Northsteel*, 1925), but it proved a complete failure. In 1927 appeared his book of village stories *Mystery of Mysteries.* In it, parallel with the general development of Soviet literature, Ivanov makes a step towards psychological Realism. His style becomes still more simple and direct, he shows us village life against the background of the psychological emotions of his characters. But his attitude to life remains fundamentally the same. Again he shows us human behaviour as senseless and aimless, and all his principal characters are possessed by dark and violent passions, which determine their actions and to which they ultimately succumb. There is a tragic note, a sense of doom and destruction, in nearly every story of this collection, and in this pessimism, this worship of blind destiny, the Communist critics saw a manifestation of Ivanov's anti-revolutionary tendencies.

Among Ivanov's stories written after 1925 there is one that differs from most of his stories in its unornamental simplicity combined with an attempt at symbolism. It has also a touch of the comic and grotesque in it. It is called *The Ferghan Cotton* and describes the enmity and competition of the representatives of two civilizations, a Russian Communist and a foreign " Imperialist " (he is apparently an Englishman, but is made to symbolize foreign colonial Imperialism in general). They are shown against the background of the tedious and monotonous life at a small station in Central Asia where the Russian Communist is engaged in buying cotton on behalf of the Soviet Government, and the Englishman in trying to thwart his plans by underhand activities. On two occasions, in turn, they nearly kill each other, but obeying some secret subconscious impulse save each other's life and end by becoming friends. It seems that in this story Ivanov wanted to show that human sentiments are, after all, above all political, social and other differences. The story is written in simple, direct language and in a humorous vein. There is also a touch of humour, but this time with a tragic concluding note, in the curious story *God Matvey*. It is a story of the Civil War, and its principal characters are a Soviet military Commissar, Denisyuk, who is a good Communist and thinks of nothing but fighting the enemies of Communism, and the peasant Matvey who calls himself " God " and invites the belligerents on both sides to stop the fratricidal Civil War. He declares himself to be invulnerable and walks under fire between the two lines. He is brought before Denisyuk, who questions him and finally decides to submit him to a test : Matvey will ride on horseback in front of the Red lines and Denisyuk's men will fire at him. During the test Matvey's white horse is killed and he himself is wounded. Here is the simple and laconic description of Matvey's end :

" God fell down. The Commissar quickly ran up to him, for some reason putting straight his revolver. God's shoulder was wet and scarlet. Smiling self-contentedly and benevolently, he tried to lift his arm but could not. On his forehead there was tied with tiny strings a broken fragment of a mirror. He saw the Commissar, smiled a still more self-contented smile, and said slowly : '.Well, my lad, didn't I say you couldn't shoot me down ? Who is going to shoot me down ? Am I God or not ? '

" And then Denisyuk (realizing that he must not do this but that he cannot do otherwise) hurriedly thrust his hand into his revolver-holster, and the fact of it not being fastened somehow encouraged him, perhaps because all this had been decided beforehand somewhere right inside him ; he hurriedly snatched out his Colt and discharged three bullets one after another at God Matvey. He looked round. The soldiers were laughing noiselessly and without themselves being aware of it. And he too laughed out without knowing this. He turned round to the dead body and fired another bullet at it. And then everybody at once grew more severe. Petrov, ruddy-faced and curly-haired, turned out to be the most agile. He ran for the spades. God Matvey was buried under a poplar-tree ; the grave they dug out for him was shallow because Denisyuk urged them on, saying that a thunderstorm was going to break out. . . ."

In the decisive battle between the Reds and the Whites that follows the Reds are victorious, but Denisyuk, who shows his troops a heroic example, is killed and the next day his soldiers bury him with great solemnity under the same poplar.

In common with other Soviet writers, Vsevolod Ivanov has been evolving towards Realism and his latest and as yet unfinished work is a long novel in five parts based partly on the autobiographical material, but stuffed with most exciting adventures. These, however, are narrated in the realistic manner. The novel is entitled *The Adventures of a Fakir.*

CHAPTER III

THE REVIVAL OF THE NOVEL

1. *The Serapion Brothers*

IN 1921–22 general attention was drawn, both in and outside Russia, to a small literary group composed entirely of very young writers who called themselves the Serapion Brothers (an allusion to the characters of the famous German Romantic E. T. A. Hoffmann). It was not a literary school held together by some programme or by any unity of manner or style. It was rather a literary fraternity whose members—poets and prose writers—were united in the first place by their youth, to a certain extent by their common training in the literary studio of the novelist Zamyatin, but above all by their interest in what was going on in Russia in those days, and by their tendency to describe the reality impartially, preserving their ideological freedom and independence and looking at the events from the outside. In form and manner of writing they belonged for the most part to the dominant current of descriptively-dynamic prose. In fact, we find among the Serapion Brothers two of the most typical representatives of that " dynamic " prose—Vsevolod Ivanov and Nicolay Nikitin. From that group came some of the most outstanding men in present-day Russian literature, like Zoshchenko, Fedin and Kaverin. In their further literary careers the Serapions diverged. But two of them at least, namely Fedin and Kaverin, played a prominent part in the revival of the Russian novel, which began in 1924 and marked the next stage in the development of Soviet Russian literature.

2. Fedin

Born in 1892, Konstantin Fedin was older than the majority of the Serapions. He began with short stories, and in his early stories one perceives the influence of Bunin's and Chekhov's manner, though perhaps in substance he is more dramatic than his masters. There is that quality of quiet dramatism in Fedin's first mature story *The Orchard* (1920)—its clear transparent outline, its well-balanced prose especially remind one of Bunin, and its theme is reminiscent of Chekhov, even though it is revolutionary. It is Fedin's favourite theme: the conflict of the old and the new in the Revolution. Its hero is the old gardener Silanty. His former masters, to whom he is devoted, have been driven away by the Revolution, and their manor house now shelters a children's colony; the new revolutionary songs sound so discordant in the old house; the orchard which Silanty looks after, and to which he is devoted, gradually falls into decay, and Silanty ends by setting the beloved house and orchard on fire. The same tragic note is sounded in the story called *Stillness* (1924), relating the pastimes of an old dispossessed squire. The quiet realistic flow of the uneventful narrative is interrupted by the almost fantastic scene of the squire's battle with the rooks for the sake of the old lady whom he once loved and betrayed—the last romantic impulse of a man beaten by life. But the story ends on a conciliatory note. *The Peasants* (1926), which tells some episodes in the life of a village shepherd and his daughter, reminds one of Bunin by its sombre portrayal of the cruel and brutal aspect of peasants' life and psychology. And the note of cruelty and gloom and despair is sounded still more clearly in *The Chronicle of*

Narovchat (1925), told in the name of a half-educated monk, and by its "*skaz*" manner reminding one of Remizov and Leskov. A new and original note was struck by Fedin in his *Transvaal* (1926), a longish story of a very curious personage, Swaaker by name, a Boer who has somehow come to be settled in a Russian village, the perfect embodiment of a cunning, enterprising, selfish and hard-hearted *kulak*, who gradually assumes almost dictatorial economic power over a whole rural district, marries the daughter of the former squire, and wields an absolute ascendancy over the peasants. This story, when first published, called forth a lively controversy in the Soviet press, many critics accusing Fedin of counter-revolutionary *kulak* tendencies. Swaaker, they said, was an idealization of the *kulak*, in spite of the fact that Fedin portrays him as an unpleasant character.

All these stories of Fedin's deal with "revolutionary" themes. There are a few others in which the Revolution does not feature at all. Such, for instance, is *Anna Timofevna* (1922), a rather long and slow-moving tale of a woman's way of sufferings and self-sacrifices, told against the background of gloomy, tedious and insipid provincial life. It belongs to a large progeny of Russian "provincial tales" and brings to mind the names of Gogol, Pisemsky, Leskov and, among the moderns, Remizov and Zamyatin. It is a bit loose in construction, but its concluding chapters are very well written. Of a different pattern, much more terse and economical, is another pre-revolutionary provincial story called *The Tale of One Morning* (1921). Its hero is a hangman, himself a former convict, a great artist in his profession, who in his non-professional life is a regular churchgoer and a sentimental lover of birds. There is a terse but extremely realistic description of the hanging of a murderer, and

all the minor characters and their different attitudes to
the execution are drawn with great mastery.

Such are Fedin's principal stories. His first big novel,
Cities and Years (1924), represented the first attempt made
in Soviet literature to depict the Revolution not in a
merely impartially-descriptive or lyrically-ecstatic vein,
as did Pilnyak, Vsevolod Ivanov and other writers of the
dynamic prose period, but in a more deeply psychological
manner. Fedin was out not only to describe but also to
grasp and disclose some of the mainsprings of the Revolution. The orthodox Soviet critics blamed Fedin for
having given a one-sided picture of the Revolution, for
having dwelt on its side-aspects and for fussing too much
about his hero, a backboneless and rootless intellectual.
Its theme is, indeed, the tragedy of a Russian intellectual
at grips with the Revolution. Its action covers a long
period of time, beginning before the War and ending in
1922. Its principal character is Andrey Startsov, a young
student who is caught by the War in Germany and
remains there as a civilian prisoner. He returns to
Russia after the peace of Brest-Litovsk and joins the
revolutionary forces. But he does not find a real place
for himself in the Revolution. His trouble is that he
puts personal interests and values before the cause which
he is serving, he is too sentimental, and this ultimately
brings about his undoing. He is killed in the end by
his friend Kurt Wahn, but he is really finished even
before physical death overtakes him. Kurt Wahn is
shown as a contrast to Andrey. He is a German, a gifted
painter. In pre-War days in Germany he and Startsov
were friends, but the moment the War is declared
Kurt's dormant German patriotism awakens and he
breaks with Andrey. He is afterwards taken prisoner on
the Russian front, and when they next meet, in 1918 in
Moscow, a radical change has been worked in him : he

is now an ardent revolutionary and a prominent member of the Council of German Soldier Deputies. He is then sent to Semidol, a small, remote provincial town, surrounded by villages inhabited by the Mordva, with the mission to supervise the return of German prisoners of War. Andrey goes with him. Here one of the important episodes of the novel takes place. A group of German prisoners of War, exploiting the nationalist separatist tendencies of the Mordva, organizes an anti-Bolshevik detachment led by a German officer, a certain Markgraf von zur Mühlen-Schönau, who plays an important part in the first half of the novel, where the action is set in Germany; he is connected both with Andrey and with Kurt, the latter having his own reasons to dislike him and the former to be grateful to him. The rebels are defeated by the Soviet punitive detachment. During this short struggle Andrey lives through something like a fit of revolutionary enthusiasm, he almost feels himself one with the Revolution; but this feeling soon vanishes and later on he vainly tries to recapture it. Moreover, he betrays the revolutionary cause and for personal reasons helps von Schönau to escape, providing him with papers which he steals from Kurt's desk. Before anything is discovered he is sent to Petrograd to take part in its defence against Yudenich's attacks. The girl who fell in love with him at Semidol follows him there. Another girl with whom he was in love in Germany comes all the way from Germany to join him, only to discover that she has a rival. She goes away, and this is a great blow to Andrey. He nearly goes mad, wandering about Petrograd, and afterwards leads a strange secluded life until ultimately Kurt's vengeance overtakes him.

The construction of this novel is very peculiar. It begins with its own *dénouement*, which takes place in 1922, after which the narrative is switched back to 1919, to

Andrey's arrival in Petrograd and the visit which von
Schönau pays him there, in disguise, on his way to Germany. Many of these incidents remain somewhat obscure
to the reader, and are intentionally covered with a veil
of mystery which is lifted only towards the end of the
book. Havoc is played with the traditional chronological
sequence of the narrative—one perceives here the influence
of Bely and Pilnyak on Fedin's composition, though in
his unusual construction there is more of a deliberately
planned order and less of instinctive looseness. It is only
with the third chapter that he takes up the exposition
of events in their chronological order. We are shown
Germany before the War, Andrey's friendship with Kurt
Wahn, their life in Nuremberg, the outbreak of War,
Andrey's life as a civilian prisoner in the small Saxon
town of Bischoffsberg, his unsuccessful attempt at escape.
There is a whole chapter of digressions, relating the
childhood and youth of the heroine of the novel, Marie
Urbach, her love affair with von Schönau, her acquaintance
and love affair with Andrey. Then the chronological
order is re-established once more, and we are told about
the revolution in Germany; the return of the prisoners,
including Andrey; his encounter with Kurt Wahn in
Moscow; their life in Semidol and the events there.
Here again there are some episodes interpolated in the
main story and some excellently drawn episodic figures.
One of these episodes, the story of the soldier Fedor
Lependin, who hails from a village near Semidol, is
taken prisoner by the Germans and interned in the same
town as Andrey, and whose end comes during the Semidol
events, when he is hanged from a tree by the rebels of
von Schönau, has even been published separately. It
forms, indeed, a separate story within the general framework of the novel. The novel ends with a chapter which
takes place in 1920 in Petrograd, and the proper

chronological place of which is between the first and second chapters.

There is a certain scrappiness—partly deliberate—about *Cities and Years*, but on the whole it is a work of considerable originality and great literary merits. In order of time it is the first big and significant Soviet novel which puts the problem of the Revolution and of the outside elements confronted with it. Fedin does not offer any ready-made solutions, he merely shows us the tragedy of a typical member of the Russian intelligentsia overpowered and swept aside by the Revolution after attempting to participate in it and to adapt himself to it. The general suffering and passive attitude of the intelligentsia is well portrayed in a memorable chapter describing the compulsory digging of trenches outside Petrograd at the approach of General Yudenich's army.

Fedin's second long novel, *The Brothers* (1928), has similar peculiarities of construction. It does not begin exactly with its own *dénouement* like *Cities and Years*, but the real place of its opening is just before the conclusion. In the introductory chapters Fedin shows us, with the effectiveness of a good dramatist (he has tried his hand at drama too and written a play about Bakunin), all his main characters in a scene saturated with the atmosphere of life and full of psychological intensity. We are shown at once all the knots of the novel ready to be untied. Whereupon Fedin proceeds to demonstrate how these complicated and intertwined knots came into being, in order to undo them in the last section of the book.

The subject of the novel may be described again as the tribulations of the intelligentsia during the Revolution. In fact it is a variant of the theme of Andrey Startsov. The principal character of the book is Nikita Karev, a composer, who becomes musician under somewhat strange circumstances and rather unwillingly. He comes from a Cossack family whose home is in Uralsk. Like Andrey Startsov he is caught by the War in Germany, and on returning home after the Revolution finds his father and his youngest brother, Rostislav, in the two opposite camps. Old Karev is a counter-revolutionary, his youngest son is a Soviet Commissar who commands a detachment for fighting counter-revolution among the Ural Cossacks and is ultimately killed outside his native house. There is a third brother, Matvey, a well-known Petersburg physician who keeps somewhat aloof from the Revolution. So, indeed, does Nikita, who is faced with the problem of reconciling his artistic vocation both with the demands of the Revolution and with his personal preoccupations, chiefly amorous. He really fails in both these tasks. He cannot find in music an adequate expression of the Revolution, and finally he loses, in turn, all the women whom he loved or who loved him.

The Brothers is without that fragmentary quality which characterized *Cities and Years*; it contains no such lyrical digressions, nor any such complicated plot, slightly reminiscent of a novel of adventure. The plot is woven round purely psychological moments, its centre is in the love intrigue, in the figure of Varenka Sherstobitova, who is loved simultaneously by several characters in the novel, who herself loves Nikita Karev but marries a friend of his childhood, the Communist Rodion Chorbov, only to leave him afterwards for Nikita. The main interest of the novel is in the figure of Nikita himself, and in the problem he has to face, in his inner conflict. The Revolution is presented as a background and the psychological motive force—not as an object of interest in itself—but there are some rather conventional revolutionary figures, the most important among them being the Communist Commissar Shering, Rodion Chorbov's chief and elder friend, whose death is made to play an important part in the general narrative, but who remains none the less a pale and somewhat enigmatic personage. Rodion Chorbov himself is another ideal Communist, of a different type however, more simple, more virile, less sophisticated. But in him, too, there is a certain woodenness. More than once it has been noted that the majority of the Soviet writers do not succeed in portraying their ideal Communist heroes and are much more successful in the drawing of the victims of the Revolution, of the downtrodden and suffering, or of those who doubt and hesitate.

The manner of *The Brothers* is much more quiet and epic than that of *Cities and Years*. Fedin really returns here to the manner of a large, realistic, social and psychological novel, though he has certainly assimilated many of the formal innovations and developments bequeathed by the age of Symbolism. He is a typical representative of the so-called " Fellow-Travellers " in Soviet Russian literature (see more about the origin and meaning of this name in Chapters V and XIII), and of all the Fellow-Travellers he stands perhaps nearest to the spirit of the traditional novel, presenting an original blend of Russian and Western European traditions. He is one of those Soviet writers who manage to maintain a close contact with the cultural life of Europe. Like his two principal characters, Andrey Startsov and Nikita Karev, he spent the War years in Germany as a civilian prisoner. Lately he spent some time in Davos undergoing a cure there, and has travelled in other European countries. He was therefore specially qualified to write a novel the action of which is set outside Russia, in Norway, Germany, Holland and other countries. This novel, called *The Rape of Europe*, is Fedin's latest. Only the first volume has so far (1934) been published. Originally it was to be called *Dumping*, and it represented Fedin's tribute to the Five-Year Plan literature. Its object is to show the decaying capitalist, bourgeois society as seen by an observant Russian traveller, a Soviet journalist, Rogov by name, who has a vague resemblance to Startsov and Karev—there is evidently something of Fedin himself in all three of them.

The bourgeois world is personified in two principal figures : Philip van Rossum, who represents the type of traditional, conservative and cultured Dutch bourgeois, and Sir Justus Elderling-Geyser, a more modern and "adventurous" type of capitalist, in whom the Soviet critics see a likeness of Sir Henry Deterding. The main feature of European life which Fedin tries to bring out is its "soullessness," but his picture looks very crude.

The weak spot of Fedin's new novel is perhaps its lack of dynamic power : in this it is unlike his *Cities and Years* and even *Brothers*. Fedin's art tends to become more static ; in *The Rape of Europe* there are too many descriptions and meditations, though some of these descriptions, these urban landscapes and *nature-mortes*, are excellent in themselves, especially the glimpses of Bergen and Amsterdam. It is, however, difficult to judge of the novel as a whole without its second volume, of which the action will be set in Russia : Fedin is a great master of construction, and he likes unexpected developments. But his strongest point is character creation—his Startsov and Lependin in *Cities and Years*, his Swaaker will live as characters. In *The Rape of Europe* the best-drawn characters are the episodic figures of Lodevijk van Rossum, the elder brother and partner of Philip, who looks disapprovingly on the latter's dealings with Communist Russia, and the phthisic hunch-backed preacher of German Fascism. As to Rogov, he is a somewhat thin, third edition of Startsov and Karev, and more of a literary device necessary for the general economy of the novel than a living character. Communist critics have accused Fedin of showing his Rogov as too much absorbed in personal affairs of the heart.

3. *Leonov*

Another typical representative of the Fellow-Travellers, and one whose name has been especially connected with the revival of the novel, is Leonid Leonov (b. 1899).

Leonov began by short stories, by clever and skilful stylistic experiments in different manners and styles, showing a versatility which even earned him the name of *pasticheur*. *Tuatamur*, a weird and beautiful Oriental poem in prose ; *The Wooden Queen* and *The Knave of Diamonds*, two charming little stories where Realism, Hoffmannesque fantasy and quaint Andersenian *naiveté* are oddly blended ; *The Memoirs of Kovyakin*, a Leskovian study of provincial life, with a touch of Shchedrin's satire in it—such are Leonov's early stories, written and published before 1924. In 1924 appeared a longer story called *The End of a Petty Man*. Though still in some respects a *pastiche* (it obviously derives from and depends on Dostoevsky), this story is very remarkable and marks a turning-point in Leonov's work, for it contains some of the most significant elements of his later mature novels. Its hero is one of the men thrown overboard by the Revolution, floating helplessly and aimlessly in the middle of its turbulent flood, the world-famous paleontologist Likharev, who is about to finish a work that must upset the existing scientific conceptions. A typical scholar, absent-minded, short-sighted, he is utterly incapable of grasping what is going on around him. The action is set during the worst years of War Communism, famine and misery. The picture of Petrograd in those days has a nightmarish effect. Likharev is joined by his sister, a consumptive old spinster who comes to help with his daily needs. He falls ill, becomes confined to bed, and is obsessed by visions and hallucinations. Every night his double, a distant relation of Ivan Karamazov's devil, comes to converse with him and to mock at him. There is a peculiar and powerful rhythm in the succession of mad and terrible scenes. One of the most effective is where a gathering of all sorts of *ci-devant* men at the apartment of the physician Elkov is described. When Likharev returns home after that gathering the truth for the first time begins to dawn upon him : he realizes that his sister is dying, that there is no bread, no provisions left in the house ; he also realizes that his country is going the way of her appointed sufferings. And suddenly there is peace and light in his soul, he is ready to die. But in order to make the sacrifice of his life complete, he must destroy his manuscripts. He does so at the instigation of his double, his demon, during their last conversation. " Let them burn," says the devil, " perhaps something will grow out of their ashes." And there is a note of mockery, of irony in the last words of Likharev's double, when he says that " now Russia will rise high, very high. The sky will be covered with concrete, tramcars will furrow the clouds. Bread will be made of air . . . people will wear velvet trousers. . . ." Upon these words Likharev flings himself at his double, slips and loses consciousness. Such is the end of the " petty man " cast away by the Revolution.

Leonov's first big novel, *The Badgers*, was published in 1925, a year after Fedin's *Cities and Years*. It was a continuation of the same tendency—away from pure verbal ornamentalism and emotional lyricism, back to psychological and social Realism. Coming as it did from the pen of a twenty-seven-year-old novelist (Fedin was five years older when he wrote *Cities and Years*), Leonov's first novel was remarkable for the wealth of its psychological and social contents and for the sureness of its handling. Leonov presented in it his favourite social theme—the clash between town and village. The novel is a diptych, it falls distinctly into two parts—the first has for its setting one of the typical merchant quarters of Moscow not long before the Revolution, a corner of the old world which still bears many traits of resemblance to the world depicted by Ostrovsky in his plays. The two heroes of the book, the two brothers Pashka and Semen, grow up amid these Ostrovsky surroundings ; by origin they are peasant boys ; they have been brought here from their native village to learn urban ways and manners and to be trained in business. Their characters are different and they soon part ways. Pashka, who is lame, sullen, unsociable and wilful, cannot stand the surroundings ; he slinks away, becomes a factory workman, a proletarian, to reappear again in the second part of the book as a Soviet Commissar. The real hero of the book is Semen. Pashka is shown only by way of contrast to him. And Semen is essentially a romantic ; although he adapts himself more easily than his brother to the new mode of life, it is powerless to delete from his mind his early village reminiscences ; at heart he remains a peasant.

In the second half of the book we are shown Semen's native village during the Revolution, a peasant rising against the Soviets, at the head of which Semen places himself. The cause of the rising lies partly in a local agrarian quarrel, but also, to a certain extent, in the peasants' grievances and discontent about the food-tax. It is ultimately crushed, and one of the reasons of its failure is the lack of any general scheme behind it, any real general purpose, any genuine fighting spirit. Semen alone rises above those petty local grievances ; he, alone of them all, has that spirit of village as opposed to town.

But he is forced to surrender, because his followers betray and desert him. The final scene shows us Semen returning from the woods, where the rebels (they call themselves " Badgers ") had entrenched themselves during the rising, and meeting his brother Pashka, now called " comrade Anton ", who heads the Soviet punitive expedition sent to repress the rebellion. Not a word is uttered between them (the brothers had, however, met and talked the matters over before that in the woods), but one feels that, although capitulating in fact, Semen does not do so in spirit. And it is not accidental that, in a new disguise and under a new name, that of Nikolay Zavarikhin, he comes to life again in Leonov's next novel, to personify the same idea and the same everlasting conflict. In *The Badgers* the conflict remains unsolved, and upon that silent meeting, rather characteristically of Leonov, the curtain falls.

The Badgers was followed in 1927 by another long novel, *The Thief*, still more ambitious in size and scope, though lacking the definiteness of the social theme of the earlier novel. The Revolution is less felt in it—in *The Badgers* we are in the very midst of its struggles—it is even difficult to situate it exactly in time, though it is obvious that its action passes during the period of the New Economic Policy. As a background the Revolution is, of course, always present in it—but then in what modern Russian novel is it not ?—Its hero, Mitka Vekshin, a curious variety of Russian Rocambol, who has at the same time not a little in common with some of Dostoevsky's characters, especially with his namesake Mitya Karamazov and with Raskolnikov, is one of the " disillusioned " of the Revolution: from a prominent figure in its early stages, a Commissar of the Red Army, he becomes, under the régime of NEP, the ringleader of a formidable gang of burglars with a world-wide reputation.

Both in matter and manner, Leonov's novel bears a close resemblance to Dostoevsky. It has a complicated criss-cross plot, a great number of multifarious characters —representatives of the underworld, Moscow gangsters, former bourgeois, small Soviet employees. Their mutual relations are often difficult to disentangle. The complex structure of the novel is still further complicated by the introduction and the very clever use of the device of a novel within a novel. One of Leonov's characters—the writer Firsov—is writing a novel about the characters of *The Thief,* and some of the incidents are reported to us in terms of Firsov's novel.

Leonov has Dostoevsky's predilection for " *nadryv* ", for painting psychological complications and perversities, for investigating the darker sides of human nature. Many of his characters have their literary prototypes in Dostoevsky's novels ; for instance, Masha Dolomanova is a direct descendant of Dostoevsky's " infernal " women, Nastasya Philippovna and others. Yet one would not accuse Leonov of merely imitating Dostoevsky. He succeeds in creating a world of his own, and his novel makes very interesting reading. Some of his character creations are quite memorable. The two that stand out as particularly attractive are Pukhov and Pugel. Pukhov, a home-made philosopher with a strong religious colouring, has many affinities with Katushin in *The Badgers.* He feels a great inward sympathy for Mitka, and when the latter starts on one of his periodical mysterious errands, he tells him " to steel himself by suffering "—again a Dostoevskian idea. Both Pukhov and Katushin have also much in common with some of Gorky's " truth-seekers ". Pugel is a circus man, a touching, sentimental and kind-hearted Russian German, and a worthy addition to the gallery of Russian Germans in Russian fiction. But where Leonov particularly excels, is in the drawing

46

of the *ci-devant* men, the downtrodden representatives of the old régime whom he pictures with great insight and plenty of sympathy. Generally speaking, " humaneness " is one of Leonov's inalienable features, and this makes him fit in well with the main traditions of Russian literature. *The Thief* has no definite political tendency, no political or social message to bring, no political axe to grind. It is true that it ends on an optimistic note— Mitka gives up his gangster life and goes into seclusion somewhere in the country, whence he emerges, we gather, a reformed character, though in what way reformed, is left intentionally unsaid.

It is a typical Leonov ending ; Leonov is not concerned with Mitka's social reformation, he is primarily interested in man and the complex mental and psychological processes inside him. The ethical problem that torments Mitka's soul, is the eternal problem of whether a man has the right to kill a fellow-being. In his revolutionary past Mitka has committed a cold-blooded murder, killing a White officer who had killed his favourite horse. That moral incident came to be the turning-point of Mitka's political career and the real cause of all his subsequent turmoil.

As a Realist, Leonov is above all concerned with life in all its manifoldness and complexity, life that is reluctant to obey any hard-and-fast rules and evolves according to its own laws. He makes one of his characters in *The Thief* say :

> " After all we [the writers] know life better than anyone else ; it has a nice taste ; one eats it and dies without noticing."

Through the mouth of Firsov it is Leonov himself who speaks here. And again, speaking of Firsov, it is of himself that he says :

" Firsov was fond of life, of its pungent and coarse smell, of its tart and bitter taste, its flimsy bulkiness, even of its wise senselessness."

To Firsov's philosophy of life Leonov opposes the ideas of a rather curious personage of his, a certain Chikilev. He is a small Soviet official, a tax inspector, a petty and insignificant man, very keen on prying into other people's affairs, who preaches the idea of a society where everything will be planned, controlled and pre-ordained, and based on a whole system of mental and intellectual espionage. This is how Chikilev formulates his idea of the future State :

" In the future State which will come in a thousand years there will be no secrets ; anyone, you see, will be able to come to anyone and watch his life at any moment of day and night be it even through a magnifying glass. For, suppose, in your mind you are planning to ruin mankind ? With those modern achievements of science—the ray of death, the sneezing gas—in one little moment you could blow into the air the whole globe. You must watch over humans, humans cannot be left unwatched. No little secrets, come out, come into the street, citizens, and make clean breast of what you are up to. Then willy-nilly everybody will be honest ; whether you want it or not you'll have to stick to it. If I, say, was the ruler of the world I would put on every man's head a sort of machine, with a kind of telegraph tape. In the morning a specially appointed official would take the reading and affix his resolution. . . . And everybody would be able to look in the same scientific way into his controller's mind. Thought—that's where the source of all suffering is. . . ."

There is a touch of a biting political satire in Chikilev's figure and a striking resemblance between his ideas and those of his literary predecessor, Shigalev in Dostoevsky's Demons. And the similarity of names induces us to think that it is quite deliberate.

It is this being in love with life which makes Leonov's novel so contagiously alive—in reading it you feel irresistibly drawn into his world, into the reality as transformed by the novelist, you begin to share the life of his characters. This, even more than any similarity of literary manner or style, is responsible for the fact that Leonov to some extent resembles both Tolstoy and Dostoevsky.

The Thief is a typical Russian novel in spite of some daring novelties in construction. Leonov's next two novels—*Sot* and *Skutarevsky*—belong to the Five-Year Plan literature and will be discussed in Chapter VII.

4. *Kaverin*

Veniamin Kaverin, one of the youngest Serapion Brothers (b. 1902), has also had his say in the revival of the novel in Soviet Russia. But even his first story, published in the almanac of the Serapion Brothers, showed that he was gravitating towards non-Russian, Western European traditions in literature, towards Hoffmann and Poe. He displayed an interest in plot which was rather unusual in a Russian writer and contrasted most strikingly with the plotless ornamentalism and constructive shapelessness of most of the writers of the dynamic prose period. This tendency became still more pronounced in Kaverin's first longer work—his *nouvelle The End of Khaza*, dealing with the life of the Leningrad underworld, burglars and anarchist gangsters. In this story the element of adventure is coupled with fine psychological portraiture. Some of the Soviet Russian critics accused Kaverin, in connection with this work, of idealizing the world of gangsters. In his next novel *Nine-Tenths of Fate*, Kaverin, without renouncing an exciting plot, set himself a more serious psychological

49

task, raising the same problem which occupied Fedin in
his two novels—the problem of the intelligentsia in the
Revolution. Kaverin's novel is, however, artistically inferior both to Fedin's novels and to his own *End of
Khaza* : he was still too young, perhaps, to cope with
his subject. He tackled a similar theme once more, and
this time with much greater success, in his next novel
which appeared in the same year as Fedin's *Brothers*
('1928). Its title is *The Trouble-Maker* or *The Evenings
on Vasily Island.* The novel depicts the spiritual discord
between the intelligentsia and the Revolution, and the
aloofness of the intelligentsia when confronted with
the problems of the day. An individualist, " counter-
revolutionary " note is distinctly sounded in this work of
Kaverin, which contains an open protest against restrictions on creative freedom, against all political chaperon-
ing of literature. In the numerous literary discussions
which took place in the years 1929–31 on the subject
of creative freedom, of the so-called " social command ",
and of the writer's place and role in the Communist
society, Kaverin came forth as a champion of artistic
freedom of creative work. His next and most mature
and original novel, *The Anonymous Artist* (1931), dealt
again with the same problem of creative freedom and
independence, and was a rather courageous defence of
Romanticism.

It bears a certain resemblance to Yury Olesha's *Envy*
(see Chapter VI). It also raises the problem of Individualism *versus* Collectivism, of Romanticism *versus* Realism,
of Morality *versus* Technique. There are two principal
protagonists in it : Arkhimedov, an artist and a crank
who embodies the romantic principle, and his friend
Shpektorov, a man of the Five-Year Plan who knows his
own mind and places technical tasks confronting the
Soviet Union above everything else. Arkhimedov's main

contention is that in contemporary Russia (the novel was
written in ·1929, the first year of the Five-Year Plan)
morality is lagging behind the technique. "Personal
dignity," he maintains, "must be an essential component
of Socialism." He comes forward as a new Don Quixote
of the old morality. The motto to the novel is taken
from Cervantes's famous romance : "They marvelled at
the intelligence and madness of this man." Arkhimedov
defends illusions. To Shpektorov who says that for
Soviet Russia "the West is a box of tools without which
it is impossible to build even a wood shed, not to
speak of Socialism," Arkhimedov replies : "A box of
tools is not enough to begin a new era." He opposes
the morality of the medieval guilds to the present-day
reign of corruption and dishonesty. He says :

"In the fifteenth century not a single workshop
would accept an apprentice until he swore to perform
his work honestly in accordance with the statutes and
the aims of the State. The weavers of those days used
to burn publicly any cloths which had an admixture
of hair. Guildsmen who were guilty of giving false wine
measures were thrown off roofs into sewers. Just
imagine the next session of the Central Executive
Committee passing a decree about labour morality.
With us there wouldn't be enough sewers for all the
unscrupulous guildsmen."

Arkhimedov openly advocates Romanticism in its
original conception. He is out to fight "the decline of
honour, hypocrisy, meanness, and boredom." But
Shpektorov's mind is directed to purely practical things.

"Morality ?—he says.—I have no time to stop and
think over that word. I'm busy. I am building
Socialism. But if I had to choose between morality
and a pair of trousers, I'd rather have the trousers.
Our morality is that of the creation of a world."

On more than one occasion Shpektorov speaks of Arkhimedov's desire "to incorporate the Middle Ages in the Five-Year Plan."

There is a remarkable scene in the novel where the Leningrad militia wants to arrest some homeless beggars who live in the sewers. Arkhimedov, a quaint figure in his old-fashioned coat and velvet striped waistcoat buttoned right up to his neck, solemn and severe, intervenes on behalf of those beggars and is arrested for disorderly conduct.

Unlike Olesha's romantics, Arkhimedov is a piteous but rather lovable creature. His controversy with Shpektorov, which forms the main theme of the book, is complicated by their personal relations. Arkhimedov's wife, Esther, and Shpektorov are in love, and the boy whom Arkhimedov believes to be his son is really Shpektorov's. But when Esther is faced by the necessity of choosing between her love for Shpektorov and her pity and perhaps secret admiration for Arkhimedov, she commits suicide by throwing herself out of a window. Arkhimedov's duel with Shpektorov ends in the former's defeat—he is even compelled to give up his last possession, his son and only prospective follower (as in Olesha's *Envy* the stress is laid on the childlikeness of Romanticism), but the epilogue to the novel suggests that perhaps after all he is not the loser, that he leaves behind something valuable : it contains a striking description of a picture by an "anonymous artist" (obviously Arkhimedov), representing the scene of Esther's suicide together with some visions seen by Arkhimedov during his aimless wanderings through the town on the same night. Here is this description :

"She is lying, with broken hands, full of shadows. Like a fishing-net they entangle the crossroads. They swing on squatting houses, in the oblique lozenges of the windows. In the desolate perspectives of the suburb they pass with the gloomy solemnity of solitary people. They fall on the kerchief which during the fall came off her eyes, on her lips bitten with effort.

" It is a twilit hour. The snow is blue, sky-blue, white.

" A hook-nosed doctor approaches her, pouting his lips with annoyance, and his hat skips on the frizzly taut springs of his hair. Strangers stand around in rigid attitudes of curiosity, indifference, and fear, some with raised hands like the terrible fools of Persian painters. All look at her. She is lying crossed by the misty stripes of shadows and light. With his mouth agape, raising his red baton, a militia-man is driving towards her in a lop-sided cab ; the horses have round, astonished faces.

" And everybody looks at her. Full of indifferent curiosity, patches of priming look at her from broken windows, and an old woman with the flat head of a snake—from a basement door left ajar. Hardly out-lined in black, a short indifferent prostitute with pressed lips peers into her eyes, telling fortunes on their glassy enamel. A beggar with a big childlike eye, wearing a battered bowler, stands gravely in the crowd. Every-body looks at her.

" And she lies as if it had been a flight, and not a fall, as if she did not crush but died because of the height. And it seems that the last man dear to her has just turned round the corner and vanished.

" Only one who with all the freedom of genius overcame the cautiousness and dishonesty of modern art which has come to be so aloof from men, could succeed in this. The mixture of the grand style with trifles, of everyday details with a deep sense of time, is a thing which one can learn neither from living nor from dead masters. Only a new vision, boldly leaning on that which all the others regard as accidental or banal, could dare upon such a return to the childlike nature of things. Next to the unconscious power of representation one feels here intelligence and memory —a terrible memory founded perhaps on a clear notion

53

of what passes before the eyes of a man falling down from the fifth floor. One had to crush to death in order to paint that picture. . . ."

This last passage echoes another earlier passage where one of the personages of the novel, a friend of Arkhimedov, thus defends artist's independence and characterizes real art :

> " There are artists who can work easily nowadays. They seize with an easy hand whatever comes their way, because in their work everything seems timely and necessary. There are among them respectable people in whom the instinct of historical self-preservation is exceedingly strongly developed ; and there are boys who come when the dinner is already eaten. . . . But real art, the only one which is wanted by its time, can dispense with both. It is a terrible, ruthless thing, with its ups and downs, with revolts against masters, with real battles in which not only canvases but men perish. It is a struggle for one's eye, for an honest eye which yields neither to laws nor to prohibitions. It is such a thing that one must be prepared to starve and freeze with cold, and suffer scorn. One must hide ambition in one's pocket or clench it between one's teeth and, if there is no canvas, paint on one's bedsheet."

The construction of Kaverin's novel is rather peculiar. The beginning of it—Arkhimedov's crucial talk with Shpektorov introducing the reader to the main theme of the book—is narrated in the third person. But from the second chapter onwards (Kaverin calls his chapters " Encounters ") the author himself intervenes, and after that we see Arkhimedov either through his eyes, or as described by those who tell him about their encounters with the half-mad artist. Now and then Kaverin brings in purely autobiographical material and tells us about his work on *The Anonymous Artist* and his other literary occupations—in other words, he constantly resorts to what the Formalist school in literary science calls "laying bare the device." This method enables him to use striking and original devices. Thus, some of his most important conclusions about Arkhimedov are arrived at during a performance of Dickens's *Tale of Two Cities* in the School Youth Theatre to which he took his two nieces, and this permits him to give *en passant* a curious critical estimate of that perfomance. In general, the theatre plays a great part in the psychological presentation of Arkhimedov—it is perhaps an application of what the school of Constructivism calls the "local method", emphasizing the romantic theme of Arkhimedov.

On the whole *The Anonymous Artist* is a curious and original piece of work and the most significant and deep of all Kaverin's novels.

His latest novel *The Fulfilment of Desires*, of which the publication was begun in 1934 in one of the new Soviet reviews (*Literaturny Sovremennik*), bade fair to become one of the literary events of the year. Kaverin is one of the most interesting figures in present-day Russian literature.

5. *Slonimsky and Savich*

Mikhail Slonimsky (b. 1897) came, like Kaverin and Fedin, from the Serapion Brothers. Like them he began with short stories. Most of his early stories (*The Sixth Lancers*, 1922) had the War for their subject and were typical of the period. His first attempt at a novel on a large scale was *The Lavrovs*, depicting the disintegration of an intelligentsia family (Slonimsky himself is a typical intellectual, a Jew by origin). The action of the novel begins before the War and goes on into the first years of the Revolution. The War, the Revolution and the life of the intelligentsia form the background. The story centres about the psychology of its principal character, Boris Lavrov, and the main problem is that of the individual's place in society. Lavrov has been described by some critics as a new variety of " superfluous man ", a type so popular in pre-revolutionary Russian literature, from Turgenev down to Chekhov and his successors, and revived after the Revolution by Fedin. He sides with the Revolution, but cannot find his place in it. Nor can he grasp the real meaning of what is going on around him, and the more he thinks about it and about his own actions the more meaningless it all appears to him. It seems to him that in siding with the Revolution he has attained full freedom. But

> ". . . much later he understood that there was no freedom anywhere on the earth, not in a single corner of it, that of all the available un-freedoms he had chosen that in which his wishes and actions coincided."

He feels himself a total stranger to the events that take place around him. To Lavrov, Slonimsky opposes Foma Kleshnev, a real Bolshevik, active, sober-minded and determined. But Lavrov remains the central and most interesting figure in the novel which is written in the manner of traditional psychological Realism.

In his second novel *Sredny Prospekt* (called after a street in Petrograd) Slonimsky's manner becomes much more terse and economical, his psychological analysis much more concentrated and subordinated to dynamic elements. It deals with the second, unheroic phase of the Revolution, with its small-bourgeois degeneration. One of the characters, Mikhail Shchegolev, is a distant descendant of Lavrov and at the same time a relation to Leonov's Mitka Vekshin. He is one of the " disillusioned " of the Revolution, a Communist turned smuggler, and utterly indifferent to everything.

An attempt to give a purely individualistic novel, without any political implications, was Ovady Savich's *Imaginary Interlocutor* (1928). It is one of the few novels in Soviet literature that go back to Dostoevsky, deal with a problem of inner life, and have a general significance extending beyond the limits of time and place. Its hero bears the symbolical name of Obydenny which could be rendered as something like " Mr. Daily " or " Mr. Everyman ". He is just an ordinary man, an average employee of a Soviet provincial trust. The background of the novel and its secondary characters are all quite real—the daily routine of a Soviet trust, Obydenny's domestic life, his relations with his insignificant colleagues. But this real-life background acquires somehow a touch of grotesque symbolism. It is a story of Obydenny's gradual transition, on his way to death, onto a different plane of life, of his meaningless, unmotivated actions, his metaphysical boredom, his estrangement from those who surround him, his communion with his double, the " imaginary interlocutor ", who represents, it seems, his own thought and foreboding of death. This double has, however, a real counterpart in the person of a young dancer, Obydenny's lodger. The novel ends in Obydenny's death, for which all the rest was merely a preparation. Curiously enough, it seems to be the only valuable work that the author has produced.

6. *Lavrenev, Malyshkin, and Lebedenko*

A number of Soviet novelists have focused their attention on the War and the Civil War. The Civil War is the subject of many of the stories and novels of Boris Lavrenev (b. 1894), but, unlike its chroniclers of the first period of the Revolution, it interests and attracts him only as the background and the determining factor of the psychological dramas of his characters. *Wind* (1924), is a

story of an anarchist sailor who gradually becomes a class-
conscious revolutionary. In *Forty-First*, Lavrenev's best-
known and most popular story, the theme is the conflict
between an ordinary human feeling and the sense of revolutionary duty : a girl Communist, member of a partisan detachment, falls in love with her prisoner, a White officer,
with whom she is left alone on a desert island. In the
end it is, of course, the sense of duty which triumphs,
and she kills the officer. Lavrenev likes to paint the
Whites, the doubting, hamletic representatives of the
intelligentsia. His attitude to the Revolution is tinged
with Romanticism. He has once complained that in
present-day life there was no place for romance, and in
the recent discussions abou. Socialist Realism (see
Chapter XIV) he championed the rights of revolutionary
Romanticism. He likes dramatic situations (*Forty-First*
is a good example) and knows how to construct a story.

A place apart among Lavrenev's novels is occupied by
his satirical Utopia, *The Downfall of the Republic of Itl*.
It is a political satire, with a strong element of the
detective novel in it, describing in terms of Utopia
foreign intervention in the South of Russia during the
Civil War. It has been influenced somewhat by Anatole
France's *Penguin Island*, but it has still more of a
Ruritanian musical comedy about it.

Lavrenev's latest novel *White and Blue* has for its setting
the Black Sea fleet during the Great War.

The pre-revolutionary fleet forms also the subject of
the novel entitled *Complete Overhaul* (1934). Its author
is Leonid Sobolev, a young and hitherto unknown writer.
It gives a vivid picture of the life of the Russian sailors,
imbued with proper revolutionary spirit.

Alexander Malyshkin (b. 1890), whose *Downfall of Dair*
(1924), describing the capture of the Crimea by the Reds,
was a typical example of the dynamic prose period, gave.

in his *Sebastopol* a long War novel written in a much more orderly and realistic manner. Its hero, Shelekhov, is a sailor from the intelligentsia, who gradually, and not without repeated setbacks, comes to espouse the cause of the Communist Revolution. The main idea of the novel is that men like Shelekhov can find their place in the Revolution only if they give up aspiring at commanding posts and accept to be its useful but inconspicuous pawns.

Another War novel, deeper and more human, written in the Tolstoyan manner and with a strong pacifist tendency is Lebedenko's *The Heavy Brigade* (1932–33). The novel dwells particularly on the last period of the War, and among its characters there are Bolsheviks, anti-Bolsheviks and neutrals. One of these neutrals, who ends by turning Bolshevik, is the principal character of the book, Andrey Kostrov. The author, in spite of his pronounced anti-militarist tendency (his book has been compared to Remarque's), does not paint the War all in black—he is capable of seeing feats of heroism and manifestations of human feelings next to all its bestiality. His anti-Bolsheviks, especially the officer Aldanov, are human and lifelike. In spite of its uneven style, Lebedenko's novel holds one of the first places in the Soviet War literature.

CHAPTER IV

1. *Chroniclers of the Revolution*

IN present-day Russian literature we may distinguish a
whole group of writers whose interest and attraction
for us lie above all in their reflection of the everyday
life of Soviet Russia, who may be called its chroniclers
par excellence. They do not belong to a single literary
school nor do they reflect the same aspects of life, the
same strata of the Soviet society. In a way it is, of course,
purely arbitrary to bracket together writers like Panteleymon Romanov, Vladimir Lidin, Mikhail Zoshchenko,
Valentin Kataev, Lydia Seyfullina, Boris Levin and
several others. Yet they have this in common that they
all chronicle various aspects of Russian life during the
Revolution and especially during its second, realistic and
constructive (or would-be constructive) period as opposed
to its first period, romantic and elementally-destructive,
of which the dynamic prose of Pilnyak, Vsevolod Ivanov,
Nikitin and others was the most faithful and appropriate
reflection. They have also this in common, that though
they choose different literary genres and manners—from
the pithy humorous or satirical anecdotes of Zoshchenko,
often one or two pages long, to the ordinary full-length
novels of Lidin or Romanov—even the novelists among
them, such as Kataev, Lidin and Romanov, can hardly
be said to have contributed to the revival of the social-
psychological novel as a literary genre. It is not the
form, but the subject-matter they are primarily concerned

60

with. And that subject-matter they have in common—
it is the everyday life and the ordinary people of post-
revolutionary Russia. If men like Fedin, Leonov and
Kaverin, who brought about the revival of the Russian
novel on a grand scale, can be regarded as Romantic
Realists, these writers of everyday life are Realists pure
and simple.

In a way, of course, this everyday-life literature has
the same source of inspiration as the dynamic prose of
the first years of the Revolution—the impartial and
faithful recording of its events and happenings. But
whereas the events and happenings of the first period of
the Revolution naturally lent the works of its chroniclers
a strong romantic colouring, the works of these painters
of everyday life are characterized for the most part by
drab realism; stylistically, they tend towards greater
simplicity, away from the romantic ornamentalism and
emotional lyricism of the dynamic prose period.

2. Seyfullina

Chronologically speaking, one of the first in this line
of everyday life Realists is Lydia Seyfullina, who is sometimes treated as a proletarian writer. She is of peasant
Tartar extraction, a village teacher by profession. She
is older than the majority of the young Soviet writers
(b. 1889); but her literary career began late. Her first
stories were published in the local press of Siberia where
she was an educational worker. They had a strong
local colour, were rather artless and did not attract
attention except locally. Most of her stories had for
their setting the revolutionary village, its social conflicts,
the Revolution as seen and lived through by the peasants.
Her first story to attract a wider notice was called *Lawbreakers*. Its principal character was a homeless boy, one

of the numerous army of the waifs and strays wandering about Russia in those years. Her next and best-known story—perhaps, it is also her best—was called *Manure*. Its action is set in the revolutionary village in the very first years of the Revolution ; its hero, Sofron, a good-for-nothing peasant, is morally and spiritually transformed by the Revolution. Parallel with his inward transformation we are also shown the material and cultural changes which the Revolution has worked in the Russian village. This story is typical of all Seyfullina's stories in outlook as well as manner. They are all written in the good old-time conscientious realist manner. They lack the verbal ornamentalism and exoticism of Vsevolod Ivanov, with whom Seyfullina has sometimes been compared, and with whom she has some aspects in common. They lack also the psychological profundity of Leonov or Fedin. In subject-matter, as well as in the stark realism of its treatment, and in the simplicity of their outlook they approach perhaps the nearest to the pre-revolutionary Populist literature. Alongside with *Manure* the best known of Seyfullina's stories is *Virineya*, showing a new type of peasant woman emancipated by the Revolution. Both these stories have been dramatized. Seyfullina's later writings have no particular literary merits, while her former popularity with the orthodox Soviet critics has given place to a feeling of guarded distrust and on more than one occasion she has been accused of petit-bourgeois tendencies, of depicting only the darker and most unpleasant aspects of village life. In her short novel, *The Encounter* (1925), there are some powerful moments of objective realistic description and some well-drawn characters, but the construction of a novel is not Seyfullina's strong point. In the longer and more ambitious novel *The Wayfarers* (1925) Seyfullina reveals her weakness as soon as she forsakes the familiar village environment.

ROMANOV

One of Seyfullina's latest stories (*Tanya*, 1934) draws
a curious portrait of a Communist child in whose mind
there is a chaos of most contradictory notions and sentiments. Written in Seyfullina's usual artless, unpretentious
realistic manner, the story raises the interesting problem
of the conflict between " fathers " and " children " inside
the Communist Party.

3. Romanov

Another writer of this group, who is also rather old-
fashioned and writes in the manner of the old school of
Realism, is Panteleymon Romanov. He can hardly be
regarded as belonging to the young literature; he is
even older than Seyfullina (b. 1884) and began to write
and was published before the Revolution, but only after
it did he really come into his own. He is a much more
ambitious writer than Seyfullina, his choice of subjects
is wider and more varied, and his work reflects different
aspects of Russian life. His longest and most ambitious
work—the novel called *Russia*—is a vast epic of the
Russian society on the eve of the War. In manner and
composition it derives from Turgenev (especially in the
portrait of the heroine) and Gogol's *Dead Souls*. It is
very long and rather dull and uninspired, though it has
doubtless its value as a document. It is also chiefly
documentary value that attaches to Romanov's two stories
(one is even a novel) which had a somewhat unexpected,
and from the literary point of view not quite deserved,
success in this country—*Without Cherry Blossom* and
Three Pairs of Silk Stockings (the real title of the latter
in Russian is *Comrade Kislyakov*). Both deal with the
problems that preoccupy the youth in Soviet Russia,
problems of love and morals and marriage, of reconciling
the romantic impulses of human nature with the new

realistic morals and with the stern demands of Communist ideology. It is the birth and the evolution of a new type of man, of a new attitude to love, to romance, to marriage, that interest Romanov most. Problems of sex particularly occupy Romanov's attention: one of his collections of stories even bears that title. He shows the new type of young men, mostly students, who have discarded all romantic notions of love. As the heroine of *Without Cherry Blossom* puts it :

" There is no love with us, there are only sexual relations, because love with us is contemptuously relegated to the domain of ' psychology ', and it is only physiology that has the right to exist."

In another story the man tells the young girl he meets in a railway carriage : " If you want to be modern, face life crudely and realistically, for such is life." And he advises her to discard the traditional notions of the moral and immoral.

In the story *Love* the principal character says to his fiancée :

" There is no such thing as mysterious and lofty love, but only a physiological process."

In *The Trial of a Pioneer* a young pioneer is censured for making " psychology " and " romance " interfere with his love affairs.

Next to his new " Sanins " Romanov shows women who, though craving for something different, show a highly developed erotic sensibility and easily succumb to " temptations ". Romanov's stories portray typical phenomena of a whole period in the life of Soviet Russia.

Romanov's latest novel, *Property* (1934), is as usual long and tedious, and its theme is the attitude of an intellectual, this time an artist, when confronted with the Revolution and its problems. The action is set in the period of

Socialist reconstruction, and the theme is treated with Romanov's customary earnestness and conscientiousness, but without any literary grace.

Romanov is not a very refined artist and cares little for purely formal achievements ; his novels are rather social documents, notations of social facts and processes, than well-constructed works of art. Most of his stories are very simply written and based on dialogues. In his " sexual " stories he often resorts to the epistolary form. His shorter stories lack the defects of construction inevitable in longer novels.

4. Lidin

Vladimir Lidin (b. 1894), who also began before the Revolution with a number of short stories written in the manner of Chekhov, is a more accomplished and cultured artist. The *milieu* he describes in his several volumes of stories is that of the Soviet employees, of the old and the new bourgeoisie, the so-called " Nepmen ", the new rich of the period of the New Economic Policy, and his subject is as often as not the seamy side of Soviet life. He is rather a short-story writer than a master of the novel, his technique reminds one of Chekhov and Maupassant. One of his first novels, *The Ships Sail*, is really a series of short stories told parallel, or rather alternately, with but loose connection, or none at all, between them, passing in Moscow, in Italy, in Germany and in the Arctic region. The two most important of these disjointed parallel stories are those of Ivan Kostrov, a thorough and sincere Communist who, after having sacrificed his health and energy to the cause of the Revolution, dies of consumption at an Italian seaside resort (before dying he falls in love with a simple Italian girl, the daughter of the innkeeper, and for a time this romantic love makes him forget his past, his work and even the Revolution) ; and of Glotov, the cashier of that factory which Kostrov runs and to which after the end of the Civil War he has entirely devoted himself. It is a story of Glotov's gradual moral downfall ; he embezzles in order to gamble at the trotting races in Moscow, and is drawn deeper and deeper into the morass until he finally attempts to commit suicide from which he is saved by a young girl who puts him on the way to moral regeneration. It is a good picture of a somewhat un-expected side of the life of revolutionary Moscow—the racecourse, the restaurants, etc. Lidin's later novels—*Marina Venevtsova* and *The Apostate*—are more coherent and have the appearance of real novels. Like Romanov, he deals here with the problems confronting the youth, the new generation. *The Apostate* is the more interesting of the two. It is more than a mere picture of everyday life—the *milieu* being that of the students and intelligentsia in general—for it also raises some vital ethical and social problems. Its hero is a young man, Kiril Bezsonov, who passes through a series of moral ordeals, commits a murder, but is ultimately regenerated. The novel ends on an optimistic note. Kiril, who had planned, with his unscrupulous accomplice Sverbeyev, to escape from Russia with the aid of some Black Sea smugglers, changes his mind and decides to go back to Moscow and make a clean breast of his part in the murder. As he does so, the beauty and attraction of life come home to him. He contemplates the waters of the sea and is suffused with joy at the thought that he is " returning to his own world," where " he would learn the values of life, of human blood, of toil, and of love."

5. Kataev

Valentin Kataev is one of the younger writers. He was born in 1897. During the Great War, when still a schoolboy, he enrolled in the army as a volunteer. Later on he had an adventurous time during the Civil War in the Ukraine. In 1918 he met Bunin in Odessa, and many of his earlier stories bear obvious traces of Bunin's influence, though Kataev himself has a strong humorous and even satirical strain which is not to be found in his master's works. Some of his short stories are written in this satirical vein, but it is in his plays and in his first novel, *The Embezzlers* (1927), that it becomes the dominant element. He also wrote a pure novel of adventures, *The Island of Ehrendorf* (1921). Of his earlier and non-satirical stories, the best are to be found in the book called *The Father*. Of this collection the title story is perhaps the best. It is the story of an old man, a man of the past, who carries on a quiet but joyless existence in one of the great Southern ports of Russia where he is employed as teacher. His only interest and joy in life is his son, a former officer who is detained in prison in the same town on a charge of counter-revolution. When the son is ultimately released he turns out to be totally unworthy of his father's care and affection. He manages to get a snug place and live comfortably, while the old man loses his job and is compelled to drag out a miserable existence. Finally the young man goes away to Moscow leaving his father to die a lone death. It is a study of two totally different types, men of two different generations. It also contains a very good picture of the humdrum everyday life in a large provincial Soviet town. Another good story in the same book is the one called *Fire*—about the tragic death of a young

Communist's wife and the husband's subsequent spiritual and moral torments and doubts.

There is in Kataev's work a strong lyrical strain which makes him stand somewhat apart from the other everyday life writers. Life is beautiful and enjoyable, it carries with it its own justification—such is one of the motifs running through a great deal of Kataev's work. It is the mood that underlies his *Father* in spite of all its apparent sadness. It is also the *leitmotiv* of another story, written in Bunin's manner, *The Russet Crosses*. Its heroine is a woman thrown overboard by the Revolution who has nothing to expect from life and decides to kill herself. She chances, however, to come upon an old letter and the faded russet crosses of lilac blossom she finds in it call back to her mind her love for her husband, the death of her child, the execution of her brother, the hunger and sufferings she had to pass through :

> " She imagined all the happy, difficult, amazing, unbearable, ordinary human life, and she realized that in life happiness and misery, love and death were the same thing, that life had no flights and falls, and that there was no need for her to die."

Kataev's novel, *The Embezzlers*, stands apart from the mass of literature dealing with everyday life. Although it deals with everyday life—the adventures of the employees of a Moscow Trust who have absconded with a sum of money—it also has a strong element of the fantastic and the picaresque. Kataev's humorous and satirical faculties come to the foreground in this work, and the adventures of the embezzlers, their peregrinations across Russia, their contacts with all sorts of queer and funny people are told in a vivid and exciting manner.

Kataev's latest novel *Forward Oh, Time !* which, like

Leonov's *Sot* and *Skutarevsky*, belongs to the Five-Year Plan literature, will be dealt with in Chapter VII.

6. *Zoshchenko*

A place apart not only among everyday life writers, but in Soviet literature in general, is occupied by Mikhail Zoshchenko (b. 1895). He is perhaps the most widely read and popular of the present-day Russian writers, and his popularity among the Russians outside Russia is not less than in Soviet Russia itself. He has evolved a style and a manner of his own which mark him off from all the other Soviet writers and make his writings easily and instantly recognizable. This style has been evolved gradually, but one of its principal elements was present in Zoshchenko's earliest works and was in fact one of the common attributes of the dynamic prose period. It is the element of " *skaz* " already referred to. But of all the numerous writers who, in the years 1920–23, used that form of " *skaz* " so lavishly and unrestrainedly, Zoshchenko is the only one to have stuck to it after it fell in abeyance with the revival of the novel and of a quieter and simpler realistic manner in short stories. But in the case of Zoshchenko it has survived in a modified form and been put to a new use.

Zoshchenko made his literary début together with the Serapion Brothers, and one of his first stories appeared in their almanac. It was a typical " *skaz* " story which later was included in the collection of *Stories Told by Nazar Ilyich Mr. Sinebryukhov*. These stories were typical of the dynamic prose period. Their subject was War and Civil War (Zoshchenko himself had taken part in both—in 1915, while a student at the Law Faculty in the University of St. Petersburg, he enlisted as a volunteer in the Russian Army, and in 1918 he volunteered to serve in the Red Army), they were told in the person of a half-educated non-commissioned officer, in a language which is a mixture of natural raciness with a most horrible acquired jargon. Even those early stories of Zoshchenko revealed his unusual literary mastery. But both the subject and the language were exotic and suited to the requirements of that period. When it ended and when the "*skaz*" manner gradually died out in Soviet literature, Zoshchenko had to think of evolving a new manner that would suit his artistic individuality. The humorous, satirical tendency was very strong in him. To-day he is the best humorist in Russian literature. But he did not arrive at once at that manner which now makes his works so individual and so easily recognizable. He passed through an intermediate period, writing a number of short stories in which the comical effects were achieved mainly through the subject-matter, through improbable and ridiculous situations and collisions, stories told in the ordinary, simple, " educated " language, in the name of the author himself. Then he began writing short humorous stories and anecdotes which stood on the border-line between real literature and newspaper *feuilleton*. Their subjects were usually topical, very often the so-called " small defects of mechanism " in various branches of Soviet administration, satirical pictures of Communist red-tape, corruption, inefficiency, etc.

Gradually Zoshchenko evolved a new manner, a combination of his earlier " *skaz* " stories and his purely comical anecdotes. It was the question of finding a proper " mouthpiece " for that " *skaz* ", a good substitute for the author, who would no longer be exotic but would fit in with the normal course of everyday life in Soviet Russia. Such a mouthpiece has been found by Zoshchenko in the Soviet man-in-the-street, the average Soviet citizen who passively accepts the Revolution, but vaguely regrets the good old times and aspires to bourgeois philistine comfort and happiness. The happily created personage of Zoshchenko expresses himself in the peculiar jargon of a semi-educated man with a strong admixture of the specific Soviet journalese which is rapidly inundating and spoiling the Russian language.

Despite the fact that Zoshchenko's situations are often highly improbable and grotesque, to him more than to any other can be rightly applied the label of writer of everyday life. He gives the truest picture of the Soviet weekdays stripped of all heroism and romanticism, of all pretension and make-belief. Some of the orthodox Soviet critics do not really know what to make out of Zoshchenko. Now they praise him for ridiculing so cruelly the petty-bourgeois vices, the spirit of *embourgeoisement* invading large circles of the Communist society, now he is himself denounced as an essentially bourgeois writer, and identified with his own characters.

Zoshchenko is one of the most prolific writers in Soviet Russia : short stories written by him form several volumes. He is also, as I said, the most popular. It is the outward, superficial comical effects, that the large reading public appreciate in Zoshchenko. But it is their second, hidden, innermost meaning, and their technical excellence, which make them real literature of the highest order. Some of them are genuine stylistic gems. At his best he reminds one simultaneously of two of the great masters of Russian literature, so dissimilar on the whole, and yet so alike in one thing—in their keen vision of the mean vulgarity and insipidity of life ; I mean Gogol and Chekhov. It is the pettiness, the vulgarity of life, the essential incomprehensibility of one man for another, that forms the psychological *leitmotiv* of a great many of Zoshchenko's stories. And in some of the best, for instance in *Wisdom*, one senses the tragedy beyond and beneath the humorous or grotesque presentation of life's vulgarity and insignificance. The most hilarious of modern Russian writers is at heart a thorough pessimist, and for an understanding reader his comical stories must inevitably leave an aftertaste of utter sadness.

To bring Zoshchenko nearer to a non-Russian reader is an almost hopeless task. His stories inevitably lose in translation the greater part of their individuality and attraction. In this respect he is rather more akin to Gogol and Leskov than to Chekhov, for his language has that individual accent and raciness which Chekhov lacked.

One of Zoshchenko's latest works, *The Restored Youth* (1933), leaves a somewhat strange impression. It is a short novel, a genre that is new to Zoshchenko—hitherto he has specialized in very short stories. But really, both structurally and stylistically, it differs little from Zoshchenko's usual stories. It is written in the same intentionally vulgar, half-educated jargon. Its very short chapters, each containing a typically Zoshchenkian episode or anecdote, make it into a succession of short stories held together by a very simple plot. Even the fact that it falls into two parts, the first, which precedes the actual novel (the first seventeen chapters), being the author's pseudo-scientific and subtly irrelevant comments and reflections on the subject of his story (Zoshchenko himself compares it rather aptly and ingeniously to an educational film) is quite in line with Zoshchenko's typical manner and merely makes of it an extended story. It is the story of an ageing, almost decrepit Soviet professor of astronomy, vaguely hostile to the existing régime though just as vaguely in sympathy with Socialism in general, who yearns for his lost youth and finally succeeds in restoring it by an effort of will. He deserts his wife, marries a young, flighty and vulgar girl, who " at the age of nineteen has already had time to change five husbands and undergo seven or eight abortions," and goes away with her to the Crimea. She soon tires of him and begins to flirt with young men. One day the Professor (nicknamed by his family and relations Vasilek which means Cornflower) finds her in the arms of one of these young men. He has a stroke and one side of his body is paralysed. But in the end he is cured, and even preserves his restored youth. He returns to his wife and family, but deep in his heart never ceases to pine after his scatter-brained Tulya. In the portrayal of characters and in the picture of everyday Soviet life there is, as usual with Zoshchenko, a strong element of the grotesque. And even more acutely than usual the reader feels all the time, beneath the story, a strong undercurrent of biting and cruel satire. The very vulgarity of Zoshchenko has an effect of great subtleness. The reader has even an unpleasant feeling that the author is laughing not only at science, at medicine, at his own ridiculous and grotesque characters, but at him, the reader, too.

This is how Zoshchenko characterizes his own work :

" Our story this time will have but small resemblance to ordinary literary productions. It will also bear little resemblance to our previous little works of art, written by a naïve and rather crude hand in the hurry of our youth and frivolity. . . .

" There will be everything which the reader expects from a book he has taken to read in the evening in order to dispel his daily worries and plunge into other people's life, other people's emotions, and other people's thoughts.

" But this on one hand only. On the other hand, our book is something quite different ; it is—shall I say?—a kind of scientific composition, a scientific work told, it is true, in a simple incoherent everyday language accessible, by dint of familiar combinations, to the most varied classes of population who have neither the scientific training, nor the courage and desire, to learn what is going on beneath the surface of life.

" This book will touch upon complicated, and even perhaps too complicated, questions, remote from literature and unusual to the writer. Such questions, as for instance the search for one's lost youth, the restoration of health, of freshness of feeling, and so on, et cetera, et cetera.

" It will also touch upon problems of reorganization of all our life and the possibilities of that reorganization, of Capitalism and Socialism and the formation of ideology. Besides, we shall touch upon other no less vital questions taken in their highest meaning and in the light of the present day.

" Well, and if this is not a scientific work, if, let us say, the Academy of Sciences or, say, the Section of Scientific Workers, having come to an agreement with the Municipal Committee and the Writers' Union, will not find here any signs of a scientific work or, while finding such signs, will not regard the author as having sufficiently mastered the Marxist-Leninist conception, then, in such a case, this book could be designated by a more neutral, a more harmless so to speak, name, which would not annoy the eyes and ears of individual citizens and organizations. Let this book be called, say, an educational film. Let it be, say, such an educational film as we have had on the screen; ' The Abortion ', or say ' Why Does It Rain ? ' or ' How Silk Stockings Are Made ', or finally ' What Is the Difference Between a Man and a Beaver ? ' ; there are such films on great contemporary scientific and industrial subjects worthy of study. Just as in those films, we shall first have a scientific argument with various footnotes, and references about this and that, and all sorts of comments definitely clearing up the matter. And only after that the reader, slightly tired and dazed by other people's thoughts, will receive a portion of entertaining reading which will be a sort of visual illustration to the above thoughts and considerations."

In the following passage describing the Professor's treatment at the hands of medical men there is a touch of a deliberate parody of Tolstoy:

" For six months he underwent medical treatment.
He was prescribed bromide and strychnine, arsenic and
phitine. He was prescribed baths and enemas. He
was wrapped in wet towels and his body was pierced
with electricity. He was questioned whether he had
had any grave illnesses or whether he had been addicted
to any excesses as a child. They talked to him about
the complications of nervous ailments, heated his head
with blue light and even tried to hypnotize him, in
order to inspire him with bright thoughts about health.
And no one told him in simple and understandable
words how his illness could have originated and how to
fight it apart from pills and potions."

Here is an ironical picture of a happy Soviet marriage,
both husband and wife being enthusiastic Communists,
and for reasons of work living apart and meeting once in
five days :

" Lida, feeling a little sorry in her heart and at the
same time surprised by the haste with which he had
married, consented to wait a little, admitting that the
search for a flat, the removal and various domestic
affairs and troubles would unfavourably affect the
course of his work. And he praised her for her common
sense and political maturity, saying that he now realized
full well that he had made no mistake in choosing her,
and that, indeed, he would perhaps be unable to find
at present a better wife. And Lida, pleased with his
praises, looked at him with admiring eyes, saying that
she too, perhaps, could have no better husband. They
were happy in their own way, and in no hurry to
disturb their happiness by kisses and embraces."

In the description of the Professor's pastimes after his
final recuperation there is the same touch of irony :

" He ran about the garden and the park in his cellular
vest, he played volley-ball, he rowed, and soon it
was simply impossible to recognize him. And in the
autumn, having started his work, he told Lida, slightly

embarrassed, that he had enrolled in a shock-workers'
brigade and that he no longer had any political dis-
sensions with her. As to some trifles, he was, perhaps,
ready to look at them now in a somewhat different
way. Perhaps he was alluding to his circumvented old
age. Yes, he was out for a new and beautiful life, for
the new world in which all human feelings will be real
and genuine and not to be bought. Lida, clapping
enthusiastically her hands, said that she could not find
a better father.

" The professor's wife had bucked up too. She
refused to do the gymnastics, saying that for some
reason her legs were stiff, but then she walked a lot
about the garden carrying a cat in her hands. And
in the evening, putting on her yellow dressing-gown,
she would walk briskly about the rooms wishing good-
night to the inmates of the house—to her husband and
Lida, and Lida's husband when the latter, once in six
days, came to see them."

It is therefore simply remarkable and amazing to see
this new work of Zoshchenko taken quite seriously by
the Soviet press as an attempt to introduce science into
literature, to bring the two together. Several discussions
were organized on this subject with the participation of
some of the most eminent Soviet scientists, such as
Professor Yoffe and others, and nobody suggèsted that
Zoshchenko was pulling their legs.

7. Ilf and Petrov

In the works of Ilya Ilf and Evgeny Petrov (*Twelve Chairs,
The Little Golden Calf*) the everyday life of Soviet Russia
is subjected to a humorous, satirical treatment, together
with a slight touch of fantasy. The world of Soviet
gangsters, bootleggers, and unscrupulous Government
officials, gives the authors rich material for their gay
picaresque novels. *Twelve Chairs* (translated into English
under the title of *Diamonds to Sit On*) describes the

farcical adventures of a cunning and ingenious rogue, Ostap Bender, in search of some diamonds which their pre-revolutionary owner hid in one of twelve chairs. Bender reappears in their next book *The Little Golden Calf*, which, though quite as entertaining, has a decidedly more serious satirical angle and a neater and better balanced plot. In many respects Bender resembles Gogol's Chichikov, and both books, especially *The Little Golden Calf*, are strongly reminiscent of *Dead Souls*. Though seen through a grotesquely distorting mirror, it is a picture of everyday Soviet actuality that the two authors give us.

8. *Levin and Others*

Among the younger writers of everyday life describing the period of the Five-Year Plan and after it is possible to single out Boris Levin, the author of *There Lived Two Comrades* (1930) and *A Youth* (1933). The former, though without any literary distinction and rather carelessly written, gives a vivid picture of the life of the young Communist intelligentsia, their normal and intellectual doubts and collisions. Unable to throw off the burden of his past and to overcome his doubting, sceptical nature, one of the two " comrades ", a former White officer Debetz, ends by committing suicide. The novel contains a curious description of a periodical " purge " in a students' Communist nucleus, and in its absence of pretentiousness has an altogether engaging accent of truthfulness about it. The latter novel raises also some of the problems confronting an artist in Soviet Russia.

Everyday-life literature of these ten years is vast and manifold. To give even a partial list of it would be a hopeless task. Some works are, however, worth mentioning in addition to the authors discussed above. N. Ognev (real name Mikhail Rozanov, b. 1890) had a great success with his *Diary of a Communist Schoolboy* (1927) which gave a vivid and life-like picture of Soviet school life; it was followed by the *Diary of a Communist Undergraduate*, but this had less merit both as a literary work and as a picture of life. Student life and student morals form also the subject of Sergey Grigoryev's *The Mar-Mila Commune* (1927). The life of a small provincial town is graphically depicted in Sergey Zayaitsky's *Vegetable Marrows* (1928). This novel is especially interesting inasmuch as it touches upon that aspect of life which is rarely to be met with in Soviet literature, namely the religious and ecclesiastical life, and portrays the curious figure of a priest working in Soviet conditions. Nikolay Nikitin (b. 1897), one of the original " Serapions ", whose early work was closely akin to that of Pilnyak and Vsevolod Ivanov, but who also wrote some more neatly-constructed novels (*The Flight, The Spy*), gives in his *Crime of Kirik Rudenko* (1928) a sombre-coloured picture of the *moeurs* of the Young Communist League: drunken debauchery, rape and murder form an essential part.

CHAPTER V

1. *From the Proletkult to the Five-Year Plan and after*

THE problem of creating a special proletarian culture, and as one of its branches a special proletarian literature, occupied the revolutionary Communist Government of Russia from the very outset. It soon became a subject of fierce and violent discussions, different solutions, sometimes diametrically opposed, being put forth both by the political leaders of the Soviets and by men directly concerned with literature. On the whole, one can distinguish, up to 1932, three stages in the development of this problem, and to those three stages correspond three stages in the evolution of the proletarian literature itself which, roughly speaking, ran parallel to the general line of development of post-revolutionary Russian literature. But in each of the first two stages two conflicting tendencies manifested themselves and fought for supremacy ; it was only in the third stage that some kind of uniformity was attained. In the first stage, which coincided with what I call the transition period in the history of Soviet Russian literature, one of these conflicting tendencies was represented, by Futurism with its claim to speak on behalf of revolutionary proletarian art. The claim that failed to substantiate itself, as became especially apparent when the place of Futurism was to some extent taken by Imaginism and there began the so-called " café period " of literature. On the other hand stood the " Proletkult "

79

(an abbreviation of " Proletarian Culture "). This body
came into being at the very beginning of the Revolution
in 1918. Its leading spirit was a certain Bogdanov, one
of the theoreticians of Russian Marxism, who even before
the Revolution had concentrated his attention on the
problem of the proletarian culture. At the basis of
Bogdanov's theory of a specific proletarian culture lay
the thesis of three parallel and independent roads for the
working class towards Socialism. Next to the economic
and political road Bogdanov placed the cultural road—
the struggle for a proletarian culture. Moreover, he
insisted on exempting this struggle from the control of
the political mechanism of the Communist Party. Therein
lay the *raison d'être* of the Proletkult as a separate organization using its own methods. In the first year of the
Revolution the Proletkult displayed a feverish activity—
it published its own magazine called *The Proletarian
Culture*; it organized a multitude of literary and artistic
studios or training centres for workers, where the latter
were trained by bourgeois literary specialists and taught
how to write verse and stories; and it succeeded in
drawing into its sphere of influence fairly large con-
tingents of workers and peasants. With this Proletkult
movement was connected the first organized group of
proletarian writers, which called itself *Kuznitsa* (Smithy).
The principal nucleus and the most talented element in
this group was represented by several poets, for the most
part workmen (Gastev, Gerasimov, Kirilov, Kazin, Obradovich, Alexandrovsky and others), some of whom had
begun writing and publishing prior to the Revolution.
Yet, leaving aside the thematic element, the revolutionary
message of their poems, there was little that was specific-
ally proletarian in them. Their form, their technique,
their methods were derived from Symbolism, and only
slightly renovated by borrowings from Futurism and

Imaginism. As for the message of their poetry, it was naturally revolutionary. But in keeping with the general tone prevailing at the time, this revolutionary element was strongly tinged with romantic heroism and far removed from everyday realities. Some of these Smithy poets even created a special genre of revolutionary Cosmism, transposing revolutionary conceptions and industrial phraseology into the cosmic plane. They erred on the side of excesses, of hyperbolism, of grandiloquence ; they were guilty of some of the worst sins of Symbolism, the only difference being that the old Symbolist dishes were served up by them with a new revolutionary sauce, disguised in revolutionary terminology. This movement opened no new avenues for the advance of proletarian literature.

The period of the Proletkult was over by 1923. The Proletkult did not succeed in calling to life any real proletarian literature. And Bogdanov's idea of fighting for the proletarian culture independently of the political and economic organisms of the Communist Party, by means of literary and artistic training, met with disapproval on the part of the responsible Soviet leaders. Both Lenin and Trotsky condemned what became known as " Bogdanovism ". Looking back, the Communists now admit the good which Bogdanov and his Proletkult did in initiating workers and peasants to the cultural and artistic life, but on the whole they regarded the experiment as a failure. Towards 1923, the fundamental idea of Bogdanov, the idea of the necessity and expediency of a specific proletarian culture, was subjected to revision. There were Communists who disapproved of the idea of a special class culture of the proletariat. The most drastic expression of this negative view is to be found in the articles of Trotsky collected in his book *Literature and Revolution*. Here is what Trotsky wrote in his article on the relations between the bourgeois and the proletarian culture :

> " There can be no question of the creation of a new culture, that is of construction on a large historical scale during the period of dictatorship. The cultural reconstruction, which will begin when the need of the iron clutch of a dictatorship unparalleled in history will have disappeared, will not have a class character. This seems to lead to the conclusion that there is no proletarian culture, and that there never will be any. . . . Such terms as ' Proletarian literature ' and ' Proletarian culture ' are dangerous, because they erroneously compress the culture of the future into the narrow limits of the present day. They falsify perspectives, they violate proportions, they distort standards and they cultivate the arrogance of small circles which is most dangerous. . . ."

Bogdanov's theory of separate proletarian culture was somewhat vague and ambiguous in its attitude to the art of the past. But in any case it did not reject that art wholesale, it called upon proletarian artists to learn from the old masters and to make use of their achievements in the interests of the proletariat as the new ruling class. Lunacharsky, the first Soviet Commissar of Education, who played a prominent part during this first period of implanting proletarian culture, was particularly keen in insisting that the proletariat should learn from the bourgeoisie and preserve the values the latter had created.

With the revival of literature, which became marked after the end of the Civil War, the antagonism between the proletarian and non-proletarian literature reached a new and acute stage. The main part in that revival was played by non-proletarian and non-Communist writers who had, however, in one way or another, accepted the Revolution as a fact. They were the writers whom

Trotsky had nicknamed " Fellow-Travellers "—a name which stuck to them for many years and came to be widely used in Soviet literary terminology, in spite of its vagueness. Trotsky defined them as writers " who fail to grasp the Revolution in its entirety, its final Communist aim being alien to them." These Fellow-Travellers, who included most of the leading writers, such as Fedin, Leonov, Zoshchenko, and others, had from the very beginning their own literary organ in the shape of *Krasnaya Nov*, the first big Soviet monthly founded in 1921. Its editor, principal literary critic and general instigator was a man called Voronsky. He befriended the Fellow-Travellers as a literary movement and became their principal champion in Soviet literature. Voronsky with his *Krasnaya Nov* and the Fellow-Travellers were soon opposed by the group called *October*, which consisted of Communist writers and advocated proletarian purity in literature. From 1923 on, it began issuing its own periodical called *Na Postu* (*On Guard*). The " On-guardists " (" *napostovtsy* "), as they were called, took an intransigent attitude towards the Fellow-Travellers. They regarded the latter not as the painters and chroniclers of the Revolution, which Voronsky and some other Soviet critics represented them to be, but as its disfigurers and detractors. They spoke of the " rotten fabric " of the Fellow-Travellers' literary creation, of their attempt to build an æsthetic bridge between the past and the present. They were extremists, who believed in the necessity and possibility of creating immediately a new proletarian art. They insisted on a sound and clear ideology in proletarian literature, and proclaimed all political doubts as inadmissible. " A clear, firm and severely consistent Communist policy in art and literature will be the leading principle of our review," said the editorial manifesto of *On Guard*.

The ideas advocated by the " Onguardists " had much in common with Bogdanov's theory of proletarian art. But the methods they used were different. Whereas Bogdanov tried to emancipate all cultural work from the State apparatus, that is from the Communist Party, the " Onguardists ", on the contrary, wanted to make it completely subordinate to the Party, to utilize the latter's political and economic monopoly for fostering proletarian art and ruthlessly exterminating all overt and covert counter-revolutionary tendencies in literature. According to one Communist critic, they were out to win the game not through the superiority of their artistic creation, but thanks to the superior means of organization which the Communist Party had at its disposal. As the same critic (Vyacheslav Polonsky) figuratively put it, they wanted to open the doors of literature not with a key, but with a *passe-partout*. The main thesis of the *On Guard* group ran that " in a class society imaginative literature serves the objects of a definite class, and only through that class of the mankind." Hence there must be a sharp antithesis of proletarian and non-proletarian literature.

" The main criterion for estimating a literary current or a literary fact," ran the programme of the *October* group, " is to be found only in their social significance. Only that literature is socially useful in our days which educates the psychology and consciousness of the reader, and in the first place of the proletarian reader, towards the final tasks of the proletariat as the organizer of the Communist society, *i.e.* the proletarian literature. Any other literature encourages a revival of the bourgeois and petty-bourgeois ideology." This statement of the *October* group was directed against both the Fellow-Travellers and nearly all the old, so-called classic literature. Violent discussions arose, in the ranks of the Communist Party and in Soviet literature, round these drastically formulated theses. According to a Soviet critic, Russian literature had not witnessed such a fierce struggle for quite a long time. " People proferred against each other accusations which did not lead to judicial proceedings only because it was thought that in literary controversies everything was permissible. Fellow-writers treated each other as if they were class enemies. All those who took part in literature had to choose—for or against, that is with the ' Onguardists ', or with the ' capitulants ' as the ' On-guardists ' called their adversaries." The most prominent theoreticians of the extreme wing were the critics Lelevich, Gorbachev and Averbach. Of the older Marxist critics, Kogan, Fritsche and Olminsky, as well as the former leaders of the Proletkult movement, Lebedev-Polyansky and Pletnev, took side with the " Onguardists ", while not only Trotsky and Voronsky, but also Lunacharsky, Bukharin and Radek, as well as the writers of the *Smithy* group, were in the opposite camp. The decisive battle took place at a special conference convoked by the Press Department of the Central Committee of the Communist Party in May 1924. The " Onguardists " were defeated and a resolution was passed which served as material for a more detailed resolution officially confirmed by the Political Bureau of the Communist Party in 1925. This resolution laid down the main principles of the literary policy of the Soviet Government. It will be dealt with in greater detail in Chapter XIII ; suffice it to say here that the Political Bureau refused to recognize the supremacy of the proletarian literature as a fact and reaffirmed its previous policy of considerate attention to the Fellow-Travellers and non-proletarian elements. The result was a split in the ranks of the VAPP (Pan-Soviet Association of Proletarian Writers) and the foundation of a new review entitled *On Literary Guard*, with the critic

Averbach and the young novelist Libedinsky at its head.

The position established by the resolution of 1925, which gave the non-proletarian and non-Communist elements a certain elbow-room for creative work and resulted in a fresh crop of literary works, lasted till 1929, when, in connection with the Five-Year Plan, it was decided to bring to an end that compromise with the " bourgeois " literature, and there was a sharp swing to the Left. Certain Communist critics insisted now on comprising art and literature within the scope of the Five-Year Plan. " Literature should help the Five-Year Plan," was the slogan of these critics, who met with the approval of the official party organs. These groups soon saw themselves masters of the situation in the literary sphere and laid their hands on the editorial boards of reviews and magazines. Their headquarters was the Russian Association of Proletarian Writers (so-called RAPP), and their chief exponent the critic Averbach.

Literature is lagging behind, said Averbach in one of his articles. It must participate in the general movement. The depiction of the Five-Year Plan is the one and only problem of Soviet literature, proclaimed the organ of RAPP in 1930. Writers were not to remain indifferent or neutral, but to fight on the literary front.

Thus began the third period, that of forcible proletarianization of literature. A wide campaign was set on foot. Averbach and his lieutenants began to exercise an almost unlimited censorship. Writers who did not unhesitatingly profess their allegiance to Communism were violently attacked. Those who did not comply with the demand for topical themes were labelled counter-revolutionary. The result was that even Fellow-Travellers began writing Five-Year Plan novels. Voronsky, Polonsky and other moderate Communist critics, who had patronized the Fellow-Travellers, were dismissed and some of them banished. Writers were also encouraged to fulfil useful functions, to pay visits to new industrial centres and collectivized farms and describe them afterwards, and a vast literature of Five-Year Plan descriptive sketches sprang up.

What did the proletarian literature produce during its second and third periods ? Before answering this question we must see what were the sources of proletarian fiction, its pre-history so to speak, and what influences it had undergone. Four principal elements went to its making. First, the old Realist writers of the *Znanie* group with Gorky at their head ; secondly, the so-called Populist literature ; thirdly, a small group of pre-revolutionary writers of proletarian extraction who wrote proletarian works ; and fourthly, a group of young writers which joined the ranks of proletarian literature after the Revolution and underwent the influence of modern Russian prose.

Of the *Znanie* writers, Gorky and Serafimovich were the two who exercised the greatest influence on the proletarian literature. But Gorky never was, strictly speaking, a proletarian writer, and his influence was above all personal. The same applies to Serafimovich before the Revolution. But his post-revolutionary work, and especially his novel *The Iron Torrent*, describing the Civil War in the South of Russia in the orthodox Communist spirit, entitles him to be regarded as a proletarian writer. Yet he did not exercise any real influence on the younger generation of proletarian literature. The outward form of his works—his orthodox descriptive Realism —was too old-fashioned.

More numerous were in the proletarian literature the Populist or semi-Populist elements. Writers of this type had formerly published their stories about villages, town

87

slums, or the life of proletarian brain-workers, in the Radical monthlies, especially in *Russkoe Bogatstvo*, which was the bulwark of Populism in Russian literature. At the beginning of the Revolution these writers were strongly represented in the *Smithy*. They had much in common with the peasant literature and also some points in common with the first Fellow-Travellers. Their most typical representative was Alexander Neverov (1886–1923), the author of *Tashkent*. Finally, a few writers from the working class who used to write stories of workers' life permeated with revolutionary ideology—like Bibik, Lyashko, Bakhmetyev—went on writing after the Revolution. Among them Bibik (b. 1878) still enjoys great popularity with workmen, and his novels are in great demand in workers' lending libraries.

2. Gladkov

To the same group may be said to have belonged also Fedor Gladkov (b. 1883) whose name is now well known even outside Russia. His literary career began before the Revolution, but his pre-revolutionary works attracted no attention: they did not rise above the average and rather low level of the Populist magazine fiction.

One of his earliest post-revolutionary works, the novel *The Fiery Steed* (1926), was a mixture of revolutionary ideology with a cheap imitation of Dostoevsky in the presentation of morbid amorous psychology. Even in his later works Gladkov could not quite rid himself of this latter tendency. His literary reputation was made in 1924 when his *Cement* was published. This was an outstanding event in the history of proletarian literature. On the general plane of development it was a fact parallel and similar to the novels of Leonov and Fedin, it signified a transition from purely descriptive works to a work of grand style, of great psychological and social significance. So it was meant to be at least. Soviet critics have praised Gladkov's novel beyond all measure; it was translated into several foreign languages and had a great success outside Russia, its sales reaching an unheard-of figure of 500,000 copies. On its title-page one could see the inscription reminding of the good old times when certain books used to be approved by the Ministry of Education or some other competent authority and recommended for inclusion in school libraries. On Gladkov's *Cement* we read: " Recommended by the Head Department of Political Education for mass public libraries. Admitted by the State Learned Council into school libraries."

It is certainly an interesting novel. Its subject is the transition of Communism from the Civil War, which had disorganized and disintegrated the life of the country, to the period of peaceful but unromantic reconstruction, and more particularly the resumption of work on a big cement factory (it is easy enough to recognize that the action of the novel takes place in Novorossiysk with its well-known cement works). Parallel with this we are shown the disintegration of the old framework of life, the dissolution of family relations, the birth of a new morality and new ways of life. The novel is full of enthusiasm for revolutionary construction, but one cannot reproach Gladkov for looking at the things through rosy spectacles. He does not shirk from branding that which he dislikes or disapproves in the conditions which prevailed at the time, even though he does so within the reasonable limits of so-called " self-criticism ", so popular once among the Communists.

The principal characters of the novel are the workman Gleb Chumalov and his wife Dasha. Chumalov has spent nearly the whole of the Civil War at the front and has been decorated with the Order of the Red

Banner; he now plays the main part in restarting the cement factory. A good Communist, he has not yet succeeded in overcoming in himself some of the old moral instincts and "prejudices". This conflict between his political and his moral nature is one of the psychological pivots of the novel. His wife Dasha, on the other hand, personifies a new "ideal" emancipated woman with whom political convictions and moral views go hand in glove. But as is often the case with "ideal" characters, she is the least convincing, the least plausible, the most wooden in the whole novel, and some of the incidents in her career touch on melodrama. There are in the novel many well-drawn secondary characters, simple unsophisticated workmen, disillusioned Communists from the intelligentsia who after the ascetic period of War Communism believe that the country is going to the dogs because of the iniquities of the newly introduced NEP. But in the depiction of the two principal characters, especially in the dialogues, there are many notes that sound false and unnatural. The novel is certainly too long-drawn, especially as there is no real plot and the author does not succeed in making the story of the resumption of work at the cement factory sufficiently exciting. Yet as a document, as a picture of conditions of life and of moods prevailing in the Communist Party at a certain period in its history, it is valuable. Its weakest point as a work of art is its style, an irritating mixture of old-fashioned Realism with ill-digested modernist devices. Gladkov, who came originally from the school of Gorky and the Populists, has been influenced by the technical methods of the modern Russian prose. But he has not assimilated them properly, he seems to parade, to flaunt them, and most of his descriptions and dialogues make an irritating reading—they are affected, unnatural. This defect is not so noticeable in translations which probably accounts for the success of Gladkov's novel outside Russia, but in the original it spoils the effect of the whole. As a literary work Gladkov's *Cement* is no doubt greatly inferior to the novels of Fedin, Leonov and Kaverin. The colossal figure of its sales need not deceive us, if we remember the official recommendation ; its enormous success was certainly to a great extent artificial ; on the other hand, it was due to the fact that here was the first modern proletarian novel written on a grand scale, going beyond pure description, attempting psychological analysis and yet quite orthodox from the political, ideological point of view. It came as an answer to the demands of the *On Guard* group, and they used it as a proof of the existence of proletarian literature. Gladkov's second big novel *Power*, dealing with the Five-Year Plan, failed to arouse the same response.

3. *Panferov*

Another colossal success of the proletarian literature was Fedor Panferov's (b. 1896) *Bruski*, of which three volumes have appeared so far (the third volume appearing after a few years' interval), but of which there are more to come ; it is the kind of work that can go on indefinitely. Its official success after the appearance of the first and second volumes (1930) was still greater than that of Gladkov's *Cement*, the figure of its sales reached 600,000 —a record figure for Russia. It was the most discussed book of the year and the Soviet press was unanimous in praising it. Every literary group—and the number of these groups was at the time quite considerable—seemed to hail Panferov as its spokesman. Officially he stood nearest to the group of Libedinsky—*On Literary Guard*. *Bruski* is a book about the collectivized village. It can hardly be called a novel. It is a long-winded, tedious chronicle whose object is to show the advantages of collective farming over individual tenure of land. There is no plot. It is rather a collection of crude sketches, ill-constructed and written in the most primitive natural- istic manner. Its descriptions are tiresome in their minuteness. There is a multitude of characters, but Panferov has no real gift of characterization and most of his characters do not come to life. There is no unifying purpose behind the novel and it falls into a series of disjointed descriptive scenes.

The subject is, as I said, the benefits of collectivization. " Bruski " is the name of an estate on the shores of the Volga. Its owner died before the Revolution and it was on the point of falling into the hands of a rich peasant, a kulak, but after the Revolution was seized by the village paupers who organized a collective farm on it. The principal organizer and the principal character of the book is a certain Kiril Zhdarkin. Demobilized after the War he comes back to his native village and is struck by his fellow-villagers' poverty and ignorance. He takes to his farming with great zeal, but gradually comes to realize that if he limits his interests to it he might himself degenerate into a kulak. He gives up his farm, goes to town and becomes a factory workman. Here the revelation comes to him—he understands that the only salvation for the peasants lies in doing away with individual owner- ship of land and organizing farming on collective lines. Zhdarkin returns to his village and organizes a commune in Bruski. Panferov's novel contains much valuable documentary material. Speaking of the third volume of his novel, at which he was then working, Panferov said in an interview that he had more to learn from technical books on peat industry than from either Tolstoy or Dostoevsky. Although biassed, his novel is not grossly one-sided ; it portrays faithfully and minutely the class conflicts and differentiation among the peasants. But its artistic value is nil—it is only a vast heap of undigested prime material. This seems to have been realized at the time of its appearance even by Panferov's most ardent admirers, yet it did not prevent the great majority of Soviet critics from proclaiming it a classical work of Soviet literature. Lunacharsky even went to the length of saying that he saw no artistic shortcomings in it. But . . . *habent sua fata libelli.* This very book, Panferov's *Bruski,* which had been praised to the skies in 1930, when everyone had to admire it and those who did not had to hide their real feelings, became in 1934 the principal target for attacks on the part of some of the leading Soviet writers and critics. The signal was given by Gorky himself, who in his recent campaign for improving the quality of Soviet literature (of which more in Chapter XIV) hit upon Panferov's *Bruski* as a glaring example of the low standard of Soviet literature. A violent controversy ensued, in which Gorky was opposed by Serafimovich and some others, but the great majority of Soviet writers, including some *bona fide* Communists and proletarians, encouraged by the fact that the criticism had come from such a high and influential quarter, took Gorky's side, and a veritable hurricane of criticism and even abuse swept down upon Panferov and his novel. In 1930 it was fashionable to swear by *Bruski* ; in 1934 it became more fashionable to swear at it. Pages and pages of Soviet literary periodicals were once more devoted to the discussion of *Bruski,* but its purport had totally changed.

4. *Libedinsky*

The young Communist novelist Yury Libedinsky (b. 1898), who in 1923-24 was one of the principal leaders of the *On Guard* group, was the first to begin the realistic period in young proletarian literature. His first novel (*A Week*) appeared in 1922. It was followed by *To-Morrow* and *The Commissars*. He is a Realist without any claim to originality. His style is simple and direct, his construction ordinary, his language rather colourless. The centre of gravity in his works is always in their contents, not in their form. He was one of the first writers to paint the Communist Party and its work from inside, and that is why his first novel was so warmly welcomed by official Soviet criticism. His heroes are for the most part Communists, not the upper leading layer of the Communist Party, nor the working mass, but its middle stratum, the average Communists either coming from the intelligentsia or those who from being simple workmen have worked their way into it. Libedinsky shows them in their social and political work rather than in their purely personal affairs and preoccupations. These latter interest him inasmuch as they are connected with and affected by that political work. In *A Week*, of which the subject is a peasant rising, we see the Communists engaged in suppressing it, the inner workings of the Extraordinary Commission, a meeting of the Provincial Executive Committee. In *The Commissars*, which depicts the critical period of transition to the New Economic Policy, there is a picture of a typical party meeting. In *To-Morrow* there is a description of a Communist demonstration and of propaganda among the workers. In those early novels of his Libedinsky appears as the novelist of the Communist Party *par excellence*. He does not raise any big problems, nor does he go very deep in the psychological analysis of his characters. Usually they are very numerous and sometimes there is no central outstanding character to hold the author's attention and the characterization is somewhat fleeting and superficial. But the characters themselves are sufficiently varied; and Libedinsky shows us a wide range of types of Communists. Although both *A Week* and *The Commissars* are quite in accord with the official general line of party policy, Libedinsky does not err on the side of undue optimism and conceal various shortcomings in the inner life and organization of the Communist Party. In *To-Morrow*, however, he deviated both from that general line and from his own strictly realistic manner. It was written at the time when the Communists in Russia fully expected a Communist revolution to break out in Germany. Libedinsky took it for granted and chose that revolution and its repercussion in Russia, then entangled in the contradictions of the New Economic Policy, for the subject of his novel. He was blamed for pessimism and pusillanimity, for linking up the destinies of Russian Communism with a problematic revolution in Germany. The style of that novel also differed from the usual style of Libedinsky : it was much more hurried and dynamic. The easy-flowing, rounded sentences gave way to short, rapid, staccato ones.

In Libedinsky's later novels the social and political element, in keeping with the general line of development of Soviet literature, is being gradually ousted by the psychological analysis, by problems of morals, of sex. His *Birth of a Hero* (1931) has been attacked for portraying a prominent member of the Communist Party from the point of view of his love affairs.

5. *Fadeyev*

Still more prominent is the psychological element in the works of such a writer as Alexander Fadeyev (b. 1901), especially in his two great novels *The Rout* and *The Last of the Udegeyans.*

Though not strictly speaking of proletarian extraction

(his father was a surgeon's assistant in the Far East), Fadeyev is regarded as one of the leading lights of proletarian literature and is one of the principal theoreticians of its latest phase. He has contributed many articles on literary matters to Soviet periodicals and taken part in numerous literary discussions that have been going on of late in Soviet Russia.

His early stories, *The Flood* (1923) and *Against the Current* (1925) were not as yet characterized by that Tolstoyan psychologism which he has consciously·adopted in his later works. *The Flood* is still an immature story and from the point of view of construction rather a failure. *Against the Current* shows great improvement as compared with *The Flood*, its narrative is terse and dynamic, but the presentation of characters is almost purely external. The theme of both stories, as in the great majority of Soviet fiction, is the struggle of the old and the new. But Fadeyev deals only with single episodes in that struggle. The subject of his next novel *The Rout* (1927),[1] which at once placed him in the ranks of the leading Soviet novelists, is also only an episode. Moreover, it is a subject that has more than once been treated before in Soviet literature (in the works of Vsevolod Ivanov, Shishkov, Seyfullina)—the guerrilla warfare in the Far East. But while those writers treated it purely descriptively or lyrically, Fadeyev approaches it in a quite different spirit, in the spirit of Tolstoyan psychologism ; he shows us different members of his guerrilla detachment from the point of view of their psychology, their inner experience. The characters of the novel are living, many-sided people, each having his or her individuality. Quite apart from the resemblance in manner this work of Fadeyev carries on the tradition of humaneness, of sympathetic attitude to one's own characters, so strongly

[1] Translated into English as *Nineteen*.

rooted in the nineteenth century literature. As regards its form, it is obviously influenced by Tolstoy. Fadeyev consciously emulates the great Russian novelist, not only in his method of psychological analysis, but also in composition and style. In general there has been of late in the proletarian literature a strong tendency to learn from the classics of the Russian novel and to imitate them. This is encouraged by Gorky. Gladkov has more than once spoken of the necessity for the proletarian writers to learn from the old masters of literature, especially the Russians. And Fadeyev has consciously chosen Tolstoy for his master. Some over-enthusiastic Soviet critics have gone so far as to place Fadeyev on a level with Tolstoy. Fadeyev, they say, has mastered Tolstoy's technique, but at the same time succeeded in enriching it with something of his own, in giving it the proletarian orientation. To believe these critics, he is nothing short of a proletarian Tolstoy. This is, of course, a gross exaggeration, and other more sober and cautious Communist critics refuse to see in Fadeyev anything more than a gifted disciple of Tolstoy.

Fadeyev's latest work, *The Last of the Udegeyans*, the publication of which was begun in 1928 and has not yet been completed, is a work of vast social and psychological scope. It is no longer an episode, but a whole world, with a great multitude of different characters. The action takes place again in the Far East of Russia, among a curious small tribe of Udegeyans, and Fadeyev displays in its treatment a thorough knowledge and understanding of local conditions and psychology. One of the principal characters is a romantically minded young boy from a bourgeois family, who is trying to discover the meaning and justification of life.

6. Sholokhov

The "back to Tolstoy" tendency in the proletarian and semi-proletarian literature is not accidental. It is very pronounced in the case of Mikhail Sholokhov (b. 1900), who is often regarded as a proletarian writer, although he is a Don Cossack by origin. His novel *The Still Don* (in English translation *And Quiet Flows the Don*) is a vast epic of Cossack life before and during the War and the Revolution. Three volumes have appeared so far and the fourth is in preparation. In manner it consciously follows the path of Tolstoy, especially in the War episodes. It is a kind of a Cossack *War and Peace* with Revolution added to it. It was Sholokhov's first great work and on its appearance it was greeted by several people, including Gorky, as a tremendous literary event. Both in Russia and elsewhere it met with enormous success. It is essentially a realistic novel, a book brimful with life. Sholokhov is particularly good where he describes the Cossacks, their life, their part in the War. His language is racy, full of original imagery. Much weaker is his portrayal of everything that is non-Cossack. And it is here that one feels what a distance there is between Sholokhov and Tolstoy, how narrow after all is Sholokhov's range, how weak his grip on the material he has to deal with. For *The Still Don* is also an historical novel in the same sense as *War and Peace*, inasmuch as alongside a multitude of lifelike fictitious characters it introduces a number of real-life historical personages like Generals Kornilov, Alexeyev, Kaledin, the Bolshevik Podtelkov and other chief actors in the Civil War drama. This historical background is never lost sight of by the author, and he often quotes actual documents of the period, especially in the parts dealing with War and Revolution. What distinguishes him from Tolstoy is the absence of a deliberate anti-historical bias which constitutes the kernel of Tolstoy's philosophy of history. Sholokhov avoids philosophizing about history and is certainly right in doing so. On the whole Sholokhov is truthful and objective in his historical presentation. He does not paint all his Reds as heroes and all his Whites as villains. One of the most idealized figures is Bunchuk, the Communist agitator and afterwards leader of the machine-gun detachment, who ends by being shot by the Cossacks gone over to the anti-Bolsheviks. But even he is shown to us, towards the end of his career, primarily as a man with all human weaknesses, and not as a paragon of Communist virtues. Nor does Sholokhov try to deny heroism to the opponents of Bolshevism, and there is a touch of grandeur in the description of the death of the Cossack officer Kalmykov at the hands of Bunchuk. The Cossack Ataman Kaledin, who sided with the leaders of the White Army, is also portrayed without the usual hostility, and there is a sense of real tragedy in the chapters of the book dealing with him, especially in the scene preceding his suicide. Nor is it accidental that Sholokhov makes his principal character, Grigory Melekhov, for whom he seems to feel a particular sympathy, change sides and desert the Reds for the Whites : in the third volume we see him actually fighting the Bolsheviks. But it is quite possible that in the volume to come he will once more turn Red, for in a recent interview Sholokhov gave utterance to his dissatisfaction with the first three volumes.

Sholokhov's second big novel, *The Upturned Soil*, promises to be almost as long and bulky. Two volumes of it have so far appeared, but more are to come. It deals with the collectivization of farming in the Cossack regions and belongs to the Five-Year Plan literature (see Chapter VII).

7. Malashkin and others

In the works of Sergey Malashkin (b. 1890) (*The Moon on the Right-Hand Side, Two Wars and Two Peaces, The Work of Evlampy Zavalishin about a People's Commissar and about Our Time, The Slut*) the psychological element is also very pronounced, but it proceeds from Dostoevsky and not from Tolstoy. Malashkin has a distinct predilection for morbid subjects. His construction is also more complicated and capricious and there is always freshness and originality in the way he unfolds his plot. His *Moon on the Right-Hand Side*, which appeared in 1927, was one of the sensational successes of the year and went through several impressions. Its subject was the demoralization of certain elements of the Communist Youth (*Komsomol*) and in some of its outspoken scenes and descriptions it beat all the records of Russian pornographic literature established before tne Revolution by Artsybashev and Anatoly Kamensky. All the same it is an interesting work, revealing Malashkin as a writer of uneven but undoubted talent. Still more interesting is his story *A Sick Man*, portraying a Bolshevik Commissar who, after killing a man, goes mad and ends by committing suicide. His madness, his nightmares and hallucinations, and the intermingling of reality and fantasy, are described with remarkable power. Malashkin's later and longer works, however, did not justify the expectations engendered by those early stories.

Another proletarian writer of social - psychological tendencies is Tarasov-Rodionov. His *Chocolate* is an interesting and piquant work, though full of affectation. His vast historical epic of the Revolution *The Heavy Steps* is rather a failure.

Among the proletarian writers we may also include the

late Dmitry Furmanov (1891–1926), the author of the half-truthful, half-imaginative chronicles of the Civil War written by one who took an active part in it (*Chapaev, The Revolt*).

In the works of Arosev (b. 1890), who is also known as a Soviet diplomat (*Recent Days, Memoirs of Terenty Zabyty, The Chairman*), are portrayed the experiences of the Communist leaders during the Civil War. In his novel *From the Yellow River* (1926) he dwells on some of the darker aspects of life of the Communist Party.

Sergey Semenov (b. 1893), first attracted general attention by his *Hunger* (1922) which contained a very realistic description of the starving workmen in revolutionary Leningrad. It has even been translated into several foreign languages and compared to Hamsun's work of the same name. His later novel *Natalya Tarpova* (1927), illustrating the psychology of the new Communist working woman, is very long and rather tedious.

Alexey Demidov's (1883–1934) *The Whirlwind* had the hardly deserved distinction of being translated into French and German : it is an average, well-intentioned, proletarian novel.

The young proletarian writer Leonid Grabar specializes in his novels (*Lakhudrin Lane, On the Bricks, The Commune of Eight*, and others) in portraying different types of Communists gone astray. The demoralization of a Communist is also the subject of Nikiforov's novel *Either-Or*. Some of the younger proletarian writers (Tveryak, M. Karpov, Korobov) concentrate their attention on the class strife in the village.

It is impossible, however, to mention even by name the host of second- and third-rate proletarian writers producing chiefly descriptive stories and sketches of little artistic merit : they are legion.

The place apart among the proletarian prose writers

belongs to Artem Vesely (b. 1900). In many respects he is diametrically opposed to the dominant tendency in proletarian literature, the tendency towards classical Realism. His manner is akin to that dynamic prose which proceeds from Bely and Pilnyak and which prevailed in the first period of the Revolution. He is a thorough ornamentalist. His rhythmic prose often reads like poetry, his rhythms are quick and breathless, his composition broken, plot is altogether absent. He has a predilection for the colourful, picturesque speech of the peasants and sailors, and in this he is also akin to the writers of the " skaz " manner. Like Pilnyak, he is fond of painting the elemental aspects of the Revolution, its " sound and fury ". His most interesting and effective works written in this manner are *Russia Washed in Blood* (first published in complete book form in 1932) and *The Native Land* (1927). He also wrote an interesting historical novel, in the same style, called *Gulyay-Pole*.

To sum up : Trotsky was right in thinking that the Soviet Government would be unable to create a special proletarian literature. The proletarian writers are now tending more and more towards the general line of Soviet Russian literature. And inasmuch as the Fellow-Travellers began to carry out the " social commands " and write production novels, even the thematic difference between the proletarian and non-proletarian, Communist and non-Communist, literature tended to disappear. The effect of the latest developments in Soviet literature comprised under the name of " Socialist Realism " has been to produce a certain levelling process, to do away with individual distinctions of style and manner. It is the same effect which the Plan in general has had in other domains of life.

CHAPTER VI

YURY OLESHA AND HIS "ENVY"

1927 saw the appearance of one of the most remarkable and arresting works in the whole of Soviet
literature. Its title was *Envy*, and its author Yury Olesha.
Born in 1899 in Odessa, he was until 1927 quite unknown,
his literary activities being almost exclusively confined
to daily journalism. *Envy* enabled him to establish his
literary reputation at one stroke. It became in fact
one of the most discussed books of the year. The main
reason of its success was its novelty and freshness. It
stood out distinctly from the general mass of Soviet
literary production : it was new and fresh not only in
its treatment of a theme that in itself was by no means
new to Soviet literature, but also in its form, in its
manner. The theme was that of the conflict of the old
and the new in the Revolution, common to so many
Soviet writers, from Leonov and Fedin down to the
third-rate proletarian novelists ; but instead of treating
it in terms of actual episodes and concrete social or
political problems in the life of Soviet Russia, Olesha
raised it to a higher philosophical plane, gave it a deeper
human and universal meaning. That is precisely what
Soviet literature, even in its best specimens, most lacks :
the Revolution has beyond any doubt narrowed down
the range of one of the profoundest and most significant
literatures in the world, has reduced and circumscribed
its themes, has deprived it of that universal appeal which
the works of Tolstoy and Dostoevsky possessed. This
in spite of the fact that, owing to the Revolution, it has

been enriched with a vast stock of concrete and novel life experience. Although directly connected with Russian revolutionary realities, Olesha's novel has also that wider universal appeal. But that in itself would not have been sufficient to ensure his *Envy* the success it obtained. Another reason for it lay in the freshness of its form, in the novelty and originality of Olesha's perception and presentation of the outside world. Not only has he a keen vision of the world, especially of its material externals, but he is endowed with a special gift for presenting it in striking and unexpected images, for making us see it as it were with new eyes. There is in his prose that quality which is possessed by the poetry of Pasternak, the greatest of Soviet Russian poets, a freshness of outlook and vision combined with freshness and felicity of expression. Olesha's art has been designated by some critics as eclectic, as a combination of different methods, of Realism, Symbolism and Impressionism. In a way that is true. But Olesha's combination of styles and methods is not purely mechanical, it is an organic blend which results in something quite new and original. If he is a Realist— and in a way he is—his Realism is unlike that of any other Realist in Soviet Russian literature, for it is modified by the impressionistic manner and projected against a symbolical background. Olesha's art has some points in common with that literary movement which was known as Expressionism and was at one time very popular in Germany, though in the end it did not produce anything of great· or permanent value. His style is dynamic, nervous but laconic ; it harmonizes well with the tempo of modern urban life—*Envy* is essentially an urban novel. Olesha has a keen vision and sense of material objects and a faculty of presenting his psychological observations in terms of those objects. Comparisons are his favourite device and they are nearly always striking and felicitous.

He enjoys mirror-like, reflecting effects, which make the ordinary habitual things look new and fresh. His hero speaks of the childlike character of his perceptions, of looking at the world through the wrong end of the binoculars. Images like these occur frequently in *Envy*:

> " The blue and pink world of the room is moving round and round in the mother-of-pearl lens of the button."
> " Clouds were racing in the sky and in the window-panes, and in the window-panes their paths became confused."
> " The day was closing down its shop. A Gypsy in a blue waistcoat, with painted cheeks and beard, was carrying, raised on his shoulder, a clean brass basin. The day was receding on the Gypsy's shoulder. The disc of the basin was bright and blind. The Gypsy was walking slowly, the basin shook slightly and the day was turning in the disc."

One of the important episodes of the novel, the encounter between Ivan Babichev and Kavalerov, takes place while Kavalerov is looking into a street-mirror and enjoying the novel, backward view of things. These instances could be multiplied if necessary, and it is obvious that Olesha's insistence on this mirror-like perception of things is not accidental. There are also characteristic, sudden and capricious, transitions from the realistic plane to the fantastic, the borderline between reality and dreams being obliterated, especially in the case of the two " romantic " characters of the novel, Kavalerov and Ivan Babichev. But the rich verbal texture of Olesha's novel is counterbalanced by the relative simplicity of plot and construction, there is even a certain algebraic baldness in the symbolical presentation of the clash between the old and the new world. The novel is quite short—in this it is rather un-Russian— and there are only six characters, of whom three stand

for the old world and three for the new. The latter are :
Andrey Babichev, a director of a Soviet Food Industry
Trust, an embodiment of physical fitness and moral and
intellectual self-contentment ; his adopted son Volodya
Makarov, a young Communist and a noted football
player, who in the eyes of Andrey personifies the new
world, a rather narrow-minded young man with a strongly
pronounced cult of machinery ; and Valya, a young girl
of sixteen, the daughter of Babichev's brother Ivan, who
combines the charms of femininity with love of physical
culture and modernity ; she and Volodya are in love.
On the side of the old world we find Andrey's brother
Ivan (Valya's father), a gifted but good-for-nothing
Romantic cast-out by the Revolution, who calls himself
" the last dreamer on earth " and wants to organize a
" conspiracy of feelings " ; Kavalerov, another dreamer
and Romantic of a somewhat different kind, with a
touch of Dostoevsky's " Man from the Underworld " in
him, and a strong inclination to buffoonery ; and Anichka
Prokopovich, an abject widow of over fifty, an incarnation
of mean vulgarity.

The book falls, from the formal point of view, into
two parts : in the first, the narrative is conducted in the
name of Kavalerov, in the second by the author himself.
At the beginning we see Kavalerov as inmate of Andrey
Babichev's house and, in his own description, the latter's
buffoon. Babichev has one night picked him up in the
street, when he was lying quite drunk on the pavement,
and taken him to his house. He did so out of sentimental memory for his temporarily absent adopted son.
Kavalerov, who is twenty-seven years old, is an individualist feeling out of harmony with his age and with the
order of things in Russia ; he dreams of personal fame,
of some way of bequeathing his name to the posterity,
but there is no such way open to him in Communist

Russia. His overwhelming emotion is envy; he is literally consumed by it. He envies and hates Andrey Babichev, the more so as he realizes that he is after all more clever, more intelligent, even perhaps more gifted in his inefficiency, than the prosperous and self-satisfied director of the Food Trust, the " sausage-maker ", as Kavalerov contemptuously calls him. Kavalerov also describes him as " a perfect male individual ". The contrast between the two is shown very strikingly, in Kavalerov's own words, in the very first pages of the book. One day, after having been snubbed by Andrey, Kavalerov decides to leave him and return to his former life. He writes a long sarcastic letter to Babichev, giving vent to his hate for him and to his sense of superiority, as well as to his belief that Volodya, whom Babichev seems to cherish so much, is in the same position too, and will not return. When he takes that letter to Babichev's flat, Volodya arrives. Kavalerov sees that Volodya is quite at home there, that his position is completely different from his own. He realizes his foolishness and wants to take back his letter, but instead of it picks up Volodya's letter to Babichev about himself and learns the real motives behind Babichev's hospitality. This intensifies his dislike of the " sausage-maker ". During the ensuing wanderings about town he comes across Babichev's brother Ivan, who is also out to fight Andrey and dreams of organizing " the last parade of human feelings " banished from the new world. He is, however, at a loss to find people incarnating those obsolete feelings. But Kavalerov is one of them—he is a perfect embodiment of envy. There is, of course, some point in Olesha choosing envy, the meanest of all human sentiments, as the corner-stone of this conspiracy of feelings. But other and better feelings must take part in it too. There is a touch of Dostoevsky in the speeches which Babichev holds before Kavalerov

in the squalid public houses of Moscow, as well as in
his long peroration before the investigating magistrate
upon his arrest by the Ogpu, when he explains the
purport of his conspiracy of feelings. The element of
fantastic unreality hovering over the whole book and
even over its ideal personages, who look more like
allegorical puppets out of a Hoffmann's tale, is enhanced
by the episode with the remarkable all-round machine
invented by Ivan Babichev, which he intends to use for
the eternal dishonour of the modern mechanized world,
and among other things for the destruction of his brother's
"Sixpence", a gigantic model industrialized kitchen
which is to provide cheap and hygienic meals for the
population of Moscow. He gives his machine the "most
romantic" name of Ophelia. In the imaginary speech
which Ivan Babichev holds at the impending inauguration
of "Sixpence", he thus addresses his brother who is its
creator :

> "Do not call upon us. Don't beckon to us, don't
> tempt us—what can you offer us instead of our capacity
> to love, to hate, to hope, to cry, to pity, and to forgive ?
> Here is a pillow. Our coat-of-arms. Our banner."

He raises his voice against that industrialized and
socialized monstrous kitchen in the name of family life,
of traditional home, and brandishes his pillow as its
symbolical expression. He speaks of turning figures,
which his brother worships, into flowers. It is true that
in the end Kavalerov and Ivan have to resign, to capitulate,
their conspiracy of feelings falls flat and they have to
admit that not all the feelings have been done away with
and discarded by those whom they fight. This becomes
especially clear to Kavalerov on the example of Valya
and her love for Volodya, for he too is romantically in
love with her and imagines himself her knight protector
in the struggle which he engages against the usurping

designs of Andrey and Volodya. In the person of Valya, Olesha seems to have endeavoured to reconcile the world of feelings with that of new realities. In spite of her earthliness (as seen especially in the scene of the football match and of the sporting exercises in the courtyard of her house) Valya is drawn in romantically ethereal colours. The sentimental romantic pink is the colour accompaniment of her theme. Behind the exterior of a modern Soviet girl interested in sport and physical culture, the author emphasizes her " ewig-weibliche " substance. The key to her personality is in Kavalerov's sentence addressed to her: " You have swept past me like a branch full of flowers and leaves," even though both Valya herself, and Andrey and Volodya laugh at it. Kavalerov's surrender and ultimate realization of his failure lead to his utter downfall and degradation: he returns into the bosom of Anichka Prokopovich. And the same fate awaits Ivan Babichev. The new thus triumphs over the old. But it is hardly possible to say that in *Envy* Olesha has solved the problem which he raised, the problem of the place of certain human feelings and values in the Communist society of present-day Russia. In the conflict between the individual and the collective, between Romanticism and Realism, the apparent triumph is on the side of the collective and of Realism, and Olesha seems to accept it as a fact, as something that has to be taken for granted. But he hardly hides his sympathy for the Romantic individualists or at least his pity for them, as he endows them, and more especially Kavalerov, with such qualities as intelligence, perspicacity, sensibility and artistic flair which give them a definite advantage over their adversaries. From the point of view of the novel's ideas and of the attitude which the Soviet critics took to Olesha's work, it is very important that we see Andrey Babichev almost entirely through Kavalerov's envious eyes. Even in the

second part, not written in Kavalerov's name, the idea
the reader has formed of Andrey is not shattered. In
fact, if Olesha wanted to denounce Kavalerov and Ivan
Babichev as obsolete, degenerate, sentimental Romantics
of the world irrevocably gone, and to oppose to them the
animal healthiness of Andrey and Volodya's machine-
like cleanliness and sportingness (there is a very good
and vivid description of a football match between Russians
and Germans of which Volodya is the hero) he has not
succeeded in making the reader really sympathize with
these representatives of the new world and look upon
them as ideal models of new men. Olesha has endowed
Kavalerov with so many of his own gifts, with such
keenness of vision and felicity of expression that the
reader is inevitably tempted to see Andrey and Volodya
as *he* sees them, to lay stress on their negative characteristics. This explains the contradictory reception which
Olesha's novel had in the Soviet press, and the heated
discussions which it provoked. At first the attention of
the critics was drawn to the negative side of the picture,
to the painting of the romantic and individualistic enemies
of the collective socialized society, who oppose it in the
name of persecuted human feelings. In the words of one
of the Communist critics, Olesha's greatest merit was in
showing so clearly what the enemies of the Soviet régime
were like, whence they came, and what weapons they
used. This negative side of the picture eclipsed the
positive, and it was not realized until later that the
representatives of the new world, whom the author
opposes to Ivan Babichev and Kavalerov, did not look
particularly attractive, that there was a fine touch of
satire in the portrayal of both Andrey with his " Sixpence "
and sausages, and Volodya with his naïve cult of machinery
and sport, that both were shown as if they were completely
devoid of all *political* interests. The Soviet critics began

to perceive a serious flaw and danger in Olesha's conception, even to suspect that at heart he was in sympathy with Kavalerov and Ivan, who come forth as champions of human feelings.

That the problem which occupied Olesha in *Envy* continued to interest and torment him is proved by the volume of stories which appeared in 1929 under the title *Love*. Two of the three stories in this volume—*Love* and *Liompa*—represent a continuation and development of some of the motifs of *Envy*. In *Love* we see a young Marxist, Shuvalov, who falls in love with a young girl and whose vision of the world is suddenly completely transformed by love. Not only does he see the world differently from the way in which he used to see it before, but he sees it otherwise than as he wants to see it. From a sober Marxian Realist he becomes a Romantic. That transformation is effected by love. His counterpart is a certain unnamed colour-blind " citizen in a black hat ", whose vision of the world corresponds to reality except for his colour-blindness. There is a moment when Shuvalov gets into such despair that he is ready to change places with his counterpart, is prepared to give up the romantic green colour of nature which has become the dominant colour of his world, and to see pears as inedible blue objects. But ultimately the feelings triumph, and Shuvalov remains with his love and his green vision of the world.

In *Liompa* Olesha takes up an allied motif of his *Envy*, that of the relations between man and the objects that surround him. In *Envy* he drew a contrast in this respect between Andrey Babichev and Kavalerov.

" Things don't like me," says Kavalerov himself. " Furniture tries to play nasty tricks upon me. Once some varnished angle literally bit me. My relations with the blankets are always complicated. The soup served to me never cools. If some silly thing, a coin or a stud, falls from the table it usually rolls under a piece of furniture which is hard to move. I crawl on the floor and, lifting my head, I see the sideboard laugh." To these hostile relations between Kavalerov and things, is opposed the latter's attitude to Andrey Babichev. Things like him and he has an easy way with them, they ply themselves to his wishes, whether it is his braces or something else. This motif is developed in *Liompa* into a whole story. It is the story of a sick man who gradually loses his hold on things and is betrayed by them. Lying on his sick-bed, the hero of *Liompa* meditates.

> " I thought that the outside world did not exist, I thought that the world would cease to exist when I ceased to exist. But here . . . I see how everything turns away from me while I am still alive. After all, I still exist. Why then don't things exist ? I thought that my brain had given them shape, weight and colour, but here they are gone from me, and only their names—useless names having lost their masters—are swarming in my mind."

To this nominalist perception of the world by the dying Ponomarev, is opposed that of a small child :

> " Objects rushed to meet him. He smiled to them without knowing a single name. He would go away and the sumptuous train of objects would flap after him."

Since 1929 Olesha has published a book of stories entitled the *Cherry Stone* (1930) which does not add any new elements to his artistic personality. The title-story once more develops one of the motifs of *Envy*. He has also written several plays, among others a dramatic version of *Envy* under the title *The Conspiracy of Feelings*.

In 1928 Olesha wrote a very good novel for children, *The Three Fat Men*, in which he also displays his inherent

Romanticism. The concluding lines of *The Three Fat Men* touch in fact on Olesha's favourite theme of emotions :

> "The three fat men ordered to me : 'Take out the boy's heart and make an iron heart instead.' I refused to. I said that one should not deprive a man of his human heart ; that no other heart—neither of iron nor of ice nor of gold—must be given to man instead of the simple, real, human heart."

This theme of the "simple, real, human heart" seems to occupy Olesha in his latest work, a "play for the cinema" called *A Strict Youth*. This skeleton of a play, almost masque-like in the symbolical delineation of characters, deals with the problems of "qualitative inequality" in a Communist society and of new morality. Its principal characters are a Young Communist, a celebrated "bourgeois" surgeon and his wife. The Young Communist, who has a great admiration for culture, science, and beauty, devises a new code of "Young-Communist" morality based on such qualities as modesty, truthfulness, generosity, hatred of egotism and even sentimentality ("To a certain extent, so that one should love not only marches, but waltzes too.") In the somewhat guarded criticisms of this work which have appeared in the Soviet Press one perceives a note of distrust—Olesha's conception of morality is said to be non-Communist and savouring of Idealism. It is in fact this undercurrent of Idealism which makes Olesha's work sound out of tune with certain important tendencies of Soviet literature.

CHAPTER VII

IN 1929, as I have already pointed out, there was a sharp change in the policy of the Soviet Government (or, which amounts to the same, of the Russian Communist Party) towards literature. This change was connected with the Five-Year Plan drawn up by the Soviet Government with a view to the industrialization of Russia and collectivization of her agriculture. It was decided to enrol literature in the service of the Five-Year Plan. The compromise with the " bourgeois " or Fellow-Travellers' literature, concluded in 1925, was over. Pressure was to be exercised on the Fellow-Travellers. They were also to make their contribution to the Five-Year Plan in literature. The leading rôle in literary matters was to belong henceforth to purely Communist and proletarian organizations. The result of all this was, in the first place, the appearance of a special literature of the Five-Year Plan, of semi-imaginative descriptive sketches. Not only proletarian writers, but the Fellow-Travellers like Kaverin and others, and the old writers like Alexey Tolstoy, contributed to this literature. Writers formed shock brigades, and paid visits to great industrial constructions and collectivized farms, in order to describe them afterwards.

But apart from this purely descriptive literature, which had not produced any works of outstanding merit (the best is, perhaps, Kaverin's *Prologue*), the Five-Year Plan gave birth to a number of bigger and more ambitious works belonging to imaginative literature in the proper sense. Such are Pilnyak's *The Volga Flows Into the Caspian Sea*, Leonov's *Sot* and *Skutarevsky*, Marietta Shaginyan's *Hydrocentral*, Gladkov's *Power*, Sholokhov's *The Upturned Soil*, Kataev's *Forward, Oh Time!* and Fedin's as yet unfinished *The Rape of Europe* which, however, seems more than likely to outgrow the limits of a Five-Year Plan novel in the strict sense.

In point of time Pilnyak's and Leonov's novels were the first. Both these authors remain in fact true to themselves in their Five-Year Plan novels and are far from carrying out the official task of glorifying the Plan. This is especially so in the case of Pilnyak's novel *The Volga Flows Into the Caspian Sea* (1930). The real, inner significance of this novel and its ultimate conclusion are almost diametrically opposed to the task of extolling the Five-Year Plan. It is true that the Five-Year Plan forms the background of the book and is its outward subject. But it is not by chance that Pilnyak conceives his industrial construction in a somewhat fantastic and hyperbolical aspect. The novel tells of the building of a gigantic dam at Kolomna, not far from Moscow, the ultimate object of which is to turn back the stream of Volga and to make the river Moscow navigable for big Volga steamers. There is a great deal of purely technical matter, and the book opens with a long passage which would be more in its place in a text-book of hydraulics. One of the chapters has even attached to it, by way of supplement, a complete issue of the wall-newspaper published at the Kolomstroy, which the readers are kindly asked to read but which from the point of view of the narrative can just as well be left unread. There is a long description of the organization and life of a modern Communist workers' city at Kolomstroy, and among the characters of the novel there are some ideal Communists like Sadykov, who from a simple workman rose to become an engineer. But the main brunt of Pilnyak's art is brought to bear, not upon the glorification of the technical achievements of the Five-Year Plan, or upon the portrayal of ideal characters, but upon the clash of the old and the new world, which Pilnyak shows us against the background of the Five-Year Plan. As an artist he focuses his attention on the portrayal of the forces which the old world arrays in this battle. Side by side with the Russia of the Five-Year Plan he shows us the half-Asiatic, pre-Petrine Russia, full of vestiges of the seventeenth century. This Russia is symbolized in the ever-recurring image of the tower of Marina Mniszek in Kolomna running through the whole book. Pilnyak develops here his favourite idea of the essential duality of Russia as reflected in her historical destinies : she has a Janus-like double face turned simultaneously towards West and East, towards Europe and Asia. It is the same idea which we meet in the novels of Andrey Bely who had exercised such a great influence on Pilnyak. The style and manner of *Volga* have been strongly influenced by Bely : the confused, intersected composition, the musical construction with recurring and intercrossing themes and motives, and numerous neologisms—such are its main stylistic features.

But Pilnyak does not confine himself to a symbolical demonstration of the essential duality of modern Russia. With a picturesqueness which reminds one of Gogol, he depicts, next to the model Communist city of Kolomstroy, built according to Plan, the little town of old Kolomna dragging on its everlasting life—sluggish, sleepy and inert, with the symbolical pigs revelling in the mud in the middle of the streets, as in Gogol's Mirgorod.

And side by side with the simple and straightforward Communist Sadykov, who of all his characters has the least interest for him, Pilnyak shows us a number of

other, more complex characters. Some of them are outspoken enemies of the Soviet régime, counter-revolutionaries and wreckers (there is a wreckers' conspiracy in the
novel—a fashionable and topical subject in all Five-Year
Plan literature) like the old Skudrin, the brothers
Bezdetnov and the engineer Poltorak who propounds
some curious nationalist ideas vaguely akin to Pilnyak's
own romantically-tinged revolutionary Nationalism. There
is Laszlo, a Communist, but of a quite different psychological pattern from Sadykov: in him the " nadryv " à la
Dostoevsky outweighs his Communism. There is also
an old crank, Professor Poletika, a mathematician of
world-wide reputation, who is the author of the fantastic
idea underlying the construction of the Kolomstroy. He
is a conscientious servant of the Soviet régime, but in
spite of that he is also a fossil, a remnant of the past,
a typical intellectual of the old pattern. His daughter
Lyubov is more of an orthodox Communist, but in her
case, too, there is a conflict between political views and
personal feelings. Finally, there is a character who is the
nearest and dearest to Pilnyak's heart—Ivan Ozhogov,
old Skudrin's brother, half workman and half tramp,
who introduces himself as " a Communist of 1919 ".
He personifies that romantic and heroic period of the
Revolution, the period of impetuous revolt, when the
elemental forces were let loose and swept like a gale across
Russia. It is the period which Pilnyak loves best, which
he has glorified in his earlier novels. It ended in 1921
with the New Economic Policy and gave way to a period
of unromantic reconstruction and solution of everyday
problems. Pilnyak's Ozhogov is not the only representative of this type of romantic Communists in Soviet
literature. In Gladkov's *Cement* two ardent Communists,
the young girl Mekhova and the typical intellectual
Sergey Ivagin, are possessed by the same mood, the same

pining after the epoch of War Communism. But *Cement* was written long before *Volga*, and the period it describes is much nearer in time to the period of revolutionary romanticism—it is the very beginning of NEP, the period of semi-bourgeois entrenchment of the Soviet Government when, from the Communist point of view, such moods were much more comprehensible and pardonable. Nevertheless Gladkov obviously disapproves of his revolutionary Romantics. In the case of Pilnyak this revolutionary romanticism is opposed not to the semi-bourgeois realism of the New Economic Policy, but to the everyday realism of the Five-Year Plan, of Socialist reconstruction. His Ozhogov is, from the point of view of an orthodox Communist, a downright anachronism, and yet Pilnyak does not conceal his sympathy for him. Ozhogov embodies for him the best elements in the Revolution, and his death in the waters of the river when the new dam is opened symbolizes the death of those best elements.

Pilnyak wanted to glorify the Five-Year Plan and to remove the bad impression which his previous novel (*Mahogany*, see Chapter VIII) had produced in official circles (some episodes of that novel, published originally in Berlin and proclaimed counter-revolutionary, have reappeared in *Volga* in a new setting), but the result has been rather a new counter-revolutionary work: the Five-Year Plan was served under a sauce of Romanticism strongly seasoned with Dostoevsky.

Leonov's *Sot* (1931), which appeared almost simultaneously with Pilnyak's *Volga*, was also meant to describe the carrying out of the Five-Year Plan, but as in the case of Pilnyak's novel, its centre of gravity proved to be not in that, but in an attempt to give a wide and deep psychological analysis of the conflict between the old and the new in present-day Russia. The Five-Year Plan is here also only a background, though in the general conception of the novel it plays a more prominent part. The subject is the construction of a huge paper-mill on a small river among the dense forests of North-Eastern Russia, in a remote, out-of-the-way corner, barely touched by civilization. Hence the title of the novel: Sot is the name of that forest river. In carrying out this industrial construction the Bolsheviks have to overcome the resistance not only of nature but of the forces of the old world. This old world, which the Communists have to fight, is represented in Leonov's novel by three elements. First, the large mass of the peasants who instinctively stick to the old and fear the new. Secondly, the monks of a desolate forest monastery, who partly inspire and direct the peasants in their anti-Communist activities. Among these monks there is also a young former officer of the White Army, an active ideological adversary of Communism and the Soviet régime with strange and confused ideas of his own; he preaches the coming of a new Attila, the destruction of the mechanized modern civilization and the resurrection of the human soul. But strange and confused as these ideas are, one feels that to a certain extent Leonov sympathizes with them, that there is something in common between those ideas and the anti-urban utterances of Semen in *The Badgers* and Zavarikhin in *The Thief*. Finally, there are some individual enemies of the Soviet Government, wreckers like the old specialist Renne.

The principal Communist in the novel, Uvadyev, combines rationalism with revolutionary instincts. " Everything is all right, everything is always all right in the world—he says—but there are still some things in it that need blowing up."

Among the several types of specialists in the novel, the most interesting is the old engineer Burago, a man of great culture and intelligence, who is whole-heartedly

serving the Communist Government but hardly shares its
ideas and mentality : the worm of culture is eating away
at his heart. But he believes in Russia as a country
where everything is possible. He tries to explain his
attitude to Uvadyev :

> "I build factories, Uvadyev, and it doesn't matter
> to me what you want to call it. I shall be with you to
> the end but do not ask from me more than I can.
> Socialism ? . . . Yes. . . . I don't know. But in this
> country everything is possible, including the resur-
> rection of the dead. . . . A new Adam is coming to
> give names to creatures that existed before him. And
> he rejoices. I can't write poetry, my business is to
> build. The philosophy of super-phosphate, you will
> say ? No, I am not Renne, I am still, let me see, how
> old . . .—he ponders and moves pensively his fingers.—
> No, after all, I am old : I remember the French
> Revolution and Icarus's disaster, and the tower of
> Babel, and the vertebrae of the Neanderthal man in some
> French museum."

Ultimately Socialism triumphs, the technical and
political obstacles in the way of construction are removed,
Vissarion (the officer who preaches the coming of Attila)
is murdered, Renne shoots himself after an unsuccessful
attempt to wreck the construction. But Leonov's interest
lies not so much in the depiction of technical triumphs
and attainments of the Five-Year Plan as in the complex
social psychology against the background of which he
weaves just as complex a pattern of individual psychology.
In the centre of it stands the figure of Susanna, Renne's
daughter, a convinced Communist, with whom several
characters of the novel, including Uvadyev, are in love.
As usual, Leonov is primarily interested in man and the
workings of man's soul, not in the evolution of the Five-
Year Plan as such.

Leonov's other novel dealing with the Five-Year Plan—

Skutarevsky (1932)—is of a more primitive pattern. The social command is more felt in it, and inasmuch as Leonov introduced here the fashionable and topical element of industrial sabotage organized from abroad (the topical character of this element in Leonov's novel is underlined by the fact that Leonov chose for the subject of his novel the wrecking activities in electrical industry— a few months before the trial of the British engineers in Moscow), its plot has acquired a melodramatic touch. Leonov's interest is, however, again primarily psychological. In the middle of the novel stands the figure of Professor Skutarevsky, a world-wide celebrity in the sphere of electricity. Himself of proletarian origin (this fact is duly emphasized), he is vaguely in sympathy with the Soviet Government and works for it as the head of a special Institute of High Frequencies created at Lenin's own wish and engaged in some secret research work (there is in the novel a curious description of Skutarevsky's interview with Lenin in the Kremlin). Nevertheless Skutarevsky's mentality is in many respects alien to the official mentality of Communism and the author is out to show—not perhaps very convincingly— how he gradually rallies to the Communist Party. A certain part in this transformation of Skutarevsky is played by his discovery of his son's implication in the electrical wreckers' plot. As usual with Leonov, the end of the novel appears to be truncated; he breaks it off on the threshold of some new stage in Skutarevsky's life-story.

Round this interesting but not very convincing central character are grouped several others. There are among them a couple of good Communists: Skutarevsky's pupil Cherimov, who knows no spiritual or ideological doubts, for whom everything in life is geometrically clear and simple; the young Communist girl Zhenia, a typical

" *komsomolka* " with whom Skutarevsky has a strange abortive love affair—one of the least successful characters in the book ; and the workman Butylkin, as straightforward a Communist as Cherimov, but more simple and unsophisticated. Among the sheep of the novel may also be included Cherimov's uncle Matvey Nikeich, in the past a bathkeeper by profession, who, from a typical petit-bourgeois instinct with the prejudices of the old régime, is all of a sudden transformed into a zealous, active Communist. Half-way between the sheep and the goats stands Skutarevsky's brother Fedor, an artist, the best-drawn and the most real character in the novel, full of complexities and contradictions ; towards the end of the novel he also seems to repent his former vagaries and take the righteous path of assisting the Socialist construction—he goes away to work as a painter at some factory in the North-East of Russia. The reverse side of the picture, the old world, is represented by a group of wreckers. Here we find Skutarevsky's brother-in-law Petrygin and Petrygin's father-in-law Zhistarev who, though not actually appearing in the novel, is directing the wreckers' activities from abroad, from a place near Paris ; and a prominent part is played in the novel by his symbolical portrait once painted by Fedor Skutarevsky. Here too we find Skutarevsky's son, Arseny, who ends by becoming disappointed in his anti-Soviet work and kills himself. As in *The Badgers* and *Sot*, the social conflict portrayed by Leonov is heightened and intensified by being transposed into the family plane too. Skutarevsky's assistant, the old Gedeonov, and a former art connoisseur and now a small broker and all-round rascal, Shtruf, complete this group. All these people are portrayed with Leonov's customary gift of characterization and his usual literary mastery, but somehow he fails to unravel and show us the real motives that actuate them. The whole story of the wrecking plot sounds rather melodramatic and artificial.

Compared with Leonov's and Pilnyak's novels, the Five-Year Plan novels of Gladkov (*Power*) and Mme. Shaginyan (*Hydrocentral*) have little literary value. They are much more orthodox, and full of technical matter which makes rather tiresome reading.

In Kataev's *Forward, Oh Time!* the production element also prevails over the psychological analysis, but it is fresher than Gladkov's or Shaginyan's novels and on the whole better literature. As distinct from the novels of Pilnyak and Leonov, the Five-Year Plan element is here devoid of the fantastic fictitious character. Kataev describes one of the real Soviet industrial constructions, the gigantic Coke-Chemical Combine at Magnitogorsck. He deliberately introduces into his novel the element of reality and prefers to call it a chronicle. And while the wall-newspaper in Pilnyak's *Volga* was a mere literary trick somewhat reminiscent of the art of those Cubists who used three-dimensional objects in the composition of their pictures, the fact that Kataev includes in his chronicle a long article from one of the Soviet papers about the production of high-grade concrete has an altogether different meaning, and there is every reason to believe that the article is authentic. In general there is a great deal of purely technical stuff in Kataev's novel. It also differs from the novels of Pilnyak and Leonov in that it is pervaded with real enthusiasm, whether sincere or affected, for Socialist construction, with that somewhat naïve Americanism, that cult of machinery bordering on fetishism, which is characteristic of a recent stage of Russian Communism. Pilnyak and Leonov deal in the first place with man and the complex intellectual and sentimental problems which confront him. Even with Shaginyan and Gladkov in their Five-Year Plan novels, human personality plays a great part in spite of the abundance of technical matter. In Kataev's latest novel technical problems are brought to the forefront and made the real subject of the novel : men are only servants of technique. The subject is the beating of the world record of concrete-mixing by an enthusiastic brigade of Magnitogorsk workers. The action of the novel takes place within one day. Round this subject Kataev has stringed up a great number of varied characters drawn up vividly but somewhat superficially, without any deep psychological probing. The description of how the brigade of one Ishchenko, under the supervision of the young Communist engineer Margulies, beats the record of concrete-mixing set up by the workers of Kharkov, is full of vividness and dynamism and reads as a description of some exciting sporting contest. The whole novel, with its quick cinematographic tempo, its constantly shifting scenes, and great variety of characters, bears traces of the influence of the American writer, Dos Passos, who at present enjoys great popularity in Soviet Russia. The wreckers, who had become almost a fixture in the Five-Year Plan literature, are absent from Kataev's novel, and this is rather a refreshing feature. By comparison with Leonov and Pilnyak, Kataev has a tendency to represent things in a much more optimistic light. One does not feel in his novel that sharp antagonism, outward and inward, between the old and the new which runs through the whole of Soviet literature, even through the works that are written by command or through such works as Panferov's *Bruski*. It is significant that to the Social-ist enthusiasm and zeal of his 100-per-cent. Com-munists, Kataev opposes chiefly the philosophy of an American industrial magnate who visits Magnitogorsk as a guest and tourist. This American industrialist lacks faith in exactly the thing which Russian Communists

have come to believe in with the zeal of converts—
in machinery, in an ever increasingly mechanized
civilization. He sees the salvation of mankind in a
return to God and Nature. It may be only a clever
subterfuge on the part of Kataev to put these unpopular
ideas into the mouth of a foreign capitalist, but among
his Russians a sceptical note is sounded only by the old
professional engineer Nalbandov; and even he is an
opportunist, who easily adapts himself to all conditions and
circumstances, rather than an active enemy of the Soviet.
And only one of the workers, Sayenko, a drunkard and
gambler, is shown as a negative character and a counter-
revolutionary at heart ; all the others are full of Socialist
enthusiasm and willing to sacrifice their interests to the
common cause, even though sometimes there is in their
behaviour an admixture of personal egoistic considerations.
Here and there, there is a slight touch of satire, but in
this respect Kataev's latest novel cannot be compared to his
Embezzlers, and one feels that he must have deliberately
blunted the point of his satire. The satirical vein comes
out especially in the conversations between the American
millionaire and Nalbandov, where the author treads on
safe ground.

A different aspect of the Five-Year Plan is treated in
Sholokhov's novel *The Upturned Soil*. Written in a
much simpler and less picturesque style than his vast
Cossack epic, it gives a striking and powerful picture of
the compulsory collectivization of peasant farms in the
Don Cossack Region and of the Cossacks' overt and covert
resistance to it, their slaughtering of their cattle, etc.
The novel does not open any new vistas before Soviet
literature. But as a picture of contemporary Russia it is
of great interest and great documentary value, especially
as it is written with the maximum of objectivity admissible
under the present conditions. There is nothing in

Sholokhov's novel of the spirit of official optimism which pervades Kataev's novel. Here the conflict of the old and the new, of the peasant inborn psychology of ownership and the doctrine of Communism, is shown in all its acuteness and reality. The majority of the characters are Cossacks and there are some well-drawn portraits of different types. The only outsider is a Leningrad workman Davydov who is sent by the Party with a view to accelerating and intensifying the collectivization campaign and whose proletarian and Communist mentality is shown in striking contrast to that of the Cossacks.

CHAPTER VIII

" COUNTER-REVOLUTIONARY " TENDENCIES IN
SOVIET LITERATURE

1. The " neo-bourgeois " and " kulak " spirit
in Literature

THERE is, of course, no such thing as counter-revolutionary literature in Soviet Russia. The preliminary censorship introduced since 1922 sees to that. Under the existing conditions openly counter-revolutionary works, even if they are written, cannot see the light of day. Such was the case of Zamyatin's novel *We*. Even at the height of the liberal policy towards literature —in 1925 and after the reform of April 1932—the Communist Party continued to proclaim its intention to fight all manifestations of the counter-revolutionary spirit in literature. But if there is no such thing as openly counter-revolutionary literature, anti-revolutionary tendencies in Soviet literature do, or at least did, exist. They assume different forms and are expressed with various degrees of concentration.

In this chapter I do not propose to examine all the manifestations of such tendencies ; some of them have been dealt with in other chapters. We will be concerned here only with their more typical and systematic expressions.

Until a few years ago the Soviet critics used to regard a large category of writers as representing " neo-bourgeois " tendencies. In his book, *Contemporary Russian Literature*, the critic, Gorbachev, includes in this category such writers as Alexey Tolstoy, Zamyatin, Ehrenburg, Bulgakov, and a group of peasant novelists and poets. I do not propose to follow Gorbachev's example. In 1934 it is futile to speak of Alexey Tolstoy and Ehrenburg as " counter-revolutionary " writers, even though neither of them may be really quite in harmony with the Revolution. On the other hand, " counter-revolutionary " tendencies can be easily detected in such writers as Olesha, Kaverin and Pasternak. In what follows I propose to deal only with writers, or works, the " counter-revolutionary " nature of which was of more than passing importance. This is obvious in the case of Zamyatin whose novel *We* was banned in Russia. The same applies to Pilnyak's *Mahogany*, which does not mean, of course, that Pilnyak's work as a whole is to be treated as anti-revolutionary (its " disharmonious " notes are, however, quite obvious, especially in *The Volga Flows Into the Caspian Sea*, which is closely related to *Mahogany*). There is still less reason to regard Sergey Budantsev as a " counter-revolutionary " writer. His first novel *The Revolt* had nothing anti-revolutionary in it. But his *Tale of the Sufferings of Mind* came at a moment when the extra-literary tutelage over literature was particularly strong, and it was therefore taken as representing the worst bourgeois and counter-revolutionary tendencies. Under the régime of the Five-Year Plan Budantsev dared to raise the eternal problems of life and death, and ignore those of Socialist construction. Bulgakov's case is somewhat similar to that of Zamyatin. His novel, *The White Guard*, and still more its dramatic version, *Days of the Turbins*, and his satirical stories of Soviet life earned him the name of an " inside *émigré* ", and there was a time when he was practically reduced to silence.

Finally, there is a whole group of peasant poets and novelists whom the orthodox Communist critics often accuse of counter-revolutionary " *kulak* " tendencies, of being the mouthpieces of the peasant-bourgeois psychology of ownership. I do not intend to deal separately with these writers, but will shortly characterize them here. The most prominent among them are the poet Nikolay Klyuev (b. 1887) and Sergey Klychkov, poet and novelist. Both were writing before the Revolution and can be regarded as the elder representatives of that line which was continued in the poetry of Sergey Esenin. Though real peasants and drawing their inspiration from the village life, both were connected with the Symbolist movement, Klyuev more especially with the mystical and religious current in it, Klychkov with the ethnographical. Both are genuine poets. (Alexander Blok had a very high opinion of Klyuev's poetry.) Klyuev hails from the extreme North of Russia, and reflects the severe beauty of its nature and the austere character of its religiousness. Klychkov paints the gentler and mellower landscapes of Central Russia and the fairylike romance of its folk-lore. This folk-lore element is very strong both in his poetry and his novels. Klyuev's poetry remained fundamentally religious even after the Revolution. Like Esenin he accepted the Revolution messianically as the self-revelation of " wooden " peasant Russia. But its industrial aspect abhorred him. He severely condemned Esenin for his poems of the period of *Tavern Moscow*, and himself continued to sing that old patriarchal Russia from which Esenin took farewell in that poem. Klychkov, who as a poet was less powerful and original than Klyuev, turned his attention after the Revolution to fiction. His village novels, especially *The Sugar German* and *The Prattler of Chertukhino*, were delightful in their freshness, the raciness of their peasant diction and their naïvely charming imagery inspired by the Russian folk-lore. Even the orthodox Communist critics had to admit their literary qualities, while strongly censuring Klychkov for his " *kulak* " tendencies, for his glorification of the age-long patriarchal customs of the Russian countryside and for his incurable Romanticism.

2. *Zamyatin's " We "*

One of the most striking manifestations of the " counter-revolutionary " tendencies in Soviet literature is Zamyatin's novel *We* written in 1922–24, the publication of which was not allowed in Russia and which has therefore never appeared in the original ; it exists only in English, French, and Czech translations. The English translation was published in New York in 1925. There is not a word in the whole novel about present-day Russia or the Soviet régime, for it is a Utopian novel and its action takes place in the twenty-sixth. century. But this is how the *Soviet Literary Encyclopedia*, published by the Communist Academy in Moscow, estimates the political significance of Zamyatin's novel :

> " While fully defending the capitalist order of things, Zamyatin has produced in his novel *We* a mean libel on the Socialist future. He is in favour of a Revolution, but of an . . . infinite Revolution. . . . Zamyatin is for a universal revolution, because he does not believe in the social revolution, because he does not want it, because it spells the doom of his class. . . . Zamyatin's theories are no more than a disguise for a very matter-of-fact and quite comprehensible pining of the bourgeoisie after the economic prosperity which it has lost, and for its hatred of those who have deprived it of that prosperity. Expressing the psycho-ideology of that social group which is being swept off the historical scene, Zamyatin's art acquires, parallel with the development of our Socialist reconstruction, a more and more counter-revolutionary tendency."

So much for the orthodox Marxist critic, a certain comrade Lunin, in his article on Zamyatin in the semi-official Soviet Encyclopedia.

We is a novel that stands apart from anything else in Russian literature. It combines the methods of scientific romance somewhat in the manner of H. G. Wells—Zamyatin knows Wells's work thoroughly and in 1922 wrote a study of him—with some typical aspects of the Russian problem novel and with a trenchant political satire. The nearest thing to it in modern European literature is Aldous Huxley's *Brave New World*, although the two books are far apart in spirit because Zamyatin, with his rather strong leaning to primitivism, is more or less free from Huxley's eighteenth-century rationalism. Yet not only the general idea and presentation, but even some minor details, reveal a very striking resemblance between the two works (Zamyatin's novel was written nearly ten years and published in English five years before Huxley's).

In *We*, we are transported into the twenty-sixth century, into a perfect modern, standardized State which has no name, but is called simply " The Single State ", and whose citizens have no names, but are known by their numbers. In this Zamyatin goes even one better than Huxley: the latter was unable, I think, to withstand the temptation of displaying his wit and ingeniousness in the choice of his names. In general there is more English *couleur locale* and topical humour in Huxley's novel and more universality in Zamyatin's. All the citizens of Zamyatin's State wear identical grey-blue uniforms (the novel was written long before the widespread and almost universal vogue for coloured shirts !) with badges bearing their numbers. They are ruled by the Benefactor (Huxley's " World-Controller "), and their life is scientifically regulated down to the minutest details. Everything is mechanized and standardized in the Single State,

though not quite to the same extent as in Huxley's
Utopia : Zamyatin's men of the future have not yet
learned to procreate new human beings by means of
artificial hatching, or at any rate Zamyatin does not go
into details about it ; but love is mechanized too, and
though promiscuity is its principle, it is, so to speak,
" distributed "—special pink counterfoil tickets being
issued for its use—and confined to certain fixed hours,
just as every " number " of the Single State has at his
disposal a few " personal " hours a day, when he is off
duty, as it were, though even then he is not free to do
as he likes, for there is no freedom in the Single
State [1] :

> " Freedom and crime are as closely connected, as,
> if you like, the motion of an aeroplane and its speed.
> . . . If man's freedom is nil, he commits no crimes.
> So much is obvious "—

thus runs one of the principles of the Single State.
Freedom and happiness are in fact incompatible :

> ". . . Happiness without freedom or freedom without
> happiness—there is no alternative. Those fools [the
> men of old] chose freedom and naturally for centuries
> they yearned for chains. That is what human misery
> lay in : they yearned for chains. . . ."

The " personal hour " of the citizens of the Single
State is accordingly subordinated to the same mathe-
matically precise rules as the rest of their life :

> " The personal hour which followed lunch [all food
> in the Single State is, by the way, chemical—a synthetic
> product of oil] became as a rule the hour of supple-
> mentary walk. As usual the Musical Factory per-
> formed through all its loudspeakers the anthem of the
> Single State. The numbers, hundreds thousands of

---

[1] I was unable to procure in London the American edition of *We*, and the
quotations that follow are a re-translation from the French.

numbers, in bluish unifs, with a golden badge on their dress showing the national number of each, walked in regular ranks by fours. . . ."

Straight line is the symbol of the Single State—" it is grand, precise and wise, the wisest of all lines." In Huxley we find a *pendant* to it, when he speaks of " the geometrical symbol of triumphant human purpose."

To look after the numbers' morals and behaviour—mathematical morals and mathematical behaviour though they are—there are special guardians whose chief task is to spy upon the numbers and who are assisted in this by the voluntary zeal of the well-intentioned numbers. To the law-abiding citizens of the Single State these guardians appear as their guardian angels and the character in whose name the book is written remarks with pointed unconscious irony :

" It is extraordinary to discover the number of things of which the Ancients [he means, of course, men of the twentieth century] dreamed and which we have realized."

It is obvious that in this institution of guardians the Communist Government should see a satire of certain of its own methods.

The narrative is conducted in the name of one of the chief mathematicians of the Single State—the most privi-leged category of its citizens—No. D-503, who is ter-minating the construction of a new gigantic flying-machine called *Integral* which will enable the Single State to establish regular communications with other planets. He writes " Notes ", as he calls them, for the benefit of the inhabitants of those other planets. But as he writes them they become something quite different from what he intended them to be, and we are made to assist at a complicated psychological process taking place inside him. Roughly speaking, it may be described as a return to the ancient human psychology, to the individual consciousness. He is discovered to possess a soul, which according to the conceptions of the Single State is regarded as an incurable disease: "numbers" are supposed to have no soul and no individual consciousness. "No offence is so heinous as unorthodoxy of behaviour"— is one of its principles. But soon it turns out that he is no exception, that "something is rotten in the Kingdom of Denmark."

The psychological transformation of "D-503" is a result of his chance meeting with a woman—No. I-330 —who fascinates him and with whom he soon falls in love in the way one is not supposed to fall in love in the Single State (until then "D-503" had normal pink-ticket relations with another woman, "O-90"). He first meets "I" in the street, then sees her at a lecture on the comparative merits of ancient and modern music at which she illustrates "ancient" music by playing "a funny instrument called piano", dressed in the way the "Ancients" used to dress, that is according to twentieth-century fashion. She exercises a strange influence on him and he obeys her oddest whims, even though his sense of duty as one of the numbers of the Single State is revolted thereby. She takes him to the "Ancient House", which is preserved on the outskirts of the State as an historical monument, as an illustration of the way the Ancients used to live before the introduction of modern transparent glass houses where everything, with the sole exception of the sexual functions, is performed in everybody's sight (during the "sexual hour" the blinds are drawn). Queer and mysterious things happen in that "Ancient House". It is, however, impossible to recount here all the incidents of the novel —quite apart from its scientific and satirical aspects it is an entertaining novel and the reader's interest is all the

time kept on the alert. In the meantime the process of
" humanization ", or individualization, of " D-503 " goes
further. He is now desperately in love with " I-330 "
and has to admit that " all this crazy stuff about love and
jealousy was not confined to the idiotic books of old " ;
he says of himself : " I was no longer living in our
sensible world, but in the ancient morbid world, in the
world of the root of minus one." He breaks with "O-90"
after giving her a child at her own request, for she also
proves to have gone off the track, to love him otherwise
than in the normal and approved way. " Having a soul "
turns out to be an infectious disease.

Then something quite incomprehensible and unexpected happens. On the so-called " Day of Unanimity ",
when all the numbers of the Single State are gathered in
a huge auditorium to re-elect their Benefactor (he has
been thirty-nine times unanimously re-elected) some
people, with " I-330 " at their head, dare raise their
voice against his election. A row ensues, "I" is wounded,
but " D " saves her and escapes with her, and she takes
him through the Ancient House to the other side of the
wall which circumscribes the boundaries of the Single
State and beyond which no number is supposed to
penetrate ; nor do any numbers know what is beyond
that wall. And there is Nature untouched by technical
improvements of civilization, there live primitive hairy
men. It is really a parallel to Huxley's " Savage Reserva-
tion ". It is with these men that "I-330" and some other
" revolutionaries " propose to start revolution in the
Single State. They all welcome the arrival of " D-503 ",
for they intend utilizing his *Integral* for their own ends.
There are no very definite ideas behind the revolutionary
action of "I-330" and her accomplices except a primitive
instinctive revolt against the standardized, planned out
life, in the name of freedom, of change, of newness.

" ' What happiness '—she exclaims.—' All that was known is over. It is a new and incredible world that is opening up.' "

When " D ", bewildered by the sight of naked men living in natural and not mathematical surroundings, asks " I " what it all means, her answer is : " It is the half we have lost," and she adds : " You must learn to shudder with fright, with joy, with furious wrath, with cold, you must worship fire. . . ." His love for this strange and fascinating woman clashes with his sense of duty, with the deeply imbued doctrines of the Single State. A curious dialogue takes place between them :

" HE : ' This is mad. This doesn't hold water. You don't realize that what you are preparing is a revolution ? '
" SHE : ' Yes, it is a revolution. Why doesn't it hold water ? '
" HE : ' Because there can be no revolution. Because *our* revolution was the last and there can be no more. Everybody knows that. . . .'
" SHE : ' There is no such thing as the last revolution, the number of revolutions is infinite.' "

One can easily imagine that this dialogue must have seemed particularly offensive and counter-revolutionary to the Communist censorship : its political implications were all too obvious.

The last part of the book is somewhat incoherent and not always quite clear. The day before the proposed trial flight of the *Integral* a proclamation is published in the official paper of the Single State announcing to all the numbers that the real cause of all the recent disasters has been discovered.

" . . . You are ill,—says the proclamation.—Your illness is imagination. It is the last obstacle on the way to happiness. Rejoice ye, it has been conquered. The way is free. The latest progress made by National

Science consists in the discovery of the centre of imagination. A triple application of X-rays to that centre will cure you for ever. You are perfect, you are like machines ; the way to 100 per cent. happiness is open. Hasten ye young and old. . . ."

The proclamation invites every number to undergo the Great Operation which will deprive them of imagination, this source of all evil. " D " sees at first a salvation in this, a way out of his inner conflict. He almost decides to undergo the operation, but changes his mind on realizing that the choice is between that and " I ". The trial flight of the *Integral* takes place, but the conspiracy falls through, a woman, the caretaker of " D's " house, who is also in love with him, having read his manuscript and reported the matter to the guardians without betraying " D " himself. The Single State comes out victorious from its encounter with the revolutionaries in the name of individualism. All the law-abiding numbers, including " D ", who is also supposed to be such, are subjected to the Great Operation : their imagination is extirpated. " I " and the other active revolutionaries are subjected to torture according to the improved Single State system, namely, put under the " Pneumatic Bell " and then sent to the " Machine of the Benefactor "—the modern improved guillotine. This is how the Pneumatic Bell is characterized :

" There were fools who compared it to the ancient inquisition ; but this is just as absurd as to put on the same footing a surgeon performing the operation of tracheotomy and a highwayman. Both use perhaps the same knife with which they perform the same operation : they cut the throat : nevertheless one is a benefactor, the other a criminal ; one is marked with a ' plus ' sign, the other with a ' minus '. . . ."

Once more it is easy to read a definite political meaning into this ironical comparison. From the purely literary

point of view Zamyatin's satirical Utopia, as far as one
can judge of it by the translation, is a good piece of
writing. Its construction is perhaps somewhat loose in
comparison with *Brave New World*; scientifically it is
not so well thought out, not so elaborate in details ; but
its satire is more' pointed, more directly inspired by
actual experience, and there is in it that element of
political satire which is absent from Mr. Huxley's novel.
The Soviet critics who have written of *We* in spite of the
fact that it has not been published in Russia admit its
high literary qualities. In contemporary Russian literature
it holds a unique place.

3. *Pilnyak's " Mahogany "*

Pilnyak's *Mahogany* (Berlin, 1929) is another work
that was denounced as anti-revolutionary and banned in
Russia. During the first years of the Revolution, Pilnyak
(b. 1894) came to occupy one of the foremost places in
the ranks of post-revolutionary prose writers. His *Bare
Year, The Third Metropolis, Machines and Wolves, Ivan
and Marya*, remain the most characteristic expression of
the first romantic boisterous period of the Revolution, of
its ornamental prose. His main theme is the antithesis
between reason and instinct, between the "machines"
and the " wolves ", and—on the historical plane—between
the old and the new, the European and the Asiatic
elements in Russia. He is instinctively drawn towards
pre-Petrine Russia. His sympathy with the Revolution
has a strong colouring of nationalism and anarchism. In
terms of politics, he has a great affinity with what is
called National-Bolshevism. In the Revolution he sees
above all the loosening of the dormant national instincts. It is the spirit of Stenka Razin and Pugachev,
rather than that of the Ehrfurt Programme and dia-

lectical materialism, that appeals to him in the Russian Revolution.

Pilnyak's weak point is his lack of constructive skill—his novels are not novels at all, but loose lyrical and philosophical compositions. But he has a keen eye and, despite all his verbal excesses, a sense of words. His work after 1924 is of less importance than his earlier novels. Both stylistically and ideologically he tried to move along the lines on which the whole of Soviet Russian literature was developing—towards greater realism and greater simplicity, but his nature revolted against it, the result being such failures as *The Tale of the Unextinguished Moon* (1927) or such hybrid productions as *The Volga Flows Into the Caspian Sea* (see Chapter VII), which defeated its own end. *Mahogany* which, in an altered form, was afterwards included in the latter novel, has more unity. It is not a novel at all : there is no plot, almost no action in it. It is a static picture, drawn in the best Pilnyakian manner, of the double-faced modern Russia, of the old world encased within the new. The attention of the writer is focused on this old world. The scene is set in an ancient small provincial town—" Russian Brugge and Russian Kamakura," Pilnyak calls it—apparently Uglich (in the novel it becomes Kolomna). The principal characters are the family of Yakov Karpovich Skudrin, his wife and daughter, his brother, his son Akim, his sisters and niece. Skudrin himself is a typical survival of the past, a cunning and clever embodiment of the instinctive counter-revolutionary forces. There is a quaint irony in his words when he enumerates the Emperors whom he survived, beginning with " Nikolav Pavlovich " (Nicholas I), adding, after " Nikolay Alex-androvich " (Nicholas II)—Vladimir Ilyich (Lenin), and concluding with " I shall also survive Alexey Ivanovich " (*i.e.* Rykov, the then Chairman of the Council of People's

Commissars). Skudrin develops a counter-revolutionary theory, which has, however, something in common with Pilnyak's own views, of the imminent extinction of the proletariat as a result of the process of mechanization— " all the proletarians will become engineers ". His brother Ivan who has changed his surname to Ozhogov (he hates Yakov), is a romantic revolutionary for whom time has stopped in 1919; with a few others like himself he has founded a primitive commune—they live in a dug-out in a factory yard and preach a peculiar kind of Communism based on love :

> " Communism is primarily love,—says Ivan,—an intense attention of man to man, friendship, co-operation, collaboration. Communism means giving up things, and for a genuine Communist the primary things must be love, respect for men—and men."

He laments the loss of that genuine Communism.

Yakov's youngest son Akim, an engineer, whose short visit to his native town forms the single " incident " of the otherwise static story, is akin to Ivan. He is a Communist, but belongs to the " Trotskyist " opposition and has fallen out with the " general line " of the party. At heart, in Pilnyak's own words, he is " the flesh of the flesh " of Ivan Ozhogov. Pilnyak's sympathy lies obviously with these two Romantics of the Revolution and it was this tendency towards romantic Trotskyism that led to his book being banned in Russia. It is true that later on a great deal of it was, as a minor episode, bodily transposed into *Volga*, but then the whole episode with Akim was excluded and, secondly, it was set-off by the Five-Year Plan, while several other figures, bourgeois counter-revolutionaries and ideal Communists, were opposed to the " last of the Mohicans " of romantic Communism. In *Mahogany* we see only the representatives of the old world, the remnants of the seventeenth

century Russia, and those two antiquated Communists :
in the last lines of the book their obsoleteness is symbolized
in Akim missing his train : " Akim the Trotskyist missed
his train *just as he missed the train of time.*" For it is
hardly possible to regard Claudia, Akim's niece, an
illegitimate daughter of one of Yakov's sisters, as a type
of a new woman. She accepts the Revolution, but her
acceptance is purely egotistic, individual. She believes in
free love and is expecting a child from an unknown
father. She explains to Akim :

> " In the centre of my attention was neither love nor
> my partner, but I myself and my emotions. I chose
> men, different men, in order to learn everything. I
> did not want to become pregnant, sex is joy ; I did
> not think of the child. But I will manage it, and the
> State will help me. As to morals, I don't know what
> it means, I have been taught to forget it. Or perhaps
> I have my own morals. I am responsible only for
> myself. . . ."

But Claudia's moral attitude, which even the revolutionary Akim finds " novel and extraordinary ", is purely
physiological.

> " Life is big,—she says,—it is round, I cannot make
> out anything in it, I cannot make out anything in the
> Revolution, but I believe in them—in life, in sun, in
> the Revolution, and I feel quiet."

The old world is represented also by the brothers
Bezdetov, who travel about the villages buying up and
reselling old mahogany furniture. This mahogany furniture, which gave its name to the book, is one of the symbols
of the old world and its description shows what a lover
of things Pilnyak is. Old Skudrin's wife belongs entirely
to the pre-Petrine Russia—her mode of life, her interests
are identical with those of Russian women of the fifteenth
and seventeenth centuries.

True to his manner, Pilnyak is not content with showing us the dual face of contemporary Russia, he insists on giving it his own ornamental Pilnyakian formulæ, such as " Pre-Petrine Russia stood rigid in the house " or " Behind the eighteenth-century window-panes the Soviet provincial night was stalking past."

Apart from the two romantic revolutionaries who in 1929 sounded anachronistic and counter-revolutionary, anti-revolutionary notes crop up here and there in the book. Pilnyak emphasizes the inefficiency of the Soviet provincial administration based on the " slow squandering of pre-revolutionary riches." The trade-union card is represented as the pivot of the town's life—it is a key to its elementary comforts ; and " those who have no vote as well as their children receive no bread."

Pilnyak's *Volga* was an attempt to make good the revolutionary deficiency of his *Mahogany*. Since 1931 he has not published much, among other things a book of American impressions entitled *O.K.* His early work remains his most important and characteristic contribution to post-revolutionary Russian literature.

4. *Budantsev's " Sufferings of Mind "*

During the literary discussions which took place in 1930–31, in the middle of the Five-Year Plan period in literature, there was much talk about the novel of the young writer Sergey Budantsev (b. 1896) entitled *A Tale of the Sufferings of Mind*. Budantsev's first novel *The Revolt* (1922) was, in form and matter alike, typical of its time. Its subject was one of the episodes of the Civil War. It was full of overstrained emotionalism, of stylistic exuberance, it showed a preference for depicting mass scenes rather than individual characters. His second novel, *The Locusts* (1927), had its plot woven round the struggle with the locusts in Central Asia. In it Budantsev's manner had considerably sobered down, and he succeeded both in conveying well the atmosphere of everyday life and in creating some good individual characters. But there was nothing to distinguish it from other works of similar nature. It was only his *Tale of the Sufferings of Mind* (1931) that drew general attention to him. It was proclaimed to be one of the most reactionary and anti-Soviet works that ever appeared in Russia. Budantsev was denounced as a representative of the pernicious Right-wing tendency in Soviet literature. Some critics openly expressed the opinion that such a work ought not to have been published in a Communist State. Yet Budantsev's novel had no direct relation to contemporary Russia ; its action took place in the sixties of the last century. Its theme was politically neutral. But the book came out at a time when neutral themes were looked upon with disfavour, when writers had to write on certain set subjects and were not supposed to think save along certain approved lines. Budantsev's theme was an eternal one, not confined to any definite historical period. There are even hardly any political and topical allusions in his novel : some mention of the Nihilists, of Herzen and his *Bell*—and that is all. The action is set in a typical Swiss boarding-house. The hero who stands in the centre of attention is Grekov, one of the inmates of that boarding-house. He is a young Russian scientist, extraordinarily gifted. He attempted to commit suicide after his wife's death. He is reserved, melancholy, absentminded. He ponders over the meaning, or rather the meaninglessness, of life   Life terrifies him by its aimlessness and its cruelty, and by its inevitable end—death. It is the eternal problem of life and death that occupies Budantsev's hero and Budantsev himself.

" Man is free,—exclaims Grekov ironically.—Freedom ! What do I want it for, if I too am condemned to the humiliating torture of falling incurably ill, of swallowing my own tongue, of being poisoned with my own urine or excrement, of writhing with terrible pain, with fear of destruction ? I am doomed to see the destruction of those dear to me and to foresee my own. Sooner or later, all the same it is soon. Freedom ! "

Grekov has a friend, Kazarin, who is quite unlike him. He is gay, sociable, and talkative. One day after dinner in the boarding-house, he tells his fellow-boarders Grekov's life-story. And Grekov himself, during his hours of solitary meditations, calls back to mind some of its episodes. Thus his life is shown to us from two different angles. And its *leitmotiv* is cruelty, injustice and mutual struggle. Even Grekov's scientific career suffered from it. His successes and achievements brought in their trail envy, and intrigues. A famous German scholar, Grekov's colleague, appropriated a most important scientific discovery of his. His marriage was not acutely unhappy, but it brought him no happiness and ended in his wife's senseless and premature death. And that sense of general meaninglessness weighs down on Grekov and permeates his whole existence. He feels as if he were in a prison :

" He realized that prison was not a place but a state of mind : one could go round the globe and yet be as if in a prison cell."

He feels an irresistible laziness and disgust " to move about, to chew, to listen to his heart, to go to the lavatory, to dress in the morning and undress in the evening." His mind is all the time at work trying to solve the problem of life. But he cannot find any meaning to it and hence his sufferings. His work, the fruits of which are bound to be destroyed one day, gives him no satisfaction. And so for the second time he arrives at the idea of suicide. But this time he decides to choose a " natural " form of it. He is not going to shoot or drown or poison himself. He will catch cold and die a seemingly natural death. He takes a hot bath and then without an overcoat goes out into the cold April night. But his plan is frustrated ; he is overtaken and saved by his friend. He is going to live. But whether he will find a meaning in life and, if so, what, remains untold. Budantsev's novel was attacked by the orthodox Communists precisely for its insistence on such an " untopical " eternal theme. One of his critics said in a discussion that it was tantamount to proclaiming the watchword of " no politics ", and that this was in itself the worst kind of politics. " To separate politics from literature is a hopeless task," said the same critic. Budantsev, he added, was one of the writers who used a method diametrically opposed to that of dialectical materialism.

5. Bulgakov

Mikhail Bulgakov (b. 1891) is regarded by the Communist critics as a writer with strongly pronounced anti-revolutionary tendencies. His anti-revolutionary reputation is based primarily on his novel *The White Guard* which has been dramatized under the name *The Days of the Turbins*. But his other works—a book of stories called *Diablerie* and several plays (*Zoyka's Flat, The Crimson Island, Molière*)—only tended to enhance that reputation.

Bulgakov himself says in an autobiographical note that *The White Guard* is of all his works the one he likes best. As a literary work it is not of any great and outstanding significance. It is a typical realistic novel written

in a simple language, without any stylistic or compositional
refinements. Its centre of gravity is in its subject and
in the psychology, personal and social, of its characters.
Its action is set in Kiev—Bulgakov's native town—and
it describes the period of the Civil War during the
independence of the Ukraine under Hetman Skoropadsky,
and the events leading up to the latter's downfall and
the subsequent occupation of Kiev, first by the Ukrainian
separatist troups of Petlyura and then by the Bolsheviks.
Bulgakov's novel stands out in Soviet literature for the
simple reason that there are no Communists in it, that
all its principal characters are Whites, and that for the
first time these enemies of Communism have been shown
from the inside, as the principal characters of the drama,
and not merely episodically, as the outside opponents of
Bolshevism. What is more—they are shown sympathetic-
ally, and this is the ground for the main accusation
levelled by the Soviet critics against Bulgakov. He is
charged by them with showing the enemies of the Soviet
régime as honest, chivalrous and disinterested men who
fight Communism in the name of their ideas and not for
merely personal egoistic reasons. This applies above
all to the brothers Turbin who stand in the centre of the
novel—the liberally minded but disillusioned, honest,
chivalrous and courageous, even though not very strong-
willed Alexis, the elder brother ; and the young, romantically inclined Nikolka, who bears a certain resemblance to
Petya Rostov in War and Peace. Bulgakov does not, of
course, paint all his Whites in the same sympathetic
colours, some of them, as for instance the Turbins'
brother-in-law Talberg, are even unpleasant ; but the
Turbins being in the centre of the picture, the general
tone is that of sympathetic insight and even at times
admiration. It is true that the brothers Turbin ended
by accepting Bolshevism, but they did so out of patriotic

considerations as the lesser of the two evils, for in the struggle that was then going on in the Ukraine between the Bolsheviks and Petlyura's separatists the Bolsheviks stood for the unity of Russia.

Bulgakov's novel had a great success among the reading public in Russia. Some of the Soviet critics have tried to explain it away by the craving of the average Soviet readers for "exotic" and "thrilling" novels. The orthodox Communist and proletarian literature, they admitted, left this craving unsatisfied, while Bulgakov's novel, with the alien and "exotic" psychology of its characters, gave it a suitable food. One of the Soviet critics drew a parallel between the success of Bulgakov's novel and that of the memoirs of the Russian *émigré* Shulgin (in general the Soviet critics emphasized a great resemblance between Shulgin's ideas and Bulgakov's mentality). But this parallel can be turned against the same critic, for it shows that in the interest which the Soviet reader took in Bulgakov's novel there was something more than a mere craving for the thrilling, the adventurous and the exotic; that it was the subject itself, the psychology of the enemies of Communism that interested the Soviet public. A still greater success fell to the lot of the dramatic version of Bulgakov's novel staged by one of the Studios of the Moscow Art Theatre. Here, if anything, the "counter-revolutionary" elements of the novel, especially the chivalry and heroism of its "White" heroes, were brought into still greater relief. The success of this "counter-revolutionary" play, which included among other things the performance of the old Russian national anthem, was so great that after a time the Soviet Government found itself constrained to forbid its performances. The ban was not lifted until after the general change of policy in 1932. But, ever since, Bulgakov, who wrote several other plays (of these *Zoyka's*

Flat and *The Crimson Island* also revealed counter-revolutionary tendencies, and the performances of *The Crimson Island* were forbidden by the censorship), has been looked upon askance by the official circles and had virtually to stop writing ; since then he has published no original works of importance, but in 1933 he made an adaptation of Gogol's *Dead Souls* for the stage.

Bulgakov's book of stories, *Diablerie* (1925), has also been denounced by the Soviet critics as anti-revolutionary. It consists of five stories of which one (*The Fatal Eggs*) is fairly long. In manner and conception these stories are quite different from *The White Guard*. They all deal with contemporary Soviet life, but with two minor exceptions they do so in terms not of Realism but either of fantastics or of satirical grotesque. The elements of form and style are accordingly much more prominent. The first story, which gave its name to the whole book, begins on the realistic plane, but passes imperceptibly into the realm of fantastic satire where the real and the unreal are difficult to disentangle. At the basis of it lies a Soviet bureaucratic anecdote, a trifling mistake, which involves, however, a human destiny and has therefore a tragic accent. It is the story of the undoing of a small Soviet clerk who gets sacked because he mistakes the name of his new boss for the word " pants " and issues as a result of that mistake a nonsensical order. In his efforts to rehabilitate himself he loses his name and identity, and meets all sorts of queer and grotesque personages. His fantastic adventures give us odd glimpses of the Soviet bureaucratic mechanism. Bulgakov does not aim here at being psychological ; his characters are not living people, but grotesque puppets, and his world that of fantastic realities. In this mingling of fantasy and realism *Diablerie* resembles Gogol's *Nose*, but Bulgakov lacks Gogol's masterful restraint in the presentation of this distorted world and goes at times a little too far in his fantastic vagaries. On the satirical plane the story ridicules the bureaucratic inefficiency and disorganization of the Soviet institutions, inefficiency that leads to tragic consequences.

There is a more clearly drawn boundary-line between the real and the fantastic in the longest story in the book—*The Fatal Eggs*. It is a satirical-scientific Utopia, and the reference in it to H. G. Wells's *Food of the Gods* is not purely accidental. The story is told against the background of a satirically presented picture of Moscow life in 1925, but its plot is based on a purely fantastic hypothesis. It is the story of a scientific discovery made by Professor Persikov, a zoologist of world-wide reputation. In the course of his work he discovers quite accidentally a new red ray with enormous life-giving and procreating capacity. His experiments with it, conducted on frogs, coincide with a strange epidemic which befalls the hens in the Soviet Union and leads to their complete extinction. Against Persikov's wish and at the suggestion of a Communist whose name is Rokk (there is a pun in it. for though differently spelt it sounds like the Russian word " rok " which means " Fate "—hence the pun of the title too) it is decided to apply Persikov's discovery to the breeding of new hens in the Soviet Union. A special farm is allotted for the purpose and Rokk placed at the head of it; hens' eggs are ordered from Germany and the experiment begins. It ends, however, in a disaster. Owing to an error on the part of some Soviet institution Rokk receives, instead of hens' eggs, several cases containing the eggs of ostriches and reptiles (huge anacondas and crocodiles) which Persikov had ordered for his scientific experiments, while real hens' eggs arrive at Persikov's address after a long delay, when it is too late to avert the disaster : snakes, crocodiles and ostriches

hatched artificially on the " Red Ray Farm " come out
of those eggs, grow in the space of a few hours to gigantic
dimensions, multiply themselves with unheard-of rapidity
(such are the wonderful properties of Persikov's discovery)
and cause havoc and destruction all around. They start
by swallowing Rokk's wife and killing all the inhabitants
of the Farm. Then the reptiles invade the whole province
of Smolensk, laying eggs in thousands as they proceed
eastwards, and procreating with extraordinary speed.
All the resources of the Republic—the Red Army, the
Air Force, the chemical warfare section, the fire brigades
—are mobilized to combat this terrible invasion. Towns
and villages on the way to Moscow are seized with panic ;
thousands of people perish ; and Moscow lives in a state
of terrible expectation. The anger of the mob turns
against Persikov who is held responsible for the disaster.
A crowd headed by Rokk, gone mad after his wife's
death, takes by storm the Zoological Institute and kills
Persikov and his faithful servants. The progress of the
reptiles is finally stopped by an unexpected circumstance :
a severe frost grips Russia one night in the middle of
August, and the reptiles and their eggs freeze to death.
Nature intervenes to save the Soviet Union from complete
destruction—a climax that in itself sounds somewhat
" counter-revolutionary ".

Apart from the main improbable hypothesis, on which
the whole story is built, there is here no such mingling
of the real and the fantastic as in *Diablerie* ; but the
reality is presented on a satirical plane. Beginning with
Rokk, an antiquated Communist wearing in 1928 the
symbolical leather jacket, who, in the past, had been a flute-
player in a cinema orchestra, and down to the episodic
figures of Soviet journalists, all the characters of the story
are portrayed satirically. Behind the whole story one
feels Bulgakov's irony, but it is difficult to make out his

real attitude ; he uses this all-round irony as a sort of safety-valve.

The third important story in this collection is entitled *The Adventures of Chichikov*, the sub-heading being " A Poem in Ten Points with Prologue and Epilogue ". It is told in the form of the author's dream and introduces Chichikov and several other characters from Gogol's *Dead Souls* to Soviet Russia, the implication being that in contemporary Russia there is plenty of scope, both for the cunning rascals and swindlers like Chichikov, and for some of Gogol's inefficient bunglers. Bulgakov's main thesis seems to be. that beneath the surface, beyond the Communist appearances, life in Russia remains much as it was in Gogol's days. On entering the gate of that very hotel from which he had departed a hundred years ago, Chichikov finds that everything there is exactly the same :

" . . . Cockroaches were looking out of the crevices and even seemed to have become more numerous. But there were some slight changes too. . . . Thus, for instance, instead of a signboard with the word ' Hotel ' there was a poster bearing the inscription ' Hostel No. So-and-so ', and—this goes by itself— dirt and filth were such as Gogol could never have imagined."

Chichikov's adventures are wittily and humorously described. He easily adapts himself to the new surroundings and circumstances and plays a number of cunning tricks on the silly and inefficient Soviet administration. The first thing he is asked to do is to fill up a questionnaire containing a hundred tricky questions. He does so in five minutes, but when he hands it in his hand trembles :

" ' Well,—he thought—in a moment they will read it, and see what a bird I really am, and . . .'
" But nothing whatever happened.

" First of all, no one read the questionnaire; secondly, it got into the hands of the filing lady-clerk who did the usual thing with it : she entered it as an outgoing document instead of incoming, and then immediately shoved it somewhere, so that the questionnaire vanished into the air as it were.

" Chichikov grinned and started upon his job."

It was only after Chichikov had played all sorts of ingenious tricks and after these had been disclosed thanks to Nozdrev, that his questionnaire was with great difficulties unearthed, and this is how it read :

" Name : Paul. Patronymic : Ivanovich. Surname : Chichikov. Social standing : · Gogol's character. Pre-revolutionary occupation : Buying dead souls. Relation to military service : Neither this nor that nor devil knows what. To what party do you belong ? Sympathizer (but with whom no one knows). Have you been under trial ? Curved zigzagging line instead of an answer. Address : Turn into the courtyard, third floor on the right, ask at the enquiry office for the officer's wife Podtochina, and she will know."

Finally, the author intervenes, offers to catch Chichikov, orders him to be dissected, finds inside him " people's milliards " stolen by him in the shape of diamonds, and orders him to be drowned in an ice-hole. As a reward he asks for Gogol's Complete Works. And then comes the ironical epilogue :

" . . . of course, I woke up. And there was nothing : no Chichikov, no Nozdrev, and what is most no Gogol. . . .

" Well, well, I thought to myself, and began to dress, and again life started flaunting before me in its everyday attire."

It seems, however, to be no accident that in the best satirical pictures of contemporary Russia the " Gogolian " traits stand out so prominently—one is especially reminded of the picaresque novels of Ilf and Petrov, and of Kataev's *Embezzlers*.

CHAPTER IX

THE HISTORICAL NOVEL

STRANGE though this may seem at first glance, the historical novel as a literary genre is quite flourishing in the country which tries to look to the future and do away with the past. Some of the historical novels published in Soviet Russia during the last ten years represent a new development in this genre and constitute an interesting contribution to literature.

The early Russian historical novel—before Pushkin— was entirely dependent on foreign models and, moreover, was, strictly speaking, scarcely historical. In the thirties and forties of the nineteenth century the historical novel as a genre received a new impetus from the influence of Walter Scott which was quite considerable in Russia where it took on a national-patriotic colouring. In its purest form this influence was to be seen in the historical novels of Zagoskin who was often called the Russian Walter Scott, though he was certainly inferior both in talent and in scope of historical vision to the famous Scottish novelist. But Pushkin's historical novels (*The Captain's Daughter* and the fragment of *The Nigger of Peter the Great*) and Gogol's *Taras Bulba*, however they may differ from each other and from the novels of Zagoskin, ultimately go back to the same common source and represent a Russian variety of Scottism. In the words of the famous Russian critic Apollon Grigoryev, the whole of the National-Romantic period in Russian literature was rooted in the influence exercised by Walter

153

Scott. The art of the historical novel, as introduced by Walter Scott and developed by Victor Hugo and other French Romantics, was in Russian critical literature of the thirties and forties the subject of a lively and curious controversy between Belinsky and Senkovsky, Belinsky coming forward as a great admirer of the Scottish novelist and Senkovsky as his detractor and in general an opponent of the historical novel as a literary genre—he called it " counterfeit art ". Zagoskin had his continuators, of whom the best known was Lazhechnikov, but the traditions of Scottism were not carried on in great Russian literature, though towards the end of the nineteenth century there was a considerable crop of second-rate historical novels which were very popular and widely read (among others those of Vsevolod Solovyev, the brother of the great Russian philosopher). Turgenev's novels were, of course, historical in a sense, inasmuch as they covered and reflected a whole period in the history of Russian society and its mentality, were so to speak a mirror of Russian social life and ideas. Turgenev himself said that he had attempted to reflect what Shakespeare called " the body and pressure of time ", but he did so in terms of imaginary and not of real historical characters, and therefore his works do not come within the strict meaning of the term historical novel.

Thus, the only instance of the historical novel in great Russian literature of the second half of the nineteenth century was Tolstoy's *War and Peace*. But *War and Peace* is a genre and a world in itself. It is, of course, a historical novel, but it is also something infinitely more ; it is both a vast epic of Russian life and a masterpiece of individual psychological analysis. What is still more important, this " historical " novel is eminently anti-historical in spirit, it sets out to shatter and destroy the traditional conception of history. Tolstoy's remarkable work has remained a solitary, isolated fact in Russian

literature, though the influence of his manner—purely
outward, however—can be perceived in the case of some
second-rate historical novelists like Count Salias.

After Tolstoy, there was a long gap when the historical
novel as a genre was relegated to the lower regions of
literature. An attempt to resuscitate it, to give it a
higher status, was made by the Symbolists—in the novels
of Merezhkovsky and Bryusov. These two writers' conception of the historical novel and the motives that
actuated them in choosing this genre, were however quite
different.

Merezhkovsky did not write historical novels out of
any artistic impulse, and in his case the novelist is subordinated to the philosopher, the thinker, who in terms
of historical facts and characters gives expression to his
historical, philosophical, and religious ideas. This is
both an advantage and a drawback : it gives his novels
a unity of conception, an ideological backbone, but it
also makes them biased, deprives them of historical
objectivity and truthfulness—this is especially obvious in
the third and last part of Merezhkovsky's famous trilogy—
Peter and Alexis. With Merezhkovsky the reader is all
the time aware of the author's intention not only to show,
to describe, but also to teach, to prove, to demonstrate
his thesis. It was quite natural that Merezhkovsky should
give up the form of historical novel and of late turn to
non-fictional historico-philosophical works (his *Napoleon,
Atlantis, Jesus the Unknown*).

The impulse behind Bryusov's historical novels—*The
Fiery Angel* (a novel of the Middle Ages in Germany)
and *The Altar of Victory*, where the action is set in the
fourth century B.C.—was purely literary and artistic : it
was an expression of the general craving of the Symbolists
away from everyday realities, from contemporary life
which in their eyes lacked sufficiently inspiring themes.

Thus they sought refuge in the past or in exoticism, or in both. This is true even if we take into consideration that, as has recently been demonstrated by a Russian critic, the psychological skeleton of Bryusov's *The Fiery Angel* was in fact autobiographical. But apart from the novels of Merezhkovsky and Bryusov and some stylistic experiments of Kuzmin, Symbolism did not produce anything in the way of historical novels. It has to be remembered, however, that the age of Symbolism was an age of poetry *par excellence* and the novel played only a subsidiary part in it. After Merezhkovsky's *December the Fourteenth* and Bryusov's *Altar of Victory* there came a new interval which lasted until after the Revolution, when the historical novel was once more revived, both in Soviet Russia and in the *émigré* literature (Aldanov).

In dealing with the historical novel in Soviet Russia it is necessary to distinguish between two different sources of inspiration. They are in fact diametrically opposed, though both go back ultimately to sociological causes. It has been said that revolutions are propitious to historical studies and to the spirit of historism. It is certainly true that inasmuch as the literature of the revolutionary time tends to grasp the meaning of events, and not merely to record them, it is bound to examine and treat them in historical perspective. Hence the birth of the historical novel bearing on the period of the Revolution itself, on the one immediately preceding it and on its more distant antecedents. There is a whole category of works in Soviet Russian literature belonging to this type of historical novel. I have already mentioned, for instance, Tarasov-Rodionov's cycle of novels dealing with the history of the Russian Revolution of 1917 as a whole and bringing in a number of historical personages such as Kerensky and other members of the Provisional Government, the late Emperor, General Kornilov and others. Here too belongs Sholokhov's *The Still Don*, which also brings in several historical characters and episodes. Sholokhov tries to be objective and impartial and to a great extent succeeds in it—partly because, though consciously he is on the side of the Revolution, his subconscious sympathies seem to lie with the Cossacks and their traditional mode of life, which the Revolution has upset or destroyed. The number of such contemporary historical novels in Soviet literature is very great. One of the most recent is Mikhail Kozakov's *Nine Points* which starts during the War, not long before the Revolution and describes the political circles of the Duma and the events immediately preceding the Revolution, to pass on probably to the Revolution itself. The first Russian Revolution of 1905 has also attracted the attention of Soviet novelists. Roman Gul's vivid but superficial *General Bo* deals with the terrorists' activities of the Social-Revolutionary party. Its hero is the well-known revolutionary Boris Savinkov, who has sometimes been described as the " adventurer " of the Revolution.

Some writers go in for the subjects of their historical novels to the revolutionary movements of a more distant past. Such novels are therefore more strictly historical, but they are also essentially revolutionary in inspiration. Such are, for example, Ilya Ehrenburg's *The Conspiracy of the Equals*, the subject of which is the Baboeuf movement in the French Revolution (Ehrenburg wrote also some " contemporary " historical novels which, like some of his ordinary novels, verge on sensational thrillers) ; Olga Forsh's *Clad With Stone*, dealing with the Russian revolutionaries of the seventies and eighties ; and Chapygin's *Stenka Razin*, a vast novel in three volumes of over 1000 pages, of which the anarchist leader of the popular movement of the seventeenth century is the central figure, but which gives a large picture of Russian life of

G   157

the period in its historical setting. It is, perhaps, a little too static and abounding in minute descriptions of externals, but it gives a vivid picture of Russia in the time of crises and general turmoil. Chapygin not only knows, but feels his seventeenth century Russia, has a keen sense of that life. He is not a newcomer in literature. His first book of stories, *Those Who Keep Aloof*, written in Gorky's manner, and his early novel *The White Hermitage* (1915), describing the peculiar and slightly exotic life of the Russian Far North, with its wild forests, its silent and obstinate peasants, its Old Believers' hermitages scattered in the woods, appeared before the Revolution. In *The White Hermitage* there was something of a Russian Jack London. Since the Revolution Chapygin has written comparatively little ; apparently he did not feel inclined to reflect the contemporary revolutionary events, and his attention was turned to the past—*Stenka Razin*, published in 1927, was his first big post-revolutionary work. Since then he has been working on another historical novel, also situated in the Russian seventeenth century and dealing with the Dissenter movement.

Olga Forsh (b. 1875), the author of *Clad With Stone*, wrote also several other historical novels. In *The Contemporaries* (1927) the principal historical characters are Gogol and his friend Alexander Ivanov, the famous religious painter : the novel describes their life in Rome in the forties of the last century. In *The Symbolists* (1933) the subject is recent literary history and the principal characters some of the leading Symbolist writers. It gives, however, a rather distorted picture of that important movement in modern Russian literature. Olga Forsh's latest novel, of which only one volume has appeared so far, takes us back to the age of Catherine the Great. Its hero is Alexander Radishchev, the famous author of *A Journey from Moscow to Petersburg*, often regarded as one of the " fathers " of the Russian intelligentsia and first Russian " revolutionaries ". The first volume of her *The Jacobin Leaven* (1934) describes Radishchev's " Lehrjahre " in Leipzig.

With Olga Forsh's *Contemporaries* we come to the second category of historical novels in Soviet literature, those of which the impulse is not to reflect the Revolution or its precedents in the past, but rather to escape from the everyday and the contemporary, as the Symbolists once did. This time, however, the reason for this escape seems to be of a sociological nature. This tendency is manifested by the writers who do not feel inclined or capable to portray contemporary life and its problems in the spirit desired by those in power. It is interesting to note that the most successful specimens of this kind of literature bear a literary-historical character and come from the pen of the well-known historian of literature, Yury Tynyanov, one of the leaders of the Russian Formalist school and an authority on the minor writers of the Pushkin period. His first historical novel had for its principal character the curious figure of Wilhelm Küchelbecker, one of Pushkin's school-fellows at the Lyceum, himself a poet and playwright, a Quixotic idealist, who was implicated in the Decembrist conspiracy and exiled to Siberia. There was in his life-story a tragic quality—it was the tragedy of a Russian literary and political Don Quixote, the inner tragedy of inefficiency, of incongruity between the aspirations of his soul and his powers of self-expression. Tynyanov's novel is based on an excellent knowledge of the period and a thorough study of its documents ; it has hardly any element of fiction, being a kind of novelized biography in the genre which Lytton Strachey, and André Maurois in France, have made so fashionable. Its " historicity " is unquestionable, it conveys well the spirit of the time and introduces several real-life characters as episodic figures, including Pushkin, Griboedov and Zhukovsky; but its interest is even more psychological than biographical or historical : it is a study of a curious psychological type, of a man lovable in spite of all his ridiculousness and inefficiency—and he was, indeed, loved by his more brilliant contemporaries like Pushkin and Griboedov, with just a touch of good-humoured mockery—this muddle-headed, but kind-hearted idealist.

Tynyanov's *Küchlya* (the novel is called so after Küchelbecker's affectionate school nickname) was published in 1925 and after that other writers took to this genre. With but short intervals there were published several novels (by Pilnyak, Gul, Sergeev-Tsensky and Pavlenko) which had for their subject episodes from Lermontov's life. But these writers all lacked that combination of poetic gift with literary - historical erudition which Tynyanov possessed in a high degree, and their Lermontov's stories proved to be failures.

In 1929 Tynyanov wrote his second historical novel, in the middle of which stood the figure of Griboedov, the famous author of *The Misfortune of Being Clever*, and one of the most curious and enigmatic figures in Russian literature. He was a man of one work, for apart from his classical comedy he wrote only heavy and clumsy poetry and mediocre plays. But he was no doubt one of the most clear-headed and brilliant men of his time, with vast and ambitious diplomatic plans which were, however, thwarted by unfavourable conditions and by fate ; he was murdered under somewhat mysterious circumstances in Teheran where he occupied the post of Russian resident and was conducting at the time important and responsible negotiations with the Persian Government. Tynyanov's novel came out just in time for the centenary commemoration of Griboedov's tragic end (he was assassinated in 1829). It was not a full-length biography, but covered only the last year of Griboedov's life, its central point being his death and that which had led up to it—the book was even called *The Death of Wazir-Muchtar* (this being the official Persian title of Griboedov). It is regarded by many critics as being the better of Tynyanov's two novels, but I can hardly agree with this view. It is certainly an interesting novel— Griboedov was too interesting a man for any novel about him with some claim to real literature not to be interesting. The element of tragedy is still more felt in it: we are shown the last year of Griboedov's life, from the moment when he first returned from Persia with the treaty of Turkmanchay in his pocket and when his fame as a diplomat—so different from his posthumous fame as a writer—reached its culminating point; after that it was a steady march towards the inevitable doom. For Tynyanov, Griboedov is a man who spread about him " the pungent smell of fate ", and Tynyanov is at great pains to convey this to the reader. Where he fails, I think, is in that which Maurois holds to be the most important requisite of biography as a work of art, namely the detection in the life studied of the inner unity, of the *leitmotiv* which it must have, however complex and contradictory the object of study may seem to be. Tynyanov has not succeeded in detecting that unity, that *leitmotiv* in the life of Griboedov—he has failed to bring nearer to us and make more comprehensible this variedly gifted man. Instead of a portrait Tynyanov gives us a mirror, broken into many fragments, in which we see reflected separate features of his model, for the most part comic and petty. No synthesis is achieved. For the doom, which Tynyanov has evidently endeavoured to make the *leitmotiv* of his work, has been substituted a number of anecdotes and caricatures. Herein lies perhaps the chief reason of the failure of his second novel. It is due to its un-historicity, its tendency to caricature, to laugh, to represent historical events as a succession of ridiculous anecdotes, and historical personages as helpless puppets. It is not even the Tolstoyan attitude to history, it is a caricature of it. Tolstoy's men in their helplessness to direct the course of historical events are merely human ; Tynyanov's are caricatures of men, their ridiculous characteristics are brought to the forefront, even in the case of Griboedov himself.

The style of Tynyanov's second novel is also much more pretentious, it has been influenced by Andrey Bely, but Tynyanov's " Belyisms " are not inwardly justified, they are not subordinated to an inner rhythm, and are irritating in their pretentiousness.

Another literary historian who took to writing historical novels, is Anatoly Vinogradov. As a literary historian he had specialized himself in problems of Franco-Russian literary intercourse. An outcome of his literary studies was a novel about Stendhal (1930). He also wrote *The Tale About the Brothers Turgenev* (1932) where, using partly some unpublished documents from archives, he drew the portraits of Alexander and Nikolay Turgenev. These highly cultivated representatives of the Russian nobility of the first half of nineteenth century were conspicuous in more than one field and played a prominent part in Russian freemasonry. The latter gave Vinogradov an extremely interesting background for his double portrait. Vinogradov is also the author of a vivid and picturesque novel, set against the background of the French Revolution, which has for its centre of interest the story of Toussaint-Louverture (*The Black Consul*, 1931). It differs from the " revolutionary " novels mentioned before by its apparent freedom from any definite political purpose.

Tynyanov's and Vinogradov's literary novels are closely connected with a large non-fictional, documentary literature of literary biographies constructed on the principle of *montage*, which the revolutionary period has produced (the best known of these are Veresaev's *Pushkin in Life* and *Gogol in Life*, but there are also collective or individual " mounted " biographies of Turgenev, Ostrovsky, Griboedov and other authors). To a certain extent all this literature reflects the same tendency to escape from actuality on the part of the intelligentsia.

A work which stands out among the historical novels of the last years is Alexey Tolstoy's *Peter the First* of which two volumes have so far appeared. It is a work conceived on a grand scale and giving a wide picture of Russia's social life in the seventeenth century, when the country was torn asunder by all sorts of crises and difficulties. The painting of different social *milieux*, and, among other things, of the peasant life under the recently introduced régime of serfdom, occupies an important place in the novel, but it is primarily concerned with Peter himself, giving a human full-length portrait of this barbarian of genius. One can disagree with Tolstoy's treatment of Peter's character, as did the late Russian historian Sergius Platonov, but one cannot deny that his portrait of the great Russian Emperor, especially as a boy and youth, is vivid and arresting. Before writing his Peter, Tolstoy did not show by his work that there were in him the makings of a historical novelist. In his preliminary historical researches he was assisted by the late historian Shchegolev who has also been his collaborator in the production of some bad plays dealing with recent history. Tolstoy's historical conception may be somewhat primitive and simplist, but in the picture of the turbulent, unsettled life of the masses in that period of crises, and of the rapidly changing face of Russian society, he shows great perspicacity and acuteness. A great merit of his novel is its objectivity, its freedom from any tendency to read present-day political issues into seventeenth century Russia, or to treat Peter as a symbol, as did Merezhkovsky who made his Peter fit in with his *a priori* philosophical conceptions to the detriment of historical truth. On the whole it can be said that Tolstoy's *Peter the First* is one of the outstanding facts in Soviet Russian literature and it compares particularly well with the literary production of the last few years when there has been a decided lowering of literary quality. One of its great attractions is its excellent full-blooded Russian.

One of the latest " best-sellers " in Soviet Russia is Novikov-Priboy's *Tsushima* (1934). A peasant by origin and a sailor by profession, Alexey Novikov-Priboy (b. 1877) is regarded as one of the leading lights among the older " proletarian " writers. He began writing long before the Revolution, but his first book of stories appeared in 1917. He has been hitherto known as the author of unpretentious but vivid sea-yarns which enjoyed great popularity with the readers in revolutionary Russia ; many of them had the inevitable revolutionary ingredient. *Tsushima* is a more ambitious work. Its subject is an episode in the Russo-Japanese War. It gives an eye-witness's account of the progress of Admiral Rozhdest-vensky's fleet round the world towards its doom at Tsushima. In the first part the author draws a detailed realistic picture of the sailors' workaday life ; the second part contains a description of the battle of Tsushima itself, in which the author was taken prisoner by the Japanese. Needless to say, the whole is coloured by the author's revolutionary attitude to the old régime, but his story, though inordinately long, is vividly told. *Tsushima* can hardly be called a historical novel : it does not aim at the creative transformation of history and reads rather like memoirs.

CHAPTER X

1. *Decline of Poetry*

IT has become a truism to say that poetry nowadays, in our modern world, is on the decline. This is not the place to analyse the causes of that general decline. Here we are concerned only with poetry in Soviet Russia. There, too, it is on the decline, but in the U.S.S.R. there are, of course, additional causes which contribute to this decline. Literature in Soviet Russia, like everything else, is planned ; it is artificially reared and looked after, it cannot develop free and untrammelled. These " nursery " conditions affect poetry more than any other literary genre or form : purely planned or purely political poetry is difficult to imagine. This does not mean that there is no poetry and no poets in Soviet Russia. There are still poets—and one or two of them are great poets—but the amount of poetical production, and the part played by it in literature as a whole, are insignificant. And if we look at the line of development of Soviet Russian literature from its origins to the present day, we shall perceive a gradual but steady decline of poetry. Some of the poets who began writing either before the Revolution or during its first years still continue as poets, but there is hardly any poetical undergrowth, hardly any new poets' names to single out in the last few years.

2. *Mayakovsky and Esenin*

The very first period of post-revolutionary Russian literature stood under the sign of poetry. It was dominated

165

by two movements : Futurism and Imaginism ; and by two names respectively : Vladimir Mayakovsky (1894–1930) and Sergey Esenin (1895–1925), although neither of them was representative of the movement with which his name was associated. Mayakovsky had little to do with the theory of Futurism, but he came to be the real driving force behind it. He appeared on the literary scene about 1913 and at once set about conquering popularity in the street. He had no scruples in using extra-literary means, in organizing rows and making literary scenes, in doing everything *pour épater les bourgeois*. By the time of the Revolution he already enjoyed a certain notoriety. There was no intentional obscurity in his poetry, he was much less involved and sophisticated than some of the theoretical Futurists like Khlebnikov ; if anything he erred on the side of extreme simplicity, coarseness, and vulgarity. It is true that he tried to revolutionize poetical technique, but he did it so as to make poetry more, and not less, comprehensible to the masses. He broke and deformed the Russian syntax, but without going to extremes ; he developed some of the prosodic innovations of the Symbolists, basing his poetry not on a sequence of accented and unaccented syllables, which forms the essence of the Russian tonico-syllabic verse, but on the number of stresses in a line, paying no heed to the unstressed syllables ; thus achieving greater freedom and producing novel and not always disagreeable effects ; finally, and this was most important, he deliberately vulgarized and lowered the poetical vocabulary—to suit the vulgar unrefined taste. Among his pre-revolutionary works his long poem, *The Cloud in Trousers*, is typical of what he is capable of, so far as the powerful poetical effects and the unmitigated vulgarity of speech and coarseness of contents are concerned. Some of its passages are unparalleled for their cynical blasphemy.

The Revolution gave Mayakovsky an opportunity of bringing his poetry still nearer to the masses, by giving it a political turn, making it subservient to the political designs of the Communist Party, turning it into propaganda verse. He openly called it so, and excelled in this genre. From 1918 on, he issued his " commands " to the artists of the Revolution. In the same year he wrote his dramatic poem *Mystery-Bouffe* which glorified the October Revolution. In 1920 appeared his long poem *150,000,000*. It was full of bombastic Soviet patriotism and revolutionary propaganda, being an invective and a satire aimed at the Western capitalist world personified in the American President Woodrow Wilson. The satirical note was always prominent in Mayakovsky's work, and apart from his poetry, much of which, especially in the first years of the Revolution, was satirical, he wrote two good satirical plays : *The Bug* and *The Bathhouse*. Mayakovsky managed to retain his popularity and his privileged position with the official Communist circles even after Futurism as such had fallen into disfavour. But in his later work, inasmuch as it was not purely satirical or propagandist, there is present a strong and growing note of disillusionment, and during the last years of his life he was once more turning to lyric, even more personal than his early lyrical verse. In 1930 he committed suicide because of a romantic and unfortunate love affair. This was the apparent reason for his death, but it seems likely that the general mood of disillusionment must have played some part in it. His suicide came as a great shock and surprise in Soviet Russia, especially as five years before he had severely deprecated Esenin for doing the same thing.

During 1923–25 Sergey Esenin was the most popular poet in Soviet Russia. His popularity was different from Mayakovsky's, of a wider and more sweeping kind, and he was popular not because he was officially encouraged and patronized from above, but rather in spite of the unfavourable attitude of the official Communist circles. There was a period when "Eseninism" was proclaimed a dangerous political disease threatening the Communist body with disintegration. Numerous works of fiction reflect the grip which "Eseninism" had at one time on Soviet youth.

Sergey Esenin was a real peasant from the Province of Ryazan. All he had in the way of education was the elementary education he received at the village school. He was a genuine poet with a natural, inborn gift of song. As a child, he had, under the influence of his mother, shown strong religious leanings, and this accounts for his frequent use of religious symbols and images even after he had cast off that primitive, childish, religious faith. His first steps in literature date from 1915, when he came to Petrograd and made the acquaintance of some leading Symbolist poets who sponsored his literary *début*. Symbolist influences were strongly felt in his work, especially in the earliest and latest periods, less so in the intermediary period, when he became associated with the Imaginist movement in poetry. His connection with Imaginism as a literary movement was, however, accidental and superficial, and his later verse was characterized by the unsophisticated simplicity and genuineness of its lyrical diction. He was primarily a lyric poet who loved his country, had a great sense of nature and a fundamentally religious conception of the world, even when he tried to be blasphemous. His attempts at epic creations, such as his poem *Pugachev*, were a failure. At the beginning of the Revolution, in 1918, Esenin voiced his enthusiastic acceptance of it in a poem called *Inonia*—he hailed it as a revival of the traditional "wooden" peasant Russia. He shared that revolutionary Messianism with other poets, like Alexander Blok and Andrey Bely, and voiced the sentiments which, in terms of political parties, were rather the appanage of the Social-Revolutionaries of the Left than of the Communists. His subsequent attitude to the Revolution, when its anti-peasant, proletarian and industrial, aspects became clear, was that of growing disillusionment. He took to drink, married Isadora Duncan and became the rowdy chief of the Moscow literary bohemians. That current of rowdyism is reflected especially in his poems of 1922–23, in the book of verse called *The Tavern Moscow* and in the poems *The Confession of a Hooligan* and *The Black Man*. Esenin's popularity and influence, especially with the younger generation, were at their highest during those years, and Eseninism, with its disintegrating and demoralizing tendencies, was, as I have said, denounced by the Communist Party as one of the principal evils to be fought against. His suicide in December 1925, and his dying farewell poem written with his own blood, were a tragic but logical culmination to this mood of disillusionment.

3. *Pasternak*

Boris Pasternak (b. 1890) is regarded by many as the greatest of the living Russian poets. He is certainly, alongside with Osip Mandelstam, the most cultured. The son of a well-known painter, after finishing a secondary school in Moscow, he studied philosophy in the Universities of Moscow and Marburg. He also made a serious study of music. His literary activity began in 1913 and he started as an adept of one of the many varieties of Russian Futurism. His first book of verse *A Twin in Cloud* was followed in 1917 by *Over the Barriers*. But it was only after he published, in 1922, his third book, *My Sister Life*, written much earlier (in 1917), that his literary reputation was made. In the next year it was followed by a new book of verse *Themes and Variations*. In 1925 he published a book of stories *The Childhood of Luvers* (see below). Pasternak's next poetical works came out in 1926 and 1927; they were two long poems, one, *Spektorsky*, of an autobiographical character, and the other, *The Year 1905*—about the Revolution of 1905. In 1931 appeared another piece of prose, an autobiographical work called *The Safe Conduct*, and this was followed in 1932 by a new book of lyrical verse—*The Second Birth*.

Although Pasternak began as a Futurist, he had really little in common with the Futurists outside his will to create new poetic values. He is primarily a lyric poet, a romantic, an individualist. In its passionate intensity his verse has been compared to Lermontov's. He is not an easy poet; indeed he is often rather obscure owing to his weird syntactical turns and his sudden unexpected metaphorical jumps. He deliberately strives to be original and uses associative elliptical methods of construction. His rhythms are vigorous and infectious. But it is above all the novelty of his vision and of the way in which he conveys it to us, that make him so startlingly fresh and original. He intentionally discards all hackneyed poetical expressions and uses " vulgar " prosaic idioms and technical words or unexpected locutions. He constructs his verses on the intonation basis, that is he tries to imitate as near as possible the intonations and cadences of ordinary speech, and yet he manages to achieve wonderful musical and rhythmical effects.

Pasternak who is a man of great culture, has never ceased to be an individualist. Even as a Futurist he remained alien to the political tendency in Futurism which was represented by Mayakovsky and Aseyev. But he tried to broach upon wider social themes in his two

longer poems, *Spektorsky* and *The Year Nineteen Five.*
The former is a tale in verse, relating some episodes in
the life of a young Moscow intellectual and bringing in
some facts of Pasternak's own life. It deals with purely
subjective, amorous and intellectual, experiences of the
hero, and is told in a personal vein. Once or twice
Pasternak seems to apologize for having selected as his
hero a socially "insignificant" personage. Its verse is
very Pasternakian, full of happy discoveries, but the
narrative is somewhat involved and obscure, and it shows
Pasternak's limitations as an epic poet. *The Year Nineteen
Five* is a series of fragments presenting various aspects
of the Revolution of 1905, the most important but not
the best of these fragments being a poem about Lieutenant
Schmidt and the famous Potemkin mutiny in the Black
Sea fleet. Here Pasternak seemingly overcomes his
individualistic, anti-social tendencies which have earned
him unpopularity with the orthodox followers of Communism, but remains a lyric poet even in his treatment
of the social theme. In *The Second Birth*, however, he
once more recovers his real poetical self and shows
himself as a lyric poet of the purest kind. Nature and
intérieur rather than social events are the favourite background for his personal lyric utterances. He has something of Tyutchev's cosmic feeling. The background
of many of his poems in *Second Birth* is the Caucasus
with its majestic landscapes. One of the best describes,
with true Pasternakian felicity and freshness of expression
and an acute sense for sound-associations (which makes,
indeed, his best poems almost untranslatable), a vision
of Tiflis from the mountains. Even when Pasternak tries
to be political, as he does in some poems, he cannot help
remaining personal, as in the poem where he speaks of
the "remoteness of Socialism" being "close by."
From the majestic splendours of the Caucasus he longs

to go " back home, in the vastness of the flat inspiring sadness," he is yearning for the " sedate life, such as it is." He aspires to simplicity and even to dumbness—in a poem which echoes Tyutchev's famous masterpiece *Silentium*. He says :

" There are in the experience of great poets—The features of such naturalness—That it is impossible, having tasted of them,—Not to end in complete dumbness.—Having ascertained one's relationship with all that is,—And being familiar in life with the future,—It is impossible not to fall ultimately, as into an heresy,—Into an unheard-of simplicity."

He ends, however, on a sceptical note by saying that although this " unheard of simplicity " is most of all needed by men, they understand complex things better.

Recently Pasternak (as well as Tikhonov, of whom more below) has been engaged in translating into Russian some contemporary Georgian poets, partly apparently by way of " escape," partly in order to comply with the demand to familiarize the Russian reader with non-Russian literatures of the Soviet Union.

4. *Tikhonov*

From 1922, when poetry was gradually losing its dominating role and the revival of prose fiction began, poetical forms underwent a change, which, if not quite similar, was at least parallel, to the evolution of fiction, a change towards greater concretization, towards Realism, romantic and otherwise. It is possible to trace several phases in this process which becomes especially marked after 1923, when the influence of Futurism, and in particular of its political, rhetorical and declamatory variety, began to dwindle. One of the first manifestations of this new tendency in poetry were the books of Nikolay

Tikhonov (b. 1896) : *The Horde* (1922) and *Mead* (1923).
They showed the influence of Gumilev and of Acmeism
in general and of the English Romantics, especially in
Tikhonov's predilection for the ballad. His ballads
dealing with the Civil War were in spirit, if not in form,
the poetical counterpart of the dynamic prose then prevailing in literature. They were romantic and realistic
at the same time. After the rhetorical, high-sounding
propaganda of Mayakovsky's political verse, after the
verbal experiments of the Imaginists, after the nebulous
revolutionary symbolism of the proletarian Cosmists from
the *Smithy* group, Tikhonov's poems brought with them
a refreshing touch of real life, a glimpse of men and
the Revolution as the poet saw them ; at the same time
their lyrical tone was that of heroic Romanticism. Not
that they were out to idealize anything, but they conveyed
that spirit of romantic heroism which pervaded everyday
life at the time, when all events, however petty, were
charged with vital significance ; when, in the words of
Tikhonov, " in every drop there slept a flood, mountains
grew through a small stone, and in a twig trampled
underfoot black-armed forests made their noise " ; when
—to use again the words of one of his ballads—" coins
lost their weight and sonorousness, and children no
longer feared dead bodies," and when " we first learned
beautiful, bitter and cruel words."

Tikhonov's books exercised a great influence on the
younger poets, including some of the proletarians, who
turned from the misty symbolism of the Cosmists to
earthly full-blooded realities. Lelevich, Rodov, Obradovich, Kazin, and even Bezymensky, all were influenced
by Tikhonov. In the case of Obradovich and especially
Bezymensky (see below) this influence was, however,
complicated by the Futurist influences, that of Mayakovsky
in particular.

Tikhonov himself, of late, has been forsaking poetry and turning his attention to prose.

5. *Selvinsky and Constructivism*

The same tendency towards concretization in poetry was manifested in the movement which took the name of Constructivism. Its chief theoretician and critic is Kornely Zelinsky; its principal poet Ilya Selvinsky. It had some points in common with Futurism, but it tried to realize to the greatest possible extent the principle of organization in a poetical work introducing into it the methods of prose, creating what it called the " local method ", which consisted in subordinating the imagery and vocabulary of the poem to its subject, in " localizing " it stylistically. It broke with certain traditions of Futurism, among other things with its wholesale rejection of æsthetics, art and culture of the past. But it retained the Futurists' cult of the technique.

As a school, Constructivism remains rather vague and heterogeneous. Its poetical *maître* Ilya Selvinsky (b. 1899) has to his credit several books of poems and four longer works. He began as a dreamer and individualist, but has gradually come round to accept the Revolution and lay stress on the social function of poetry. His principal works are *Ulyalaevshchina* (1927), *Memoirs of a Poet* (1928), *Pushtorg* (1929) and *Pao-Pao* (1932). *Ulyalaevshchina* is almost a novel in verse dealing with the bandit movements in the East of Russia and portraying several cleverly drawn characters. The plot of the poem is somewhat blurred and this is one of its defects, but the tendency towards plot as such, away from purely lyrical forms, is typical of Constructivism. Selvinsky is a realist, even a naturalist : in *Ulyalaevshchina* one feels his greediness for life. One critic has aptly described him as " temperamental rationalist ". His vocabulary, his syntax and his irregular metres have been strongly influenced by Mayakovsky. In some of his works, *e.g.* in his *Gypsy Poems*, Selvinsky is making mere word-and-sound experiments, he introduces new typographical methods, he punctuates his words with full stops and queries, he mixes Latin characters with Russian—these verses are experiments merely for the sake of experiment, but in Selvinsky's longer poems and in his best lyrical verse this element of experimentation is subordinated to a wider design. In *Pao-Pao* Selvinsky has written a lyrical play. It is the story of an ape which is supposed to symbolize both the low and animal instincts of mankind and also bourgeois culture. On getting into the beneficent proletarian environment of a Soviet factory and discovering there the only true ideology, that of Marxism, Selvinsky's monkey becomes human. This lyrical play is Selvinsky's contribution to the Five-Year Plan literature. It must be confessed that it is an utter failure.

In his *Memoirs of a Poet*, which like *Ulyalaevshchina* is a tale in verse, but with a still hazier plot, Selvinsky displays his gift of parodist : some of his parodies of the principal Soviet poets are very much to the point.

6. Bagritsky

The young poet Eduard Bagritsky (born in 1896 ; died in March 1934) also belonged formally to the Constructivists. He was one of the most talented and original of the younger Soviet poets. His first book of poems *South-West* had some points of resemblance with Tikhonov's romantic Realism. It was possible to trace in him the same influences—of Gumilev and Acmeism, of the English Romantics (there were in his first book some good translations from English). He was a Romantic himself who looked upon the Revolution as something strange and alien, but inevitable. In one

of the best of his lyrical poems, in which one feels the
winds of the Revolution blowing, he speaks of "strange
constellations rising over us," of "strange banners un-
furling over us." And he feels himself to be "a rusty
oak leaf" bound to follow those strange banners. In
some of his poems he tried, however, to approach nearer
to the subject of the Revolution and to portray it otherwise
than purely subjectively. Such are his *Conversation With
the Young Communist Dementyev* and especially his *Lay
About Opanas*, the story of a Ukrainian peasant who flies
from the Communist food-detachment commanded by
the Jew Kogan, encounters on his way the "Green"
anarchist bands of Makhno and is forced to join them.
Then Kogan is taken prisoner by the Makhno bands
and Opanas is despatched to shoot him. On the way
to the execution he changes his mind and proposes to
Kogan to let him escape, but Kogan chooses death.
Later on the Mahkno bands are defeated by the Reds
and Opanas in his turn taken prisoner. Questioned by
the Red commander Kotovsky he confesses to having
killed Kogan and submits docilely to the execution. It is
a typical revolutionary heroic poem. In his later poems,
collected in *The Victors* and *The Last Night*, Bagritsky
drew nearer to the Revolution and to Socialism, without,
however, becoming didactic or doctrinaire : his sense of
life saved him from that. In his posthumously published
autobiographical narrative poem *February* the romantic
note is revived again.

Although Bagritsky called himself a Constructivist, his
connection with the group was rather loose and there was
little in common between him and Selvinsky.

7. *Aseyev*

Futurism also developed a tendency towards grand
epic forms, which tended to supersede purely lyrical or

propaganda poetry. Next to Mayakovsky, one of the principal representatives of post-revolutionary Futurism was Nikolay Aseyev. He began writing and publishing before the Revolution. Less revolutionary in form than Mayakovsky, he appeared in his first poems as a rebelling individualist, a brigand, fond of romantic " stylizations " of Cossacks. His revolutionary protest sought inspiration in the past, and assumed archaic forms. In his poems of 1914-15 there is a manifest tendency to escape from the world, to go back to primitive nature ; they are full of vitality and movement. Aseyev accepted the Revolution from the very outset, but like most poets of the time he accepted it romantically. Its romantic rebellion appealed to him and harmonized with his own moods. Like all the Romantics of the Revolution he took a hostile attitude to the New Economic Policy in which he saw a return to bourgeois life and habits. These moods were reflected especially in his poem *A Lyrical Digression*, through which there runs a feeling of bitter despair and solitude.

From 1923 on, Aseyev took an active part in the so-called LEF—" Left front of literature ", which published a review of its own under the same name. The political vein in his poetry became more pronounced, he began writing industrial lyrics and dealt in his poems with topical themes of Soviet everyday life. But he still returns at times to his romantic attitude, and in his revolutionary poems it is possible to find traces of his early " stylizations ". His three longer revolutionary poems—*The Poem of the 26 Baku Commissars*, *The Poem About Budyenny* and *Semen Proskakov* (where a Red Soldier is contrasted with Admiral Kolchak) mark the consecutive stages in Aseyev's poetical assimilation of the Revolution.

8. Bezymensky and other Proletarian Poets

Bezymensky, Zharov, Obradovich, Golodny, Ushakov, Svetlov, and other younger proletarian poets represent the realistic period in proletarian poetry, which began after 1923. They differ, both in their themes and in their style, from the earlier proletarian poets—the Cosmists of the *Smithy* group. If the style of the *Smithy* poets was obviously influenced by the Symbolists, that of Bezymensky, Ushakov, Zharov, and others, evolved under the influence of Mayakovsky's coarse and bombastic diction, though in the case of some of the proletarian Realists, like Doronin, Golodny and Svetlov, there is a tendency towards classical forms, towards greater simplicity and lyricism. While the *Smithy* poets often took for their subject the worker in his professional life at the factory, the younger generation of the proletarian writers, less organically connected with the working class (many of them do not even belong to it and have come to the Revolution from outside) concentrate their attention on the political element, on the life of the Communist Party and of the Young Communist League. This was especially the case with Bezymensky. He was the poet of the Young Communist League and the Communist Party, their recognized bard. His popularity at one time was very great and his works published in huge quantities. He was on the way to becoming the Poet Laureate of the Soviet Government—the position held from the beginning of the Revolution by Demyan Bedny (real name Pridvorov), who is however only a clever (and even this not always) political rhymster, and not a real poet. But after the change of policy in 1932, Bezymensky's influence and popularity has dwindled. Bezymensky is a 100 per cent. Communist. If the " civic " poets of the nineteenth century proclaimed that one " need not be a poet but must be a good citizen," Bezymensky went still further, saying that in his poetry he was primarily a member of the Communist Party and only then a poet. In nearly every poem he proclaims his Communist convictions. It was he who coined the formula that had such a success : " I carry my membership card of the Communist Party not in my pocket but in myself." To the traditional sentimental themes of the " bourgeois " lyric poetry he opposed the matter-of-fact proletarian realities. Let others think of spring, he said—

> But I walk on and on, and think persistently
> Of the cost price of Soviet goods.

Or :

> Some are afraid for girlish lips,
> And I for the smoking stacks.

His attitude to the world is that of joyful optimism. He says that, " if the heart of a Communist nucleus could for a moment become a fifty-kopeck piece it would contain two kopecks' worth of bitterness and forty-five kopecks' worth of joy." Life for him has " a nice tasty smell ". One of his first books was called *That's How Life Smells*. But the principal thing for the proletarian poet is " to be able to find the World Revolution behind every small trifle."

Bezymensky's verse is akin to Mayakovsky's—it is coarse, bombastic, declamatory, intentionally devoid of all musicality. His vocabulary is full of vulgarisms. In his *Poem About Love*, which is a posthumous " reprimand" to Mayakovsky for his suicide, he calls d'Anthès " that son of a bitch ". In his longer poems (*Komsomolia, A Little Town*) he uses a rapid succession of most varied metres. Bezymensky lacks the sensuous vision of the world : he explains and relates things rather than shows them. And much of his poetry is mere rhymed journalism. But if in his earlier verse the life of the Communist Party and political propaganda were his almost only subjects, later his field of vision was somewhat enlarged and his official optimism mitigated by the realization of the tenacity of the old-world instincts beneath the Communist surface of Russian life. He suddenly perceived the " Tartar face " of Russia (*Pathways*, 1925). He remains, however, in his poetry an orthodox Communist. His popularity was at its highest during the Five-Year Plan period of literature when he came forward as one of the staunchest and most intransigent partisans of the official policy in literary matters. His dramatic poem *The Shot* (1930) produced a sensation of a political rather than a literary nature. His *Night of a Chief of Politsec* is also a political poem—or rather a series of poems united by the common subject. The subject is the work of the political instructor on a collective farm. It is a curious mixture of different styles—Mayakovsky rubbing shoulders with Koltsov and Nadson. There is in it a strong strain of sentimentalism (" socialistic ", it is true), rather unusual in Bezymensky.

Another proletarian poet of the same stamp deriving his poetics from Mayakovsky and the Futurists, is Alexander Zharov, but he is much less interesting and typical than Bezymensky.

Nikolay Ushakov, author of *The Spring of the Republic*, is a much younger writer. He also proceeds from Mayakovsky but develops a lyrical strain and is less political in his choice of subjects.

Mikhail Golodny, Ivan Doronin and Mikhail Svetlov tend towards greater simplicity and look to classical poetry for their models. Of these three Svetlov is the most talented and original.

Alexander Prokofyev is turning for inspiration to Russian folk-lore and trying to create new modes of expression for his socialistic themes.

A place apart among the proletarian poets of to-day belongs to Vasily Kazin. He comes from the *Smithy* group, but has nothing of their nebulous Cosmism and Symbolism. His vision of the world is concrete and fresh, and he finds fresh and unhackneyed words and images to convey it. In this he is akin to Pasternak. But Kazin is as simple and unsophisticated as Pasternak is sophisticated and complex. There are no intellectual depths in Kazin : he gladly and simply accepts the world as he sees it, and he sees and represents it in a way that is his very own. He has, however, been writing very little of late.

Finally, it is necessary to mention a curious figure in to-day's Soviet poetry—Nikolay Zabolotsky, author of numerous " productive " and " agricultural " poems in which he often endows animals with human properties, but in a manner that has nothing of the fable about it. There is in his poems an odd mixture of hyperbolism and matter-of-factness. At times they seem too much like parodies or nonsense verse to be taken seriously. Yet he is taken seriously in Soviet Russia, and the poet Tikhonov said recently of Zabolotsky that he must either " commit creative suicide " or completely reorganize his poetics and his attitude to the world.

9. *The Poets' Prose : Mandelstam, Pasternak, Tikhonov*

Osip Mandelstam (b. 1892) published in 1928 a little book of prose, *The Egyptian Stamp*, which revealed in him an interesting and original prose writer, with a very personal style. It shows the same sense of historicity, the same feeling of time as his poetry. The central piece in this collection of semi-imaginative essays is called *The Noise of Time*. To call them autobiographical would be inexact : Mandelstam himself says that he prefers not to speak of himself, but to follow his age, " the noise and growth of time." And he succeeds very well in conveying not only the noise but the smell of it : the atmosphere of the pre-revolutionary St. Petersburg and of Theodosia during the Revolution, of a bourgeois Jewish family in which he grew up, and of one of the fashionable modern schools to which he went and which in some ways tried to imitate English schools. The slightly caricatured figure of Parnok, which gives a certain structural unity to the otherwise somewhat incoherent title-essay, and the lovingly drawn portrait of the author's friend Sinani, not to speak of some minor personages, whom Mandelstam brings to life, are excellent character creations. Mandelstam likes to generalize, and sometimes hits upon very happy " formulæ ", full of fresh and unexpected imagery. Such are, for example, his two pages on music in *The Egyptian Stamp* where, in images of startling originality, he tries to convey his impressions of different composers. One of the best chapters in *The Noise of Time* is "The Bookcase"—a description of his first bookcase and its contents. It shows that Mandelstam can remain "concrete" while generalizing. A recollection of the book of Nadson's poems, which he calls " the key to the epoch ", leads him on to a most striking, synthetic portrait of the Russian intelligentsia of the nineties. *The Egyptian Stamp* is one of the most personal, original, and enjoyable books in Russian post-revolutionary literature—it stands in a class by itself.

Pasternak's prose is unlike anything else in Russian literature. It is most certainly a poet's prose, but it is devoid of any specific poeticalness. Yet it has great affinities with his poetry—the same originality and freshness of vision and the same felicity of expression. His most typical prose work is *The Childhood of Luvers*. It is the story of a few years in the life of a girl on the

verge of puberty. There is no outward plot, the story
is really about nothing, but not at all in the way in which
some of Chekhov's stories are created out of nothing.
Pasternak is concerned with rendering the deep subconscious current of life in the soul of his heroine and
he does so just as much by noting the inner movements
of her soul, as by the description of things outside her
that take part in her life and affect her. Pasternak's
method has sometimes been compared to that of Proust,
but though a certain influence of the greatest of modern
French novelists can be traced in Pasternak's prose, the
difference is very great. Pasternak is at once more
concise and more elliptical. Another name that occurs
when one reads Pasternak's stories is that of Rainer-
Maria Rilke, the great German poet whom Pasternak
admires very much and whose influence is visible also
in his poetry.

Here is a typical passage from *The Childhood of Luvers*
describing the girl's illness :

" This was due probably to someone's heavy steps
behind the door. The tea in the glass, on the little
table by the bed, rose and came down. The slice of
lemon in tea rose and came down. The sunny stripes
on the wall-paper swung. They swung in pillars like
bottles of syrups in shops behind the signboards on
which a Turk is smoking a pipe. On which a Turk . . .
is smoking . . . a pipe. Smoking . . . a pipe.

" This was due probably to someone's steps. The
patient again fell asleep.

" Zhenia fell ill the next day after Negarat's departure ; on that very day when she learned after her
walk that in the night Aksinya had given birth to a
boy ; on that day when at the sight of the van with
furniture she decided that its owner was going to have
rheumatism. She spent a fortnight of fever, thickly
spattered over the sweat with painful red pepper which
burnt her eyelids and the corners of her lips. She was

vexed by perspiration and a feeling of hideous fatness
was mingled with the sense of a sting. As if the flame
that made her swell had been poured into her by a
summer wasp. As if its sting, thin like a grey hair,
had stuck in, and one longed to take it out, more
than once and in more than one way: now from the
purple cheekbone, now from the inflamed shoulder
aching under her chemise, now from somewhere
else."

Apart' from *The Childhood of Luvers* and a few other
shorter stories (first published in 1925; reprinted in
1933 under the title *Aerial Ways*, with a new prose
fragment added, distantly related to the poem *Spektorsky*),
Pasternak wrote a very interesting autobiographical work
The Safe Conduct—the confession of a Romantic and
individualist at grips with a fundamentally hostile world.
Of all Pasternak's stories only *Aerial Ways* has some
relation to the Revolution, but the latter is only a background to its psychological theme, necessary for a more
complete illustration of one of its characters.

"When a poet writes prose he merely extends the
range of his work,"—these words of Nikolay Tikhonov
can be well applied to his own work. In his prose he
remains true to his romantic Realism. He showed this
in his first book of stories *The Venturesome Man* (1927).
He is not content with seeing the primary superficial
truth of real life; beyond it he perceives another and
different truth: it is, in his own words, the truth of
artistic perception which merges into the subtle art of
artistic lie and consists in transforming everyday life so
that from a mere accident it becomes something many-
sided and general. Tikhonov's art is based on his vision
of reality, but he condenses that reality and turns it into
something almost fantastic. He likes sharp, definite outlines and bright colours. Neither in his descriptions nor
in his psychological analysis does he admit of any finer

shades. He likes unusual dramatic situations, and he prefers to show his characters in action. Curiously enough, while tending in his poetry to become less of a Romantic and more of a Realist (such is the tendency of his verse after *Mead*), in his prose Tikhonov is moving in the opposite direction. His latest work *An Oath in the Fog* (1933), a story with a well thought-out and exciting plot, taking place in Svanetia, a mountainous region in the Caucasus, is full of this heightened Romanticism, of adventures, of unusual characters. Yet Tikhonov's Realism is felt in the thoroughness with which he has studied his material, his background. But he knows how to give it a romantic and fantastic twist without ceasing to be a Realist. His *Oath in the Fog* is more romantic than his previous book *War* (1932) or his collection of Five-Year Plan descriptive sketches of Central Asia (*The Nomads*, 1930), although even in this latter, behind all its matter-of-factness, the reality is sometimes condensed to fantasy and romance. Tikhonov's style is in harmony with his romantic Realism : it is vigorous, virile and picturesque—in its wise economy one feels the influence of his poetical training, his Acmeist heritage. He is likewise in no small degree indebted to Kipling, both in the technique of his stories and in the spirit of romantic Realism which pervades them ; like Kipling's, many of them deal with military life ; often their action is set on the eastern outskirts of Russia.

CHAPTER XI

THE DRAMA

EVERYBODY who visits Soviet Russia comes back impressed by the fact that here is the only country in the world where there is no crisis in the theatre, where the theatrical life is in full swing, and the art of the theatre is blossoming in all its varieties. The names of Stanislavsky, Meyerhold, and Tairov are known all over the world. They stand for different and even diametrically opposed tendencies. It must, however, be noted that the tendencies they represent are not of revolutionary creation, that they were all rooted in the pre-revolutionary Russian theatre, and only some of them received a fresh impetus from the Revolution. The intense psychological realism of Stanislavsky and his Moscow Art Theatre, with its tendency to extend the psychological treatment of the characters of a play beyond its actual limits, to create personal biographies of those characters; the Constructivism of Meyerhold and his highly pronounced tendency to subordinate the author and the actors to the supreme will of the producer; the " pure " theatre of Tairov, as much opposed to psychological realism and naturalism as Meyerhold's, but differing from the latter in its tendency towards æsthetic " theatricalization " of reality—in their substance all these different theatrical currents already existed before the Revolution. In the case of Stanislavsky and Tairov the Revolution did not even affect to any considerable extent the main line of their development, but in the case of Meyerhold it instilled into his theatre new social and political contents, led him on to what Lunacharsky termed his " socio-mechanics " : the constructivist technique was sub-ordinated to the class idea.

Stanislavsky (the Moscow Art Theatre), Tairov (the Kamerny Theatre), and Meyerhold represent the three principal currents in the contemporary Russian theatre. All the other theatres, especially the new which sprang up after the Revolution, either proceed from one of them or represent an attempt to combine their principles. Thus, the Vakhtangov Theatre combines the methods of Stanislavsky with those of Meyerhold. The Theatre of the Revolution (Alexey Popov), the Realistic Theatre (Okhlopkov), and the Leningrad Dramatic Theatre (Akimov), follow more or less in the path of Meyerhold, though the latter's influence is tempered by some others. The Theatre of the Revolution especially aims at a synthesis of various methods. It is also most consistent in choosing for its productions modern plays with a definite social and political significance. The same stress on the modernity of the repertoire is laid by the Trades Unions' Theatre, but here the theatrical method is that of realism.

The Revolution undoubtedly gave a new impetus to the theatrical life of Russia. There were several reasons for this. There is no denying, of course, the efforts expended by the Soviet Government in fostering theatrical culture, especially during the first years of the Revolution, when it realized what a powerful weapon of propaganda the theatre could be. But to these conscious efforts must be added the inherent theatrical instinct of the Russian people, its love of the spectacular, which was intensified during the Revolution, because the theatre came to be one of the means of escaping from the hard and cruel realities of life. Even during the worst years of famine and general misery the theatres in Moscow were crowded. The numerical increase of theatres and theatrical audiences since the Revolution has been enormous. Factory and village club theatres, children's theatres, theatres of various national minorities (Jewish, Georgian, Armenian, etc.)—such are more or less new post-revolutionary developments in the life of the Russian theatre. The theatrical technique has progressed with gigantic strides. But the weak spot of the post-revolutionary theatre is its lack of good dramatic literature. Russian theatre as such has always been more interesting and significant than the dramatic literature on which it had to rely and to feed itself, but never was the scarcity of good dramatic literature so strikingly disclosed and illustrated as in the modern Russian theatre, and especially in the first years after the Revolution.

In an article published about two years ago the novelist Zamyatin reported the conversation he had in Moscow with the well-known American producer Cecil de Mille. " Your theatre," said de Mille to Zamyatin, " is nowadays certainly the most interesting in the world. Your actors and producers are, without any doubt, ahead of the whole world. But . . . where are your new plays which would be worthy of these actors and producers ? "

The problem of creating a new revolutionary repertoire has been tormenting the leaders of the Soviet theatre ever since its inception. Even before the Revolution, more than in any other country, the Russian theatre had to rely to a great extent on foreign repertoire, and what there was of the original dramatic literature, was, with a few exceptions, eminently undramatic and untheatrical. Such was, after all, practically the whole theatre, not only of Chekhov, but also of Ostrovsky. This explains to a great extent the fact that the aspirations of modern Russian theatre towards " theatricalization " made it go to the extreme in denying the role of the playwright in the art of theatre, in trying to do without him or in taking the utmost liberties with his texts—hence Meyerhold's well-known free and often distorted adaptations or "stylizations" of classical plays (Gogol's *Revizor*, Ostrovsky's *Forest*)—we find them ridiculed in Ilf and Petrov's *Twelve Chairs*. Meyerhold proclaimed the supremacy of the producer over the writer and the actor—and in this he was not alone : the European theatre showed the same tendency ; Max Reinhardt in Germany, Granville-Barker in England saw a few years ago the renovation of the theatre in its emancipation from the author. But parallel with Meyerhold's experiments on this "authorless" path and the development of the theatre along the line of mass performances, of revolutionary festivals, in which the elements of enthusiasm and of satire sometimes clashed, and which, in a way, were a revival of the ancient and medieval conception of the theatre as a mass mystery, the problem of a new repertoire continued to preoccupy those concerned with the destinies of the Russian theatre.

In 1927, surveying the results achieved by the Soviet theatre during the first revolutionary decade, Vladimir Wolkenstein, one of the leading Russian dramatic critics and himself a dramatist of some merit, wrote : "The problem of the new theatre is above all a problem of a new repertoire." In summing up the results of ten years of dramatic activity he was rather optimistic, emphasizing especially "the increasing interest taken by the public in the new plays." But Wolkenstein surely erred on the side of official optimism. Three or four years later Cecil de Mille was still asking Zamyatin, "Where are your new plays ?", and Zamyatin had to agree with him that there were none. In 1933 the lack of good new plays was still the keynote of Soviet Russian dramatic criticism. And if in 1927 Wolkenstein was right that the

public demanded new plays, in the last few years it seems
to have grown tired of what it was being given in the way
of new plays, and once more shows an increased interest
in classical works. This is no doubt partly due to the
fact that the great majority of the new plays produced
since 1929 has been even inferior to the new plays of the
first revolutionary decade. Most of those Five-Year Plan
plays were cut according to the same pattern and in con-
formity with the officially set up standards. They re-
sembled dramatized political sermons rather than plays.
Zamyatin ungenerously describes the Five-Year Plan
dramatic literature as " a series of prematurely born
babies." Like all babies born before their time they had
a disproportionately large head (full of first-class ideas)
and a weak, rickety body which could not support that
head. Like all prematurely born babies they were in
need of artificial feeding and though this was supplied
plentifully by the critics, it did not save them. All these
plays were constructed according to the same model ;
they all dealt with some industrial undertaking or collectivized farm, with an invariable wreckers' plot, and in
the end counter-revolution was punished and Communism triumphant—the socialistic variety of the happy
ending. Even good writers could not instil life in those
" still-born babies " : the Five-Year Plan plays of Kataev
(*Vanguard*), Nikitin (*Line of Fire*), Trenev (*Yasny Log*)
all failed. The only exception was the success of
Afinogenov's *Fear*, one of the best plays in the modern
Soviet repertoire (it was performed in England in 1932
by the Stage Society). But *Fear* was not an ordinary
Five-Year Plan play. Although it had the inevitable
element of a wreckers' conspiracy, it also raised a problem of much wider and deeper moral significance—
the problem of the Revolution's right to terror—and
it tried to solve that problem in terms of individual

psychology, and not along the lines of a prescribed social pattern.

The Soviet Russian dramatists can be, roughly speaking, divided into three principal groups. The first, and until a few years ago the most numerous, group is constituted by the writers, mostly belonging to the intelligentsia, who either began to write or at least received their general and special theatrical education before the Revolution. Various tendencies—romantic, realistic, futuristic—are represented in this group. Among the older writers who belong to it one can mention Alexey Tolstoy, Trenev, Lunacharsky, Wolkenstein ; of the younger, Fayko, Erdman, Romashov, Tretyakov, and several others. Several well-known Soviet writers for whom the drama is only a side-line can also be included in this group : Zamyatin (besides his own plays, an adaptation of Leskov's story—*The Flea*, an attempt to revive Russian popular show staged with great success in Moscow), Babel (*The Sunset, Maria*), Fedin (*Bakunin in Dresden*), Leonov (*Untilovsk*, and the adaptations of *The Badgers* and *Skutarevsky*), Vsevolod Ivanov (*The Armoured Train*— for a long time one of the most successful plays, in spite of its technical shortcomings, in the repertoire of the Moscow Art Theatre), Seyfullina (*Virineya*), Bulgakov (*The Days of the Turbins*), Kataev (*Squaring the Circle, Vanguard, The Road of Flowers*), Olesha (*A Conspiracy of Feelings, A List of Benefits, The Three Fat Men*), Lavrenev (*The Break*), Zayaitsky (several plays for the Children's Theatre). Two young romantic poets, Andrey Globa and Konstantin Lipskerov, also belong to this group.

The second group, much less numerous, is constituted by the peasant and proletarian writers, Communists in the majority. Here belong the late Neverov (*The Womenfolk, Zakhar's Death*), Gladkov (*The Band*), Bill-Belotserkovsky (*The Storm, Echo*) and some others.

Finally, the third group, more or less akin to the second, is represented by the younger Soviet intelligentsia, by men who were brought up in post-revolutionary surroundings. The most prominent among them are Afinogenov (*Fear, The Crank*), Kirshon (*Bread, The Trial, The Marvellous Alloy*), Glebov (*Zagmuk*), Vishnevsky (*The First Cavalry Army, The Last Decisive, An Optimistic Tragedy*), Pogodin (*My Friend, Snow, Tempo*), Uspensky and others.

Whereas in the first group there is a great variety of tendencies, most of the writers of the second and third group belong to the Realist school.

The evolution of dramatic literature in Soviet Russia followed more or less along the lines of the general literary development. In other words, it evolved in the direction of Realism. During the first period, which coincided with the period of the Civil War and the turbulent years of the Revolution, the first group of writers turned its main attention to historical themes interpreted in the romantically heroic and revolutionary spirit. None of these historical revolutionary plays have really survived the test of time and some of them, like Alexey Tolstoy's *The Conspiracy of the Empress* and *Azef*, were frankly bad. The best play of this early period was perhaps *The Outlaw*, a romantic tragedy of Lev Luntz, a young and very promising writer who belonged to the group of the Serapion Brothers and died prematurely in 1923. He represented among the younger writers the extreme " Westernizing " tendency. His play, too, was fundamentally opposed not only to the prevailing tendency of the period but also to the dominant traditions of the Russian theatre : it had a well-constructed plot and a real sense of tragedy. There were also some other plays of purely romantic nature, but most of them were only printed and not staged. Lunacharsky, who then played a great personal part in the destinies of the Russian theatre, tried to combine in his own plays Romanticism with revolutionary rhetoric, but the result was poor.

The second group of writers focused its attention during this early period on revolutionary propaganda plays of a rather crude and primitive nature. Many of them were a mixture of dramatized newspaper articles with political speeches, with White villains and Red heroes for personages. They were produced in thousands and staged with great enthusiasm at the front, and in the factory and village clubs. None of them were more than ephemeral creations. But there were also propaganda plays of a somewhat higher quality, coming chiefly from writers of the first group, such as Mayakovsky's *Mystery-Bouffe*, Tretyakov's *Roar, China !* or the dramatization of Ehrenburg's *Trust D.E.* Mayakovsky's *Mystery* has, however, very little dramatic quality and reads better than it acts. Tretyakov's *Roar, China !* is, on the contrary, too primitive from the literary point of view—it is pure political propaganda made into an effective spectacle. Of the leading writers of the second group Bill-Belotserkovsky, Neverov and some others began by propaganda plays.

The second period is marked by pronounced realistic tendencies on the part of both groups, the outcome being a number of plays on contemporary subjects, dealing with the Civil War, with the changed ways of life and the problems raised by the Revolution. Trenev's *Lyubov Yarovaya*, a realistic play of the Civil War, Vsevolod Ivanov's *Armoured Train* (an adaptation of his story of the same name very effectively produced and splendidly acted by the Moscow Art Theatre), Bulgakov's *The Days of the Turbins*, also an adaptation of his novel *The White Guard*, Erdman's *Mandate*, a light and vivid Gogolian comedy produced by Meyerhold, and Lavrenev's *Break*, were among the most successful plays of the second period. Of the proletarian plays of the second period the most characteristic was Bill-Belotserkovsky's *Storm*, also dealing with the Civil War. A great success was assured to Kataev's *Squaring the Circle*, a light comedy, almost a farce, on the subject of Soviet marriage and relations between the two sexes in the student *milieu*. Student life is also the subject of *Konstantin Terekhin*, a lively, though rather slipshod comedy by Kirshon and Uspensky. The comical aspects of the new revolutionary mode of life form the subject of a number of gay comedies and vaudevilles by different writers (*e.g.* Shkvarkin's *Someone Else's Child*, one of the most successful plays of the last two years, some of Romashov's plays). The same kind of themes is treated more seriously and at the same time more satirically in the plays of Bulgakov (*Zoyka's Flat*, *The Crimson Island*).

Among the numerous Five-Year Plan plays Kirshon's *Bread* was one of the greatest official successes. A still greater success was his *Trial*, dealing with social conflicts in Germany. But speaking of both in retrospect the Soviet critics now tend to emphasize their shortcomings—namely, their artificial construction, their slipshod language, their interest in externals rather than in men. And the latest slogan in Soviet theatre, just as in Soviet literature, is " Back to man ", or should we say " Forward to the socialistic man ". Soviet dramatists, just as Soviet novelists, are on the look-out for a hero. A fresh departure in the dramatic literature of the Five-Year Plan period was Olesha's play *A List of Benefits*, where, as distinct from the same author's novel *Envy* (dramatized as *A Conspiracy of Feelings*), the conflict between Individualism and Socialism is solved more definitely in the orthodox Marxian fashion in favour of Socialism : the heroine of this play, a Soviet actress, who flees from Soviet Russia to Paris in search of a more congenial atmosphere, ends by taking part in the Revolution that breaks out in France and meeting her death on the street barricades. But even in this orthodox play Olesha, unlike most of the Five-Year Plan writers, leaves room to individual psychology. His latest theatrical work, " a play for the cinema " entitled *A Strict Youth* (published in August 1934), has for its theme the problem of inequality in the Socialist society, of the place which talent and brains must occupy in it. Socialism means inequality, and one must " live up " to those who create music, pictures, ideas and beauty—such is the main thesis of Olesha's young Communist, the principal character in the play. Olesha also brings in his favourite theme of " feelings ". The same young Communist champions some of the feelings which the Communists have come to regard as bourgeois prejudices, but which, he maintains, are really all-human. On some points Olesha's play strangely echoes Kaverin's novel *The Anonymous Artist*. But there is about this short scenario an atmosphere of light and gay airiness which is altogether absent from Kaverin's novel.

Next to Olesha's play it is strange to read the ideas expounded almost simultaneously by one of the young Communist dramatists, Pogodin (author of *My Friend* and *After the Ball*, a play about collectivization), in connection with the pan-Soviet Literary Congress held in August 1934, at which he was one of the *rapporteurs* on drama. Pogodin insists on a most ruthless extermination of all the vestiges of bourgeois psychology, of bourgeois Realism in the new socialist-realistic dramas. Candidly enough, he gives examples of those vestiges of bourgeois Realism not only in the plays of other writers, but even in his own. He seems to conceive Socialist Realism not only as something different from bourgeois Realism, as an "improvement" upon it, but as something in which there is no room for any "bourgeois" psychology. But what is the positive meaning of that Socialist Realism Pogodin does not explain. It is worth noting that this same Pogodin, a year before, was praised in Soviet theatrical magazines for introducing into his plays the human touch of humour, for having put an end to the "leather-jacket-proletarian-hero" period in Soviet dramatic literature and taken the stilts from under his personages.

Gorky's *Egor Bulychev and Others*, one of the recent productions of Vakhtangov Theatre and the Moscow Art Theatre, and its sequel *Dostigaev and Others* are variations on one of Gorky's favourite themes—the decadence of the Russian bourgeoisie. Like his latest novels these plays are essentially retrospective in character. Their success is significant as witnessing certain new developments in the Russian theatre. One of the regular Soviet dramatic critics, R. Pikel, confessed, in connection with Slavin's *Intervention*, that the theatregoer in Soviet Russia was "fed up" with "didactic, edifying plays where life is fitted into ready-made schemes and political formulæ, where utter boredom reigns, vice is punished and virtue triumphs." The theatregoer in Russia, says Pikel, wants real, full-blooded life. Significant confessions to be made in April 1933 ! Is not, after all, the story of the Soviet theatre, just as of Soviet literature, and even broader—of the Soviet Union itself—a story of the incessant struggle between the claims of life and the encroachments of the cut-and-dried doctrine, in which life gradually gains ground ? Like fiction, the drama in Soviet Russia is moving towards Realism. What is more, the theatre itself seems to be taking the same direction. After many years of experimenting on the lines of Meyerhold's and Tairov's pure "authorless" theatre, with the producer's omnipotence as the main guiding principle, the need is being felt of restoring to the author his rights. When one reads the recent articles of some of the leading Soviet dramatic critics, one thinks of Pirandello's "six personages in search of an author." In the past, one of them tells us, it was the dramatists who created their theatre—the theatres of Æschylus, Sophocles, Shakespeare, Molière, Schiller, Ostrovsky, Ibsen, and Chekhov, were the creations of the authors. But if there is no dramatist capable of creating his own theatre, it is up to the theatre to create its own dramatist. "One of the principal tasks of the Soviet drama is to combat the producer's theatre in the name of the dramatist's and actor's theatre." (Amaglobeli.) The circle is completed. After sixteen years of daring modernist experiments, of Constructivism and "pure theatre", of attempts to do away with the author and even the actor, the Russian theatre comes back to the traditional realistic conception of the theatrical art, where the role of the producer is confined to the interpretation of the dramatist's idea and the direction of the actors. The dramatist and the actor are restored to their former position as the mainstays of the realistic theatre. But as yet there is no author in Soviet Russia who would seem to be capable of creating his own theatre, of becoming a new Molière, Ostrovsky or Chekhov. In the opinion of the critic quoted above, only a few recent plays can be considered as the embryos of "the new theatre of the dramatist and the actor." He cites Gorky's *Egor Bulychev* in the Moscow Art Theatre, Slavin's *Intervention* in Vakhtangov Theatre, Pogodin's *My Friend* and Solovyev's *Personal Life* in the Theatre of the Revolution, Romashov's *Fighters* and Leonov's *Skutarevsky* in the Maly Theatre. But none of these writers can claim to be the creator of a theatre of his own. The dearth of good plays continues. One of the striking features of the Soviet theatre, connected with this dearth of good plays, is the extraordinary number of " dramatizations " of novels of Russian and foreign authors, both old (Tolstoy, Dostoevsky, Turgenev, Gogol, Balzac, Flaubert, Hugo, O. Henry, Anatole France) and modern (Leonov's *Badgers* and *Skutarevsky*, two versions of Fadeyev's *Rout*, Kataev's *Embezzlers* and *Forward, Time,* Olesha's *Envy* and *Three Fat Men*, Seyfullina's *Manure* and *Virineya*, etc. Most of them have, however, proved a poor substitute for real dramas.

Pikel, the already quoted dramatic critic, makes an interesting statement when he says that the Soviet theatre is still worse off than literature is, when it comes to the element of plot. Yet the theatregoer, just as the reader, " is attracted by a narrative rich in incident, in sharp unexpected collisions, in sudden, quite unforeseen situations. Dumas in literature, Scribe in drama, abound in these. Scribe's *Glass of Water* has been holding the stage of the Maly Theatre for a score of years. . . ." Pikel sees the elements of " *dumisme* " in Slavin's *Intervention*, and ascribes to this, among other things, its attraction for the public.

To encourage dramatic literature and to foster Socialist Realism in the theatre a Government competition was organized in 1934. The result was that no play was considered worthy of the first prize. The selection committee, which, next to some politicians, consisted of writers (Alexey Tolstoy) and producers (Meyerhold, Stanislavsky, Simonov, Vladimirov and others), in its decision stated that the Soviet drama despite all its achievements was still unable to cope with the tasks imposed on it by the fact that it is the drama of a proletarian state. " We have as yet no first-rate plays which in their ideological and artistic significance would be worthy of our great age," said the committee, and it recommended the dramatists to study their life more closely, to take a more active part in Socialist construction and to master more thoroughly " the victorious doctrine of Marx-Engels-Lenin-Stalin." Whether this recipe would produce good dramas, one may be allowed to doubt. The committee, however, found some of the 1200 plays submitted interesting and significant. It divided the second prize between Kirshon, of the *Bread* fame (*The Marvellous Alloy*), and Korniychuk (*The End of the Fleet*). Kirshon's new play is a gay comedy dealing with an important invention in the Soviet aviation industry. It is better written than *Bread* but it does not open any new horizons before the Soviet theatre. Korniychuk's drama is one of the numerous plays of the Civil War, its subject being the voluntary destruction of the Black Sea fleet in 1918. It opposes the revolutionary patriotism of the sailors to the egotism of the admiral commanding the fleet. Korniychuk, who is a young Ukrainian Communist, handles his plot and dialogue quite skilfully. The third prize was divided between three authors: Romashov (*The Fighters*), Dzhanan (*Shahname*) and Kocherga (*The Watchmaker and the Hen*). Romashov's play is a simple realistic picture of the life of the Red Army officers in peace time. Dzhanan's *Shahname*, written in the Armenian language (he is himself a well-known Armenian actor), is a political interpretation of a legendary and historical subject : its action takes place in Persia and its political sting is pointed against Great Britain as the real wirepuller behind the policy of various Persian Shahs. Kocherga's play *The Watchmaker and the Hen* is a curious combination of purely farcical situations, which the author handles with some skill, and a rather shallow revolutionary symbolism which runs through the whole play, the main idea being that the Revolution is the real master of time.

Most of the characters seem to be intentionally caricatured and especially the one who symbolizes the bourgeoisie—the half-mad German watchmaker Karfunkel.
The construction of the play is rather ingenious : its
four acts take place at the same small station in the
South of Russia in 1912, 1919, 1920 and 1929 respectively.
Thus, parallel with the action of the play, the author,
who is an old but hitherto quite unknown Ukrainian
dramatist, shows us the change from the old régime to
the Revolution and the achievements of the Soviet Government by the time of the Five-Year Plan. The play is
full of the proper revolutionary spirit.

It is interesting to note that some of the Soviet dramatists
revert to plays dealing with personal life. Such is even
the title of the previously mentioned play of Solovyev.
Personal life is also the subject of the latest play of Bill-
Belotserkovsky (*Life is Calling*), who began as the author
of propaganda pieces and highly revolutionary plays about
the Civil War. This transition is very significant. It is
also significant that his play occupies the first place among
those which the selection committee recommended for
production.

But the search of the Soviet drama for an author to
restore its vitality still continues, and the problem of the
repertoire remains as acute.

CHAPTER XII

1. *Formalism*

THROUGHOUT the second half of the nineteenth century the dominant tendency in Russian literary criticism was towards the so-called " social " or " civic " (*obshchestvenny*) criticism, towards estimating literary works by their social content and appeal. The characteristic feature of this school of criticism was its severance from the great Russian literature, which, in its best representatives, developed virtually outside the influence of this dominant school of criticism. And when we come to the twentieth century it can be said, at least with regard to one of the important schools of modern literary criticism, that it was literature that influenced its development. I mean the so-called Formalism, or as some of its adepts prefer to call it, the formal method. It goes in fact back to two main sources. On one hand, it goes back to those two schools in Russian science of literature, which are linked with the names of two remarkable scholars—Professor Alexander Veselovsky of St. Petersburg and Professor Alexander Potebnya of Kharkov, of whom the first initiated in Russia the so-called school of historical poetics, and the second the school of linguistico-psychological poetics, both breaking sharply away from the traditions of civic criticism. On the other hand the formal method was greatly indebted to modern Russian poetry, to Symbolism and its subsequent outgrowths. Chronologically speaking, Formalism, as a school in the study of literature, practically coincided with the appearance of Futurism, and, especially in its Left extremist wing, was closely connected with the latter. But the basis of the formal method in the broad sense of that term had been laid down on the one hand by the literary historical studies of Veselovsky and Potebnya, as well as the kindred movements outside Russia, and on the other by the poetry and poetics of Symbolism, especially in the person of Andrey Bely whose studies of Russian prosody marked an epoch in Russian literary studies and exercised a decisive influence. In spite of Bely's errors in some particulars and of the fallacy of some of his conclusions, his work in this field still retains its value and interest. The method first applied by him to the study of Russian poetry was followed and developed by the Formalists.

What, in the case of the Symbolists, had been a more or less limited expression of their natural interest in problems of literary form, and had been confined to poetry, Formalism as a school tried to embody in a theory and apply to all the facts of literature, construing literary science along the same lines which are adopted in approaching other arts. It studied literature as an evolution of literary forms and genres and tended to reject all extra-literary—ideological, sociological, psychological, biographical and other—elements. Literature, it said, was primarily an art, and therefore literary science and literary criticism must in the first place deal with the specific *devices* of that art (the Formalists use the word " *priëm* " = *procédé*) and not with its philosophical, social, psychological or biographical contents. But almost from the beginning, different currents could be distinguished in Formalism and later on this distinction became still more sharp ; at the same time Formalism as a school underwent a certain inner evolution, tending to become less exclusive and to arrive at a combination of its original methods with some others.

The beginning of Formalism as a school dates from the first years of the War, when a group of young students of literature organized in Petrograd the so-called Association for the Study of Poetical Language (better known under its abbreviated name of " Opoyaz ") which issued its non-periodical publication. The leading role in that group was played at the time by Victor Shklovsky, who became afterwards the principal theoretician of the Left wing of Formalism. In the first miscellany published by " Opoyaz " there appeared his article entitled " Trans-sense Language and Poetry " which testified to a close relationship between Opoyaz and Futurism as a reaction against Symbolism in the name of the so-called " self-sufficient word ". The Futurists raised a revolt against literature in which words were subordinated to sense. In carrying their conclusions to the extreme they went so far as to demand a universal " trans-sense " language. One of the young Russian historians of literature, who later on joined the Formalist school, Boris Eichenbaum, says that " the main slogan which brought together the original group of Formalists was the slogan of the emancipation of poetic words from the fetters of philosophical and religious tendencies which were more and more getting hold of the Symbolists."

The principal tenets of moderate Formalism were stated with great dogmatic clarity and fulness in B. M. Engelhardt's book *The Formal Method in the History of Literature* (1927).

The main fallacy of the traditional approach to the problem of the æsthetic suggestivity of a work of art is seen by Engelhardt in our incapacity to overcome the dualistic conception of the " object expressed " and the " means of expression ", or—to use the ordinary terminology—of form and content, the result being that, instead of studying a beautiful *work of art*, we study *the beautiful* in a work of art. It is necessary to do away with this dualism. " In a work of art," says Engelhardt, " studied on the æsthetic plane, there can be neither a system of means of expression, nor an expressed object, and this not only in the sense of the famous contrast between form and content, but also in the sense of a broader antithesis of the ' language of art ' and the æsthetically significant object of expression. From this point of view there is no such thing as an æsthetically significant object expressed in one or other way in a work of art, but only that work of art as an object of æsthetic study." There are two elements to be distinguished in every such object : (1) the æsthetic significance as such, and (2) the work itself as concretely determined structural unity. From this point of view the process of artistic creation consists in the shaping of an æsthetically indifferent concrete material (the object of creation) into an æsthetically significant one (the work of art). Defining the object of æsthetic study as concrete matter *plus* æsthetic significance, the Formalists determine the boundaries of literary science and its auxiliary branches. The problem of æsthetic significance as such belongs to the competence of general æsthetics. The matter itself in the state preceding its æsthetic reshaping is studied in accordance with the corresponding non-æsthetic branch of study. In the case of literature it is to be found in linguistics. The task of the particular æsthetics of a given art is to establish the æsthetic function of different elements of the organized concrete matter. Thus, the task of the æsthetics of literature is as follows : first to define, on the basis of general æsthetics, what æsthetic significance as such means ; secondly, on the basis of general and particular linguistics, to establish the primitive characteristics of verbal material in its pre-æsthetic state, and finally to elicit the meaning of the peculiarities of that material in its æsthetically organized form. Therefore the study of a literary work consists in demonstrating how the æsthetic factor transforms original verbal material into a work of art. In defining æsthetic significance the Formalists adhere to that school in modern æsthetics (the school of Hamann and Jonas Kohn in Germany) which defines it as " self-value ". There are in fact two ways of seeing an object : the non-æsthetic with a practical purpose behind it, and the æsthetic which is purposeless. This may be illustrated by the difference in the perception of, say, a river landscape by the pilot who is piloting the boat, and the passenger of that boat who simply enjoys the view. For the pilot each detail of the river has a meaning, is interesting not in itself but because of its bearing on his task. For the passenger the whole landscape is interesting and valuable in itself. That is what this school of æsthetics means by self-value. In order to turn the raw material into a self-valuable work of art, it is necessary first to eliminate all collateral meanings connected with it, while, on the other hand, inasmuch as an object devoid of those collateral meanings ceases to attract attention in the same degree as before, it is necessary somehow to increase its power of being perceived. Thus, the process of æsthetic formation can be divided into æsthetic neutralization and æsthetic concentration, and the æsthetic interpretation of a work of art consists in explaining this double process. The problem of the other element of an æsthetically organized whole, the element of words, is solved by the Formalists by resorting to linguistics. Linguistics tell us that language is an organ of communication. This conception comprises two elements : (1) that which is being communicated, and (2) a system of means of communication. Those means or vehicles of communication are represented by words. Therefore for the Formalists a poetical work, as an æsthetically significant system, is a complex unity of means of expression. This enables one of the principal theoreticians of Formalism, Roman Yakobson, to say that poetry is indifferent to the object of expression, that it amounts to the shaping of self-valuable words, by analogy with other arts, such as music, painting, architecture, and dancing. In practice, therefore, the Formalists reduce the study of a work of art to the study of its devices, meaning by device words or separate elements of verbal structure in their æsthetic function—the æsthetically organized and valuable elements (*e.g.* the rhyming words taken as rhyme, or the syntactic figures as an element of construction ; devices in the Formalist sense include also the choice of subjects and the treatment of plots, and Formalism has done much for the study of this particular aspect of literature). The unity of devices, says one of the adepts of formal method, Professor Zhirmunsky, who does not, however, share the extreme views of the Left-wing Formalism, constitutes the style of a literary work. The principal theoretician of Formalism, Victor Shklovsky, maintains that a literary work represents " the sum of its stylistic devices " and nothing else, that it is pure form. The Formalists reject Potebnya's theory of poetry as " thinking in images ". For them words, and not images or emotions, constitute the material of poetry. Their poetics is built on the opposition of two systems of language—the poetical and everyday. To the ordinary speech, aiming at the maximum of economy, fluency and correctness, is opposed the poetical speech deliberately obstructed, complicated and twisted, aiming at overcoming the automatism of perception. In accordance with this, they lay stress in literature on the device which they call " making strange ", the object of which is to present usual things in an unusual form or from an unusual angle. This device is very often resorted to by Tolstoy. One of the Formalists, Yury Tynyanov, has developed a theory of verse language as a constant violation of automatism through the domination of one of the factors of construction of language as the constructive principle, and the deformation by it of all the subordinate elements ; thus for instance, the metre of a poem tends to deform its syntax and sense. According to Tynyanov, poetical language represents a continuous struggle of various elements, which by means of all kinds of violations, interruptions, brakings, digressions and hindrances, tends to create the impression of a deliberate verbal construction and destroy the automatism of perception.

The extreme Formalists not only ban altogether the element of contents in the usual sense, and study the naked forms of literary works, but they have a tendency to deny all causal connection between literary facts and other facts that co-exist with them. Above all they deny all connection between the work and the personality of its author. Thus, Boris Eichenbaum in one of his articles says :

> " The soul of the artist as a man experiencing some mood or other remains and must always remain outside his work. A work of art is always something made, shaped, invented, not only artistic but artificial in the good sense of that word, and therefore it has and can have no place for the reflection of the inner empiric world of its author."

Eichenbaum denies just as emphatically all causal connection between art on one hand, and life, social environment, etc., on the other. In the face of the prevailing official sociological school this denial sounded very courageously, but of late the Formalists, as will be

shown below, have gone back on some of their statements
in this respect. In the eyes of the Formalists literary
evolution consists in a succession of forms and genres.
The author of a curious *Theory of Literature*, Boris
Tomashevsky, says that the value of literature lies primarily
in its novelty and originality. "Forms of art," says
Shklovsky in the miscellany *Theory of Prose*, "are
accounted for by their artistic lawfulness. A new form
comes not in order to give expression to some new contents, but in order to replace the old form which has lost
its artistic value." The same idea is expressed by
Eichenbaum when he says that art lives "by crossing
and contrasting its own traditions, developing and modi-
fying them according to the principle of contrast, parody,
shifting and sliding." But in saying this the Formalists
do not establish the laws which govern this specific
dialectic of art, this succession of forms ; they do not
explain why this and not that form succeeds and ousts
such and such old form. This gap in the theory of
Shklovsky, Eichenbaum and Yakobson was pointed out
by their "fellow-traveller", the most moderate and
cautious among the Formalists, Professor Victor Zhirmunsky, author of a number of valuable studies of
theoretical and historical poetics, including a very good
book on Pushkin and Byron. It was he who drew the
distinction between the widely understood formal method,
and the excesses of Shklovsky, Yakobson and Eichenbaum
which he called "formalistic". In his introduction to
a little book by the well-known German specialist on
literature, Professor Oskar Walzel, dealing with the
problem of form in poetry, Zhirmunsky sets forth a
number of points on which he differs from the Left-wing
Formalists. He accepts the formula of art as device only
as a method of æsthetic study. But alongside with that
formula there can exist other equally lawful formulæ,

e.g. art as a product of mental activity; art as a social fact and factor; art as a moral, religious or educational fact, and so on. Syncretic forms of creation are to be met not only in the primitive stages of civilization. Some of the works of the German Romantic Novalis, Nietzsche's *Zarathustra*, many writings of Andrey Bely, are instances of philosophico-poetical syncretism in modern literature; here too belongs the whole sphere of the so-called tendentious literature, where the artistic object is coupled with the object of moral or social sermon. Zhirmunsky admits that " tendentiousness " in a wide sense, that is a certain moral tendency or orientation, is common to a great majority of literary works.

Once it be granted that device is not the only fact that matters in a poetic work, it follows also that it is not the sole factor of literary evolution. Zhirmunsky rejects therefore Yakobson's formula of device as " the sole hero of literature." He thinks that Joseph Bédier was quite right when, in his classical work on French heroic legends, he studied the influence of monastic culture, the tasks of monastic and ecclesiastical policy, and the life of monasteries. One is equally justified, when studying Nekrasov as a poet, in considering the influence of Belinsky's ideas on him.

Zhirmunsky objects also to the explanation of the succession of literary forms on the principle of contrast as the sole factor—it is too broad and meaningless; it does not explain the direction of historical process, for most widely dissimilar tendencies can arise by contrast. Nor does Zhirmunsky accept the view of literature or poetry as a purely formal, objectless art; on the contrary, he says, poesy just as painting and sculpture, and as distinct from music and ornamental drawing, is one of those arts which have an object. Modern poetics is wrong in giving preference to the problems of composition over those of thematic. Problems of prosody, instrumentation, syntax, and construction of plots, do not exhaust the sphere of poetics. The æsthetic study of a work of literature is only then complete when it embraces poetic themes, the so-called " content " or " message " of the work considered as an æsthetically effective factor.

Finally, Zhirmunsky establishes another and very important point of divergence between himself and the Left-wing Formalists. He refuses to put on an equal footing a purely lyrical composition and the modern psychological novel; the relationship between composition and theme in the two is quite different. While a lyrical poem is, indeed, a work of verbal art wholly subordinated to the æsthetic design, a novel by Tolstoy or Stendhal makes use of words in their neutral capacity and subordinated, as in everyday speech, to their communicative functions. Such a work, even if it be considered a work of verbal art, can be so considered only in a sense very different from a lyrical poem. Of course, there is such a thing as purely æsthetic formal fiction, in which the elements of style and composition are prevalent. As examples of such fiction in modern Russian literature Zhirmunsky cites the stories of Gogol, Leskov, Remizov and Andrey Bely—it is what is sometimes called " ornamental " prose. But it is precisely when confronted by such ornamental works, that one becomes fully aware of their fundamental difference from the novels of Tolstoy, Stendhal or Dostoevsky, in which words are neutral elements or, using the Formalist terminology, are perceived not in their self-valuable meaning, but with all the collateral meanings attached to them.

All the above refers primarily to Formalism as a school in literary science, and not in literary criticism properly speaking. But, as a matter of fact, the theoretical views of the Formalists have naturally influenced their critical activity, that is their judgments on contemporary literature, inasmuch as they engaged in it. This is admitted by Engelhardt in his book quoted above, even though he draws a distinction of principle between the study of literature and literary criticism. Criticism, he says, does not investigate art but is its complement, its final stage. Its object is to assimilate a given work of art to the artistic consciousness of the modern public. The criterion of scientific objectivity cannot be applied to criticism. Criticism is always subjective, for the criticized work has to pass through the personality of the critic as the representative of a certain historical and social environment. Therefore Engelhardt admits that the critical essays of the Formalist school leave a strange impression. Yet it would be absurd to deny the inevitable connection between literary science and literary criticism, to demand that they should use totally different criteria. Literary criticism need not be quite objective, it can introduce certain modifications into the hard-and-fast rules laid down by the literary historian, it can take into consideration facts and elements which literary history leaves out. But how can a literary critic, who accepts in principle the theory of Formalism, resist the temptation of applying purely formal criteria in his own critical appreciations ? In the second half of the nineteenth century Russian literary historians were strongly influenced by the " civic " tendencies of literary criticism ; now it is the turn of literary history or science to exercise its influence on literary criticism. If this process is not as noticeable as it might have been, it is due to the fact that in the sphere of literary criticism, to an extent still greater than in the sphere of literature itself, one feels the pressure of the official doctrines. And the official school of literary criticism in Soviet Russia, the so-called Marxian or sociological criticism, is openly hostile to

Formalism in its pure form. There was a period—the period of general relaxation of pressure—when the Formalists could express their views more or less freely; but gradually, and to some extent under pressure, Formalism underwent a certain inner evolution, more especially in connection with its attitude to contemporary literature. It began about 1927 and went in the direction of comprising within the scope of its studies problems of social and historical genetics of literary facts. This evolution was partly due no doubt to outside causes. Until then Formalism was the only movement, the only school to take open and courageous stand against the official Marxist doctrine of historical materialism, for which literature is merely one of the superstructures of the underlying economic basis, and which approaches literary facts from the class point of view. During the period of NEP and after 1925 in view of the Government's policy towards the peasants, when in general a more lenient attitude was taken to non-Communist literature, Formalism was tolerated as one of its varieties. But even before that some of the Marxist critics, including Trotsky and Peter Kogan (*Literature of These Years*, 1924), took a definitely hostile attitude to Formalism, declaring it to be one of the worst expressions of the bourgeois spirit.

On the other hand, some of the Left-wing Formalists (the most important among them was Osip Brik) tended to conclude an alliance with the proletarian writers and to direct proletarian literature into their channels; an expression of this tendency was the review *Lef* of which Brik and Mayakovsky were the principal collaborators. It was an attempt to enroll Formalism in the service of the revolutionary art without betraying its principles. A similar tendency was displayed by Constructivism.

But the vast majority of the Orthodox Communists remained openly hostile to Formalism, and their principal organ, *On Guard*, waged a consistent war on them. This hostility to Formalism became particularly pronounced after 1929, and was no doubt one of the reasons why the Formalists changed their attitude and began to take an interest in the social aspect of literature, in the social environment of literary work. But this outward reason was not the only one. Doubtless some of the Formalists, and especially Eichenbaum, realized the insufficiency, narrowness and futility of the purely formalistic method. This change in their attitude found an expression in a number of articles by Eichenbaum, in Shklovsky's work on Tolstoy (1929), and in some others. But this inclusion of sociological criteria in their method did not imply that they became Marxists or even gave up their formal method, and critics of the sociological school remain very critical and suspicious of the Formalists' "sociologism". Thus, Professor Efimov of Smolensk, in his essay on *Formalism in Russian Literary Studies* (1930), is very sceptical about the value of the Formalists' sociological method. It is not real, he says. It denies the causal, genetic connection between social and economic facts on the one hand, and literary facts on the other. It is willing to admit only a relationship of interaction and influence between these two series of facts—the literary and the extra-literary.

"From the point of view of literary history—says Eichenbaum in one of his articles—the conception of 'class' is important not in itself, as in economics, and not for the determination of the writer's views which often have no literary significance ; it is important in its literary and literary-professional function, and therefore it acquires importance whenever the class idea as such becomes prominent in this function."

Efimov quotes Shklovsky's book on Tolstoy, in which Shklovsky studies the problem of Tolstoy's connection with his social environment, his class, and describes *War and Peace* as a miscarried expression of Tolstoy's aristocratic class - consciousness. Efimov sees the theoretical fallacy of Shklovsky in that he attributes to social causes, not the literary work itself, not the execution of it, but only its idea, its plan. According to Shklovsky this socially determined idea is, in the process of creation, defeated by the style which is not a result of social factors.

Whatever may be the errors and excesses of extreme Formalism, with its one-sided and purely abstract neglect of all but form in the literary work, there can be no doubt that on the whole the effect of Formalism on Russian literary studies and literary criticism has been beneficial. Formalism drew attention to problems of form hitherto almost completely neglected by Russian literary historians and critics ; it studied concrete literary facts instead of indulging in extra-literary meditations and generalizations ; finally, it tried to put literary history and literary criticism on a more solid scientific footing, and do away with literary dilettantism. At one time it was the dominant school in the Russian study of literature, and it exercised a great influence even on the currents that were opposed to it, namely on the sociological school in its different aspects. Nowadays, with a few exceptions, the followers of that sociological school, including its purely Marxist variety, pay infinitely more attention to problems of form, than did their " civic " predecessors of the nineteenth century. At no other period was the study of literature in Russia so productive, so rich in both theoretical and historical works, as at the time when Formalism was the dominant critical school. Whatever its intrinsic merits, its influence was fruitful and stimulating. Here is a selected list of new works on literary history and theory published during the period 1921-27 : Zhirmunsky :

Rhyme; Shklovsky: *Theory of Prose*; Tynyanov: *Problem of Verse Language*; Eichenbaum: *Melody of Verse*; Vsevolodsky-Gerngross: *Theory of Intonation·*; Zhirmunsky: *Structure of Lyrical Poems*; Reformatsky: *An Essay in the Analysis of Novelistic Composition*; Zhirmunsky: *Poetry of Valery Bryusov and Pushkin's Heritage*; Eichenbaum: *The Young Tolstoy* and *Lermontov*; Grossman: *Poetics of Dostoevsky*; Tseytlin: *Dostoevsky's Tales About a Poor Clerk*; Grigoryeva: *The Scenic Structure of Chekhov's Plays*; Vinogradov's and Eichenbaum's studies of Akhmatova's poetry; Wolkenstein: *Dramatic Art* and *The Law of Dramatic Art*. Studies of foreign and comparative literature include Zhirmunsky's *Byron and Pushkin*, Piksanov's *Griboedov and Molière*, Shklovsky's *Pushkin and Sterne*, several articles by N. Yakovlev on Pushkin and the English literature and by Tomashevsky on Pushkin and the French literature. Among the works which deal with general methodological problems one may mention Zhirmunsky's *Problems of Poetics* and Tomashevsky's *Theory of Literature*.[1] Not all of the above-mentioned books come from the pen of the Formalists proper; but it was Formalism which originally gave the stimulus to all the studies of this kind, and therein lies its great merit.

2. *The Sociological Method*

The sociological method in literary criticism and in the study of literature, which is the principal method

[1] This list is very far from complete; those who are interested in the problem will find further references in the bibliographical section of Tomashevsky's *Theory of Literature*, in Vladislavlev's bibliography *Russkie Pisately* (Moscow, 1924; special section entitled "Problems of Poetics", pp. 433–438) and in an article of A. Voznesensky in *The Slavonic Review* (June 1927). The literary output of the Formalist school, especially in the field of theory, has been less considerable after 1927. But the number of Soviet Russian works studying the literary past is still very great. Numerous new literary documents and memoirs of great value have also been published during these years.

opposed to the school of Formalism, comprises several varieties, of which Marxism is only one. Among its followers are (or were) to be found some of the older literary historians like the late Professor Sakulin, author of an important work on the methodology of literary studies and of a *Synthetic Construction of Literary Studies* ; or Professor N. K. Piksanov ; both of them, though they adopted the sociological method, are not strict Marxists. Among the orthodox Marxist critics we find Mme. Axelrod-Orthodox, Fritsche (died in 1929), Kogan, Lunacharsky (died in 1933), Trotsky, Voronsky, Polonsky (died in 1930), Gorbachev, Polyansky and many others. They all vary however in their attitude to the problem of form and content.

Kogan (author of *A History of Recent Russian Literature, The Literature of These Years* and other books) expresses the extreme anti-Formalist view when he says :

"I am little attracted by formal investigations. I have no interest in Mayakovsky's syntax, in discussions about the composition, the image, the epithet, etc. I was never able to understand why these boring questions should be thrashed out in public."

This view is the nearest to the old traditional attitude of Russian civic criticism with its utter contempt for form. There are other Marxists, however, especially of the younger generation, who have imbibed something of the Formalist attitude and pay more attention to questions of form and style, even though they explain them by economic and social causes. The extremist wing of Marxist criticism is represented among others by V. F. Pereverzev, author of long works on Dostoevsky and Gogol, who is inclined to regard literature as an expression of the productive process in the strictest sense of the word. He does not neglect problems of form and style, the study of compositional and verbal devices, but he seeks an explanation for them in the process of production as the basis of everything. Dostoevsky's art, in his interpretation, becomes an expression of the social grievances and aspirations of the lower-middle class. Some of the leading orthodox Marxist critics have, however, accused Pereverzev of " vulgarizing " Marxism.

All these differences apart, there is something common to all those who adopt the Marxian method. It has for its starting-point the doctrine of historical materialism. As distinct from the æsthetic method in all its varieties, which *describes* the sum of æsthetic facts, the Marxist method aims at *explaining* and *interpreting* literary creation. It deduces a given complex of literary facts from the social environment in which the literary work is produced. It implies, therefore, three consecutive stages. First, it analyses the economic structure of the given society. Then it proceeds to explain, from this economic foundation, its social conditions and its class division. Thirdly, it deduces from the preceding two studies its social psychology, its mental and intellectual state, which is the result of the complex reactions of the economic and social factors. But where the Marxists vary is precisely in the question of the interaction and relative importance of those three elements—the economic foundation, the social conditions and the social psychology. For some of the Marxians the social psychology of a society is the immediate source of its art and literature. The economic and social facts have no direct bearing on literature, they act through the intermediary of the psychological factor, they merely condition the society's psychology. But other Marxians take the economic factor, especially " the dominating form of production," for the immediate starting-point of their studies. Besides Pereverzev, this view is taken by Fritsche and Kogan.

Some of the Sociologists (*e.g.* Sakulin) tended towards

a fusion of the sociological and formal methods; they tried, without giving up the sociological basis of their appreciation of literature, to appropriate certain conclusions arrived at by the Formalists and to utilize them in the study of literature. They accept the theory which says that history of literature is a history of styles and forms, but they look for a *sociological* explanation of that succession of styles and forms.

One of the younger sociologists, Efimov, in his controversy with the Formalists insists that from the point of view of historical materialism production is not *one* of the aspects of social life, but a process representing the source of all social changes. The economic foundation in its relation to the superstructures is not mere " outside material ", as the Formalists believe it to be, but a creative and formative principle : each of the superstructures (law, morals, art, and literature) is only a specific manifestation of that basis, each is social throughout and that is why it is possible—to use the expression of Plekhanov, one of the founders of Russian Marxism, and one of the first, long before the Revolution, to apply it to the study of literature—" to translate the works of art from the language of art into the language of sociology." Another exponent of the sociological method, Medvedev, expresses the same idea when he says that " the language of art is only a dialect of a single social language."

As in the case of Formalism, it is necessary to distinguish between the application of the sociological method to the study of literature, especially of its past phenomena, and its manifestations in current literary criticism. As far as the former is concerned, the sociological school has produced some interesting and valuable works (by Sakulin, Piksanov and others). Its purely critical output is of little value, influenced as it has been by the constant variations and vicissitudes in the official literary policy of the Communist Party on which it felt itself to be dependent. There are several Marxist histories of recent Russian literature : by Kogan, Lvov-Rogachevsky, Gorbachev, and Lezhnev and Gorbov. The latter, written jointly by two authors, though short, is perhaps the best ; it gives a vivid and succinct account of the first ten years of Soviet literature. Polonsky's book *Outline of the Literary Movement of the Revolutionary Age* (1929) deals more particularly with the Soviet Government's and the Communist Party's policy in literary matters. Of the books of critical essays coming from the pen of the Marxist critics the best are Trotsky's *Literature and Revolution* (1926), Voronsky's *Literary Types* (1927), and Polonsky's *Essays on Contemporary Literature* (1927 ; second edition, 1930). Trotsky's book, though somewhat dilettantist, displays a natural critical acumen.

CHAPTER XIII

GOVERNMENT POLICY IN MATTERS OF LITERATURE

1. *From 1918 to the Five-Year Plan*

GOVERNMENT interference in all domains of life in Soviet Russia is such an important factor that it is impossible to discuss the development of literature since the Revolution without analysing the bearing which this purely political factor had upon it. As has already been said, the Soviet Government and the Communist Party of Russia had from the very outset intended to subordinate literature to their political designs, to the ultimate aim of creating a Proletarian State. But in the actual accomplishment of this object they had to take into consideration numerous outside circumstances, to adapt themselves to the changing political and economic conditions. The line of the Soviet Government's literary policy is therefore by no means straight—it is a zig-zagging line.

What were the principal stages in that policy?

During the first period of the Revolution, the period of the Civil War and War Communism, the Government and the Party were too much beset by more urgent and vital problems to pay proper attention to literary questions. Literature was more or less left to take care of itself. This practically resulted, as has already been pointed out, in Futurism making a bold bid to establish its literary monopoly. Its theoreticians openly spoke in their principal and more or less official organ *Iskusstvo Kommuny* (*The Art of the Commune*) of their dictatorship in the field of art parallel to the dictatorship of the proletariat in the domain of politics and economics. In the article entitled " The Draining of Art ", printed in the first number of *Iskusstvo Kommuny*, one of the leading Futurists, O. Brik, stated the main principles of the Futurist programme. The new art, he said, must break completely with the bourgeois art of the past. The aim of art was to produce new and unprecedented things. Artists should go to factories and workshops : Futurism was tantamount to the proletarian art. In another article the same author proclaimed : " Art will be proletarian or there will be no art at all." The tendency of the Futurists to get hold of the commanding posts under the new Government was, during the first months of the Revolution, encouraged by the late Lunacharsky, who was the first Soviet Commissar for Education and thus had all the matters of literature within his direction. Some of the prominent Futurists, like Brik, Punin and others, were appointed to the leading posts in the Commissariat of Education and were in charge of its literary, artistic, theatrical and other departments. But very soon the Soviet Government realized that this tendency of Futurism to identify itself with the proletariat and to speak in the name of the Government was dangerous. As early as December 1918, Lunacharsky wrote in *Iskusstvo Kommuny*: " It would be a nuisance if the advanced artists were definitely to imagine themselves to be a State school of art, representatives of the official art dictated from above, even though revolutionary." Two features, he said, of the extreme Left school of art were alarming—their destructive attitude to the art of the past and their tendency, while speaking in the name of a definite school, to speak at the same time in the name of the Government. Lunacharsky himself, in spite of all his sympathy for the advanced school of art and the encouragement he gave to Futurism, was one of the few Soviet leaders who always advocated a reverent attitude to the art of the past, insisted on the necessity of preserving its monuments and enjoined the new proletarian artists to learn from the old masters. In this he differed not only from the revolutionary adepts of Futurism, who wanted to throw Pushkin and Michelangelo overboard, but also from the theoreticians of the Proletkult, although on the whole he sympathized with the latter's efforts to build up separate proletarian culture (see Chapter V). In this respect he was at variance with the principal leaders of Communism, for both Lenin and Trotsky looked with disfavour upon the attempts of the Proletkult movement to assert its independence from the political and economic action of the Communist Government. With the literary revival after the end of the Civil War, with the growth of literary production, of which a great part was politically neutral, impartial, descriptive ("The work of art must be organic, real, must live its own special life," it "may but need not reflect the epoch "—proclaimed, for instance, the Serapion Brothers in their literary manifesto signed by the young and gifted playwright Lev Luntz), it became necessary to take a definite attitude to that growing literary production. The problem of the opposition between the proletarian and non-proletarian, the Communist and non-Communist literature was also becoming more acute. The attempts to foster artificially proletarian literature failed. The non-proletarian writers, the so-called Fellow-Travellers, easily asserted their superiority owing to the superior quality of their work, and the literary stage in those years practically belonged to them. But the proletarian writers were becoming more and more arrogant and insistent in their demand for hegemony. With the foundation of the groups *October* and *On Guard* (cf. Chapter V) and of the All-Russian Association of Pro-

letarian Writers, their activities became more organized
and systematic and their campaign for hegemony assumed
a more violent character. In the resolution passed by
the first Pan-Soviet Conference of Proletarian Writers on
the report of Vardin, it was openly stated that the rule
of the proletariat was incompatible with the prevalence
of non-proletarian ideology and therefore of non-proletarian literature. In a class society, said the resolution,
imaginative literature had no right to be neutral, it must
actively serve the ruling class, and all talk about the
possibility of peaceful co-operation and competition of
different literary and ideological currents was sheer re-
actionary Utopia. Literature was an arena of class war.
The resolution insisted that the proletariat had already
created colossal material and spiritual cultural values, and
that now its task in the domain of art was to seize power
and establish its hegemony. The literature of the Fellow-
Travellers was declared to be fundamentally anti-
revolutionary, exception being made only for a few of
them. The last paragraph of this resolution insisted on
the principle of hegemony of proletarian literature being
officially recognized.

Throughout 1923–24 violent battles were fought round
this cardinal problem of literary policy, many political
leaders of the Soviets taking an active part in them. The
point of view of the opponents of the proletarian hegemony was well formulated by Bukharin: " First you
must build, and then you can receive "—was his retort
to the " Onguardists ". The same was the attitude of
Lunacharsky, Radek and Trotsky, the latter taking
even a more negative view of the proletarian literature
and its prospects (cf. Chapter V).

On 19th May 1924 a conference, specially convoked by
the Press Department of the Communist Party, passed
a resolution confirming the Party's policy with regard to

the Fellow-Travellers and their literature. It avoided any
mention of the proletarian literature, preferring to speak
of the "art of workers and peasants who become, in the
process of cultural elevation of the large masses of the
people, workers' and peasants' writers." The resolution
criticized the methods of the *On Guard* group and rebuked
it by proclaiming that "no literary current, school or
group must come forward in the name of the Party." This
resolution was embodied in that of the 13th Congress
of the Communist Party dealing with the problem of the
Press. In 1925 it went a stage further, when its Central
Committee passed its famous resolution which became a
kind of literary Magna Charta Libertatum, a literary
constitution which for some years to come was officially
to govern all literary relations in U.S.S.R. Of course,
the liberties which this constitution granted to Soviet
writers were only relative; there could be no question
of full creative freedom. This was clearly stipulated
in the first paragraph of the resolution, which was almost
identical with the basic principle proclaimed by the
conference of the proletarian writers. It said, namely,
that in class society there was and could be no neutral
art. It is true that this statement was qualified by a
reference to the infinitely more varied forms in which
the class nature of art, and of literature in particular,
manifests itself, as compared with politics and economics.
The resolution went on to say that in the period of
proletarian dictatorship the Party was confronted by the
problem of finding a *modus vivendi* with the peasantry
and of gradually transforming the latter; the problem
of admitting a certain amount of co-operation with the
bourgeoisie and then gradually ousting it; the problem
of enrolling the intelligentsia in the service of the Revolution and of winning it over from the bourgeoisie. The
task of conquering the positions in the domain of literature,

said the resolution, was a very complicated one, for
" while the proletariat already possessed unfailing criteria
for estimating the social and political value of any work
of art, it had no such ready-made answers to all the
questions of artistic form." The resolution denied the
existence of the hegemony of the proletarian writers.
The party, it said, must help those writers " to earn for
themselves the historical right to such a hegemony." It
insisted on the necessity of a friendly attitude being shown
and unconditional support given to the peasant literature,
and on respect for its peculiarities. As regards the
Fellow-Travellers, it was necessary to bear in mind :
(1) their differentiation ; (2) the part played by many of
them as skilled " specialists " of literary technique ; and
(3) the existence of vacillations within that category of
writers. The general attitude towards them must be that
of tactful care, so as to ensure their speediest adherence
to Communism. With regard to the proletarian writers
the resolution recommended that all possible support
and assistance should be given to them and their organizations, while discouraging all manifestations of " Communist snobbery " on their part. " Just because the
party sees in them the future deological leaders of Soviet
literature, it must fight by all means against the frivolous
and contemptuous attitude to the old cultural heritage as
well as to the specialists of literature." " The party must
also fight against the attempts at purely hot-house ' proletarian ' literature." While proclaiming the necessity
of ruthlessly combating all counter-revolutionary manifestations in literature, the resolution recommended an
attitude of tactful and cautious tolerance to all literary
groups " which can and will go with the proletariat."
The Communist critics were told to give up their tone of
literary command. Paragraph 13 of the resolution laid
down that the party as a whole was not in a position to

tie itself up by preference to some definite school of literature. " Everything leads to suppose that a style congenial to the epoch will be created, but it will be created by different methods. . . . All the attempts to bind up the party in this respect at the present stage of the cultural development of the country must be rejected." The resolution therefore advocated free competition of various groups and currents in the domain of literature ; any other solution of the problem, it said, would be " a bureaucratic pseudo-solution. While morally and materially supporting the proletarian and peasant-proletarian literature, helping the Fellow-Travellers, etc., the Party cannot grant a monopoly to any of the groups, even the most proletarian from the ideological point of view : this would mean, in the first place, the undoing of the proletarian literature."

Such was this Magna Charta of Soviet literature. It gave the Fellow-Travellers a certain scope of freedom and something like a sense of security. It led to a split within the ranks of the *On Guard* group, the extreme advocates of proletarian hegemony. The bulk of the group accepted the resolution of the Communist Party as the guiding principle, and decided to direct its activities along new lines. Its slogans became " learning, creative work, and self-criticism." It began to talk of raising the quality of literary production. The unrepenting extremists, with the critic Gorbachev at their head, left the group, and the latter changed its name, inserting the word " literary "—*On Literary Guard*. In its new work it was led and inspired by the young novelist Libedinsky.

This state of relative freedom lasted till 1928, and it was the most fruitful period in the history of Soviet literature : it saw the appearance of such works as Leonov's *Badgers* and *Thief*, Fedin's *Cities and Years* and *Brothers*, Olesha's *Envy*, etc. The " Onguardists " did not, however, renounce their final aim, which was the "proletarianization" of literature, and, headed by the inapt but aggressive critic Leopold Averbach, were ready at any moment to attack all more or less independent artists. A new campaign against the Fellow-Travellers was started in 1929. There were two famous incidents, as a result of which Pilnyak and Zamyatin had to resign from the All-Russian Writers' Association. Pilnyak's resignation was a result of the publication of his tale *Mahogany* in Berlin—the novel was proclaimed to be counter-revolutionary, full of pernicious, "Trotskyist", petty bourgeois tendencies. In the case of Zamyatin the reason was the appearance of the fragments of his novel *We* (see Chapter VIII) in a Russian *émigré* review in Prague. Although Zamyatin himself proved conclusively that he had nothing to do with that publication (it was, indeed, obvious from the fact that those fragments were published in a re-translation from the Czech, that it was done without Zamyatin's knowledge), a violent campaign was launched against him in the Communist Press, and the All-Russian Writers' Association was obliged to pass a vote of censure on him, as a result of which he resigned his membership, saying that it was impossible for him " to belong to a literary organization which, albeit indirectly, takes part in the persecution of a co-member." He came to be regarded as an "inside *émigré*" and a secret enemy of the régime and soon went to live abroad.

In the same year there was a lively controversy in the Soviet Press about the so-called "social command" in which a number of prominent critics and writers (among the latter Fedin, Pilnyak, Gladkov, Selvinsky and others) took part. Most of the writers, even the Communist Gladkov, pronounced themselves against the expediency of giving writers "social commands" or of setting them

definite literary tasks. One of the most significant utterances against such a policy came from the moderate
Marxist critic, Vyacheslav Polonsky, at one time the
editor of two important Soviet periodicals—*Novy Mir*
(*The New World*) and *Pechat i Revolyutsiya* (*The Press
and the Revolution*). This is what Polonsky wrote in his
article in *Pechat i Revolyutsiya* :

> " The theory of ' social command ' marks an attempt
> on the part of a group of writers and artists of the
> extreme Left, who are severed from the proletariat, to
> establish a link with it while retaining their own in-
> dependence as creators of ideological values. Having
> assigned to the working class the role of ' social com-
> mander ' and inspirer, they themselves retain the
> humble role of ' artisans ' of artistic craft, of custodians
> of the devices of creative art, of producers of ' ideo-
> logical' things. . . . They address themselves familiarly
> to the proletariat, they strive to dispense with inter-
> mediary critics who prevent them from conversing face
> to face with the proletariat. It is easy to notice that
> while throwing a bribe to the working class, they in
> reality still remain on the other side. For the theory
> of ' social command ' does not create that *organic link*
> with the proletariat, that close relationship which would
> psychologically debar their contrast of ' you ' and ' I '.
> . . . This organic welding with the working class is
> precisely what the epoch demands of the master who
> aspires to be the proletarian artist of the proletarian
> revolution, and the proletarian mouthpiece of our
> wonderful age."

Polonsky opposed the theory of social command from
the Marxist, class point of view. But before a few months
passed he was himself proclaimed a counter-revolutionary
and divested of his leading position in the Soviet reviews.
The theory of social command on a large scale received
official approval and was given a new and much more
definite form. It was no longer a question of fulfilling
the implicit " command " of the ruling class ; it was

decided to place literature in the service of Five-Year Plan, to give writers explicit social and political tasks to perform, to instil new political blood into a literature that had become much too free and objective. It was a triumph for the Russian Association of Proletarian Writers led by Averbach, Bezymensky and other 100 per cent. Communists, who began to exercise a virtual dictatorship in all literary matters. The dream of the " Onguardists " was realized. The result was a drying up of the creative sources of Russian literature and a narrowing-down of its themes. For about three years the Five-Year Plan became the only subject of Soviet literature ; it produced a few interesting novels, which, however, were the more interesting the less they complied with the official plan. But side by side with those few novels there was a vast crop of dull, purely descriptive writings coloured by official optimism. Recently it was officially admitted that 75 per cent. of the literature of this period was not good for anything except the waste-paper basket.

2. The " Reform " of 1932 and After

This position lasted till 1932, when, by a new resolution of the Central Committee of the Communist Party, the organizations of proletarian writers were abolished and all the writers united in a single Union of Soviet Writers. This step was motivated by the " successes of Socialist construction," which made the existence of separate proletarian literary organizations superfluous. It was tantamount to raising the Fellow-Travellers to the rank of full-fledged allies. The Government decided that, having succeeded in breaking in the literature and sub-ordinating it to its plan, it had achieved a sufficient degree of homogeneity which could be maintained for the future. A great part in this reversal of policy on the part of the Communist Party was played by Gorky and since then his voice has become especially authoritative in all literary matters.

The resolution emphasized the considerable growth, both in quality and quantity, of literature and art in the past few years, which it ascribed to the achievements of Socialist construction. It called to mind how, some years before, when the alien elements were still active in Soviet literature and the ranks of proletarian literature still lacked the sufficient strength, the party helped, by every means in its power, the creation of special proletarian organizations in the sphere of literature and art. " But now "—said the resolution—" that the rank and file of proletarian literature has had time to grow and establish itself, and now that the new writers and artists have come forward from factories, mills and collective farms, the framework of the existing proletarian literary and artistic organizations is becoming too narrow and hinders the proper development of artistic creation." This, it went on to say, was pregnant with the danger of these organizations being turned into a means of cultivating exclusive coteries and of alienating considerable groups of writers and artists from contemporary political problems.

.   .   .   .   .

What, then, was the effect on Soviet literature of this new turning in the literary policy of the Soviet Government and what was its real meaning ? The literature of the Five-Year Plan has given way in the last two years to so-called Socialist Realism (see Chapter XIV). The transition, however, took place rather imperceptibly and it is difficult to draw a line between the works belonging to one and the other.

But in any case, by comparison with the period 1929–32, the interference of the official circles with literature is felt less. The organizations of proletarian writers, which then voluntarily performed the functions of supervision, investigation and censorship, have been suppressed. The Union of Soviet Writers comprises all those writers, living and writing in Soviet Russia who adhere to the platform of the Soviet Government, support Socialist construction and accept the method of Socialist Realism. Though ill-defined and apparently admitting of a certain breadth and variety of styles and forms (see below in Chapter XIV), this method none the less circumscribes the writer's scope by imposing on him the obligation to deal in his works with the Socialist realities. By the very fact of adhering to the Union of Soviet Writers (this, though formally a voluntary act, is too closely bound with material and other advantages to be really regarded as such), a writer working in Soviet Russia limits, of his own accord, the range of his creative work and accepts to serve the Communist State in his capacity of writer. In a way this means going back even on the amount of freedom which the famous Resolution of 1925 accorded to the then Fellow-Travellers, not to speak of the earlier period of more or less spontaneous literary creation when such a thing as the manifesto of the Serapion Brothers was still conceivable. It suffices now to prove that a work is incompatible with the spirit of Socialist Realism, that it contains a slight admixture of poisonous idealism, to place it outside the pale of Soviet Russian literature. This *a priori* must make the writers very circumspect in their choice of subjects and their treatment of them. The political factor still remains decisive, and although the writers are no longer supposed to portray nothing but the Five-Year Plan or to write purely political novels, they are nevertheless expected to write in the spirit of Socialist Realism, whatever that may mean. The critics in their turn approach the works they criticize in the first place with this criterion. Thus, Sholokhov has

231

been proclaimed a typical representative of Socialist
Realism and his works, especially *The Upturned Soil,*
are in great favour with the official circles and the
critics. With regard to Fadeyev, in connection with
his novel *The Last of the Udegeyans,* some doubts were
expressed on this point, and a curious incident, typical
for Soviet literary *mœurs,* took place recently. Mr.
D. S. Mirsky allowed himself, in his article on Fadeyev
(*Literary Gazette* of 24th June 1934), to reproach the
latter for trying to win back the sympathies of the
intelligentsia whom he had " offended " by his portrayal
of Mechik in *The Rout.* Soviet literature, he said,
has reached its present high level without Fadeyev's
participation. Fadeyev must recognize his latest novel
as an " artistic blunder ". Nearly a month later (22nd
July 1934) and obviously in connection with some new
instructions to critics—to be milder and more tolerant—
The Literary Gazette was obliged in its leading article
to back out and " accept the responsibility for Mirsky's
blunder." At the same time Mirsky was taken severely to
task by some of the official Communist critics who pointed
out that a recent convert from "White-Guardism " had
no right to criticize proletarian writers. The fact that
Mirsky's criticism of Fadeyev was " ultra-proletarian "
in its inspiration, and that he showed himself to be
plus royaliste que le roi, was somehow disregarded. For
a time Mirsky's name disappeared from the *Literary
Gazette*—to reappear in it quite recently, in January 1935,
when, somewhat belatedly, Gorky himself came to his
defence saying that Mirsky was quite right, because
" everyone knew " that Fadeyev's novel was bad, and
it was not Mirsky's fault if he was born a prince. In
reply to this Panferov, the author of *Bruski,* published
an article in *Pravda* and *Izvestia,* once more accusing
Mirsky of unfair methods of criticism. This episode is

only one of the many instances illustrating the conditions under which Soviet critics have to work.

A greater amount of freedom accorded to literature is felt also in the fact that nowadays Soviet writers and critics are much more free to estimate critically the achievements of Soviet literature. Under the Five-Year Plan régime the superiority of Soviet literature over the bourgeois, whether past or present, was an axiom for the whole of Soviet critical opinion. New works of Soviet literature, which satisfied the requirements of the moment, as Panferov's *Bruski*, were easily proclaimed masterpieces. Now, as we already know, nearly everyone criticizes *Bruski* for the low standard of its literary technique, which cannot be made good by any ideological qualities. And in the course of the first six months of 1934 Soviet writers and critics (encouraged by Gorky) were heard to talk more and more often about the " general low level " of Soviet literature. It has not yet created, they said, anything of great significance, anything worthy of the great revolutionary epoch. The intrinsic literary qualities of a work, its technical merits, the quality of its language, began to play more and more part in critical estimates. A campaign was started which insisted on raising the technical quality of literary production, on learning from the classics, both Russian and foreign.

One of the features of this last period is also the encouragement given to writers' participation in *collective* works. Several such works dealing with political and social subjects have been undertaken or accomplished within the last two years, with the collaboration of some of the leading Soviet novelists and poets. One can cite, for instance, such works as the description of the construction of the White Sea Canal, *Men of the First and Second Five-Year Plans* and *A History of Factories and Workshops* (edited by Gorky and Mirsky).

Let us sum up the principal stages in the evolution of Soviet literary policy :

1. 1918–20 : Parallel attempts to make use of Futurism and kindred movements, and to create proletarian literature by means of " Proletkults ".

2. 1921–24 : Patronizingly friendly attitude to the Fellow-Travellers, and support of the proletarian literary organizations which, as they grew stronger, began to claim literary hegemony.

3. 1925–28 : Disavowal of the proletarian organizations and allowance of greater freedom to the Fellow-Travellers ; promulgation of the literary " Magna Charta Libertatum ".

4. 1929–32 : Subordination of literature to the Five-Year Plan policy ; dictatorship of the proletarian literary organizations ; strict control and pressure from above.

5. 1932–   : New relaxation of pressure and recognition of relative freedom within the limits of Socialist Realism. Struggle against group spirit and attempts to make Soviet literature more homogeneous.

But throughout all these changes, these ebbs and flows of the Government's literary policy, one thing remains unchanged : in Soviet Russia politics preside over the destinies of literature, literature is no more than an *ancilla rei publicae.* This has been demonstrated once more with full clarity, though in a milder form than during the dictatorship of the RAPP, without an obvious pressure from above, spontaneously as it were, at the pan-Soviet Literary Congress which took place in Moscow in August 1934 under the auspices of the pan-Soviet Writers' Union and the protection of the Soviet Government. The Soviet writers were once more urged to accept the Communist Party's programme as a guide. In the present conditions, the speakers at the Congress maintained, it was impossible for a Soviet writer, whether Communist or non-Communist, to avoid taking sides.

The Government spokesman at the Congress, comrade Zhdanov (who since then has acquired notoriety through his appointment in the place of the murdered Kirov), stated quite plainly that literature in Soviet Russia could not help being tendentious. The writers, one after another, subscribed to this thesis asserting the " Bolshevist tendentiousness " of Soviet literature. One of the most emphatic statements to this effect was made by Vsevolod Ivanov, once a member of the group of Serapion Brothers, which in its manifesto of 1922 flatly rejected all tendentiouness in literature and said that they demanded " one thing : that the voice should not ring false." Now Ivanov confessed that life had taught them to be wiser, and they realized that " Bolshevist tendentiousness " was a *sine qua non* of the literary equipment of any Soviet writer. The same keynote rang in the speeches of several other writers : the whole Congress was, among other things, a manifestation of loyalty to the Soviet Government on the part of literature. Some went even further. Thus the playwright Vishnevsky gave vent to his martial Soviet patriotism and urged his " friend Olesha " not to forget, " in his dreams about a better future," the more immediate need of being ready to defend, arms in hands, the Soviet Union against the imminent Imperialist aggression. He promised henceforth to devote his energies to the production of special " defence literature " destined to keep up the martial spirit of the Red Army.

In its address to Voroshilov, the Commissar for Defence, the Congress undertook " to arm the country and the Red Army with new specimens of literature," depicting on the one hand the Red Army as it is, in its heroic simplicity and incomparable strength, and on the other, the

eventual enemies, the quality of their effectives and their
" anti-human aims."

There were, however, some speeches that struck a
different note. One of the most interesting was that of
Yury Olesha. He had the courage to say that every
artist could create only within his powers : " A writer
can write only what he can write." He candidly admitted
that it was impossible for him to put himself into the
shoes of an average workman or of a revolutionary
hero, and therefore he could not write about either of
them. He was primarily interested in man and, above all,
in the modern young man of Soviet Russia, in whom he
saw the embodiment of the moral aspect of Communism,
for him the all-important one. He developed a purely
moralistic conception of literature, insisting on its educational value, on the writer's task of teaching people to
" be better." He declared that youth and its aspirations
were to be now his principal theme.

The growing interest in man as such was stressed in
several other speeches, and thus the new period in Soviet
literature opposed to the Five-Year Plan period. The
Formalist critic Shklovsky spoke of the birth of " a new
proletarian humanism," of the period of " new sensibility."
The poetess, Vera Inber, emphasized the failure of Soviet
literature to portray " positive " characters, the reason,
for which she saw in the tendency to draw them
flat, without all their human flaws and blemishes. A
curious document was quoted by the Georgian novelist
Dzhavakhishvili[1]—a " letter of instructions " to the Congress from a group of readers, subscribers to one of the

---

[1] National minorities' delegates played a great part in the Congress, and the
latter proclaimed as one of the urgent tasks the greater interpenetration of Russian
and other national literatures of the Soviet Union. The difference of languages
must not conceal the *ideological* unity of the Soviet literature thus widely understood. Similarly, a closer intercourse with international revolutionary writers
was urged.

municipal lending libraries in Rostov-on-Don, urging the writers, among other things, to

> "write more about love, about marriage, paint the way of living, without exaggerating, but also without underrating its importance. . . . Give striking unforgettable types of heroes of our days, both positive and negative. . . . More historical novels are wanted. The reader feels a great need of them. . . . Besides, we want to laugh. Give us the chance to burst out laughing, and not only to smile gingerly. . . .We are against ready made patterns. . . .We want a literature which would be read and which one should want to read. . . .Write in a simple correct language. Learn that from the classics."

This document seems to be a fair statement of the widespread desiderata of the Soviet reading public bored with the "ready-made patterns" of a great deal of Soviet literature, which, in the words of Dzhavakhishvili, sometimes overdoes the political and ideological element, turning works of art into propaganda pieces. He would stop, he said, all talk of "forbidden subjects" which was still sometimes heard : to his mind all subjects were good *if* treated in the spirit of Socialist Realism. Does not, however, this latter formula of incantation considerably vitiate his sweeping dismissal of "forbidden" subjects ? This depends on what is really meant by Socialist Realism.

CHAPTER XIV

LATEST DEVELOPMENTS : SOCIALIST REALISM.—NATIONALISM
versus "WESTERNISM", AND "CLASSICISM" *versus*
"MODERNISM"

THE principal object of the literary "reform" of
1932 was to do away with the group spirit in Soviet
literature, to put an end to the exclusiveness and mutual
competition of various literary organizations, and to achieve
the maximum possible degree of unity and homogeneity.
Its practical outcome in the sphere of organization was
the foundation of a pan-Soviet Writers' Union. This
Union differs from all similar bodies in bourgeois countries
in that it is not merely a professional organization, but
its members are held together by certain common political
and literary principles. The statute of the Union provides
that all its members shall adhere to the political platform
of the Soviet Government, and that in their works they
shall apply the method of Socialist Realism. In the
Statute of the pan-Soviet Writers' Union its aim is
defined as " the creation of works of high artistic significance, saturated with the heroic struggle of the international proletariat, with the grandeur of the victory of
Socialism, and reflecting the great wisdom and heroism
of the Communist · Party . . . the creation of artistic
works worthy of the great age of Socialism."

Although, by comparison with the situation prevailing
during the period of 1929–32, the " reform " of 1932 may
be regarded as " Liberal " in spirit, it is obvious that, as
compared with the state of things created by the resolution

of 1925, the explicit demand of adherence to the Soviet political platform imposed on all the members of the pan-Soviet Writers' Union was a step backwards. But from the literary point of view the second of the above-mentioned stipulations is even of more importance for it signifies an attempt, unique in the history of literature, to impose on the whole body of writers of a given country a definite literary method. The unique character of this measure is made still more obvious by the fact that this literary method—designated as Socialist Realism—is not an invention of that body of writers itself, but has been dictated to it by the political leader of the country, a man who has not and never had anything to do with literature. The catchword of Socialist Realism—this has been especially emphasized on the occasion of the first pan-Soviet literary congress in August 1934—was coined by Stalin, and it was he who formulated the role of Soviet writers as " the engineers of human souls."

It remains to be seen, however, what is really meant by Socialist Realism and what are its practical manifestations in present-day literature. In interpreting the meaning of this newest catchword the leading Soviet literary commentators seem to admit that it must be taken in a rather broad sense, and that it includes a great variety of styles. But in their theoretical disquisitions they fail to define it more or less precisely even as a broadly understood method, and when it comes to its practical manifestations the position becomes still more confused. Inasmuch as the stress in this latest literary formula is laid on the word " Realism ", its point is directed against Romanticism on one hand, and against certain formalistic and stylistic innovations which tend to subordinate the description of real life and living men to formal and stylistic designs. But inasmuch as this is so, the new method merely sanctions the tendency which has been

dominant in Soviet Russian literature ever since 1924–25.
" Back to Realism ", such has been in fact the implied
slogan presiding over the evolution of the Russian novel
since its revival in 1924. And the further away from 1924
we are, the more pronounced is the tendency to clothe
this Realism in its traditional classical garments. Fedin's
Brothers is more realistic and more true to tradition than
his *Cities and Years*, while most of the novels of the
Five-Year Plan and of the proletarian Realists are nearer
to the old-fashioned realistic school than the earlier works
of Fedin and Leonov. It seems paradoxical at first
glance that, as soon as the proletarian literature outgrew
its infancy, the period of its revolutionary transports, it
became even more conservative, more traditional and
old-fashioned than the literature of the Fellow-Travellers.
But it will appear natural if we remember that the champions of proletarian literature always laid stress on the
content to the detriment of the form. It is significant
that the invitation to learn from the classics has come
not only from Gorky, not only from the Communist
novelist Fadeyev, who takes Tolstoy for his literary master,
but also—and in point of time even earlier—from
Bezymensky, who in his early poetry tried to combine
revolutionary ideas with the revolutionary technique
borrowed from Mayakovsky. In the fragments of his
poem *Guta* he deliberately adopts Pushkin's epic metre
and form and calls his fellow-poets back to Pushkin.
Simplicity is a great thing, and we must learn the secret
of it from the classics—such is the gist of the numerous
articles of Gorky and the brunt of his advice to his
younger contemporaries who, in his opinion, spoil their
work with stylistic innovations. This latter tendency
has become very prominent since the Revolution. A
number of younger writers, especially those of peasant
and proletarian extraction, have brought with them into

literature their local dialects or occupational slang. Works like Panferov's *Bruski* abound in words and locutions for which the great majority of readers require a special glossary. Hence the significant fact of a campaign for the purity of the Russian language launched, after sixteen years of Revolution, by Gorky and other Communist writers.

Most of the critics and writers now writing about the failure of the post-revolutionary literature to produce anything really great and urging the necessity of learning from the classics are merely repeating what one of the most broad-minded Communist critics, Voronsky, the former editor of *Krasnaya Nov*, said seven or eight years ago when the champions of proletarian literature ran him down for his " bourgeois " tendencies. In the preface to his book *Literary Types*, Voronsky wrote :

". . . Alas, we are still very far from Pushkin, from Tolstoy or from Gogol. . . . For the time being we are confronted with the task not so much of over-coming and doing away with the art of the past, as with that of critically assimilating, studying and adopting it. And after all, will our transitional period produce any Tolstoys, Gogols and Dostoevskys ? No doubt that with us at present intelligence, talent, and will are focused on the social struggle and construction. It is not an accident that our age has produced Lenin, but is so far powerless to oppose its own artists to the brilliant pleiad of classics. . . . The ' hero of our days ' comes from Lenin, and not from Tolstoy, Belinsky and Pushkin. . . . To find and embody him in art is the main task of contemporary literature. It has by no means been solved yet. Our novelists and poets see at present only some of his features ; the synthetic image has not yet been recreated. What we want is less scolding, less officialdom and clichés, and more of individual interpretation. We must learn from the masters of the past to look and see with our own eyes."

In the period 1929–32 this pronouncement of Voronsky was regarded as a downright heresy, now it is exactly what the official Soviet Russian critics and literary leaders have come to admit, after several years of "scolding and officialdom" in literature. The same longing to be able to look with one's own eyes is expressed in the words of the young Communist writer Poshekhonov when he protests against those who demand that all writers should go to factories, and says: "It is bad for a writer to see everything as it is and have no power to say what is good and what is ugly." Or when Leonov, in an article entitled *Appeal to Courage*, thus characterizes the recent period in Soviet literature :

"And there you have books of nondescript colour and form, without the 'upper floor', without that indispensable hormone which would save them from death for at least a quarter of a century. A standard type has been created for an industrial sketch, a novel, a play (with the inevitable disaster in the middle and the heroism of the masses), for a collective farm epic (with the inevitable cunning peasant who is at first 'for' and then 'against'), for a current newspaper or magazine poem (where the revolutionary thought of the poet is replaced by the beating of some rather inaudible witch-doctor's tambourine). Titles are prepared in advance just as labels : the birth of a guild, the birth of a hero, the birth of a factory, the birth of an artisan, the birth of a woman : this sounds majestic and saves the author's mind all trouble. Many pages of such books are known to the reader long before they have been written. A friend of mine, a voracious reader, told me while perusing on the counter of a bookshop a well-known book : 'I think I've already paid for it.'"

But if the proclamation of Realism as the dominant school of the age does no more than consecrate the *status quo* that has long been in existence, its qualification by the word " Socialist " hardly helps make the matters clearer. Wherein lies the difference between Realism pure and simple, and Socialist Realism ? Is it only the Socialist contents of a work, its Socialist " message ", that makes all the difference ? But then why speak of a new literary *method* and *style* ? Some of the Soviet critics draw a parallel between Socialist Realism and what a Russian critic of the seventies of the last century, Shelgunov, called " Popular Realism " (in this connection one recollects the movement of " Populism " started a few years ago by a group of French writers) which he opposed to the " aristocratic Realism " of the majority of Russian writers of the nineteenth century (Turgenev, Tolstoy, Goncharov, Pisemsky). As a typical representative of Popular Realism Shelgunov took one of the minor " Populist " novelists of the sixties, Reshetnikov. He described the essence of Popular Realism as the pre-occupation with social psychology above all. Instead of individuals and representatives of the upper classes it focused its attention on the " masses ", on the middle class and the peasants. According to the Soviet critics, Popular Realism, which in different forms has survived till the October Revolution, ceased to satisfy the requirements. And just as in the sixties, after the peasant reform, the Realists were now confronted with the task of discovering a new realistic method that would fit in best with the historical realities of the moment. First of all they were bound to realize that this new form of Realism must oppose itself to popular Realism as a lower and obsolete form expressing the small-bourgeois mentality. Socialist Realism is called upon to reflect the Socialist realities and the socialistic mentality. It is thus, historically speaking, a lawful successor of Popular Realism. The value of this term, says the critic in question (Pereverzev), lies in that it naturally and inevitably presupposes its historical antithesis and at the same time its inevitable premise—" Popular Realism ". But this really leads us nowhere.

Some other critics, who have tried to explain the meaning of Socialist Realism, have opposed it to bourgeois Realism, as a positive form may be opposed to a negative. The traditional bourgeois Realism in all its varieties was rooted, according to those critics, in a critical, more or less negative, attitude to reality. It was born of a protest against that reality and was potentially revolutionary. Socialist Realism, on the contrary, is founded on a positive attitude to the new realities of a collectivized society. It is fundamentally optimistic, it says " yes " to life, while the pre-revolutionary bourgeois Realism was fundamentally pessimistic and often led to a morbid and unhealthy attitude to the world. Drawing the antithesis a little further, we may come to the conclusion (though this conclusion is not to be found in the discourses of the Communist critics) that Socialist Realism is potentially conservative, and in doing so we should not be wide off the mark.

Finally, there was a tendency to oppose Socialist Realism to revolutionary Romanticism which had been prevalent during the first years of the Revolution and which still characterizes the work of some of the Soviet writers. But the outcome of the long and heated discussions in the Soviet literary circles on this subject has been the admission of revolutionary Romanticism as a necessary component part of Socialist Realism. Gorky went still further when, in one of his articles published in the summer of 1934, he proclaimed revolutionary Romanticism to be " a pseudonym of Socialist Realism." A formula was thus found to solve the problem and to reconcile the contending literary factions, but it did not add to our understanding of Socialist Realism as a literary method.

SOCIALIST REALISM

Recently a Soviet critic (Nusinov) has discussed Socialist Realism as a method of psychological presentation essentially antithetical to the psychological methods of Dostoevsky and Tolstoy. The object of Socialist Realism, he said, was the exact opposite of Dostoevsky's psychologism which reduced man's actions to the struggle of eternal forces of good and evil within him and sought a religious solution and explanation. Some of the Soviet writers, went on Nusinov, seemed to think that the psychological method of Tolstoy was much nearer to Socialist Realism than that of Dostoevsky. But in fact Tolstoy was nearer to it only in one point—in his moral optimism. Both Tolstoy and Dostoevsky showed human beings in their individual, not their social aspect. With Tolstoy, a man is an embodiment of good so long as he is left to himself, but becomes an agent of evil whenever he is, or feels himself to be, a part of a social collective. Therefore, according to Nusinov, Tolstoy's method is even more dangerous than Dostoevsky's, for Dostoevsky at least " shows the man of the past in all his iniquity." If a Socialist writer wants to assimilate Dostoevsky's and Tolstoy's psychological methods, he must needs replace their non-class and non-historical, religiously-pessimistic and abstractly-ethical, attitude to man and his emotions, by a social and historical interpretation. Therefore, of the classics of bourgeois Realism, Balzac and Stendhal, with their social and historical approach to their themes, are nearer to Socialist Realism than either Tolstoy or Dostoevsky. At the end of his article, however, Nusinov lets the cat out of the bag and brings us back to the starting-point by disclosing the essentially political nature of Socialist Realism. He says :

" The main task of Socialist Realism is the struggle for the destruction of the world of property and the triumph of Socialism."

One of the tasks of Socialist Realism in literature has been described by some of its exponents as the creation of *types*, of typical personages of the revolutionary epoch. These exponents of Socialist Realism admit that till now Soviet literature has been unable to create such types. On the other hand there are other partisans of Socialist Realism who insist that it must look out for *heroes*, that it must reflect the *heroic* features of the great revolutionary age. And again they maintain that on the whole Russian post-revolutionary literature has failed to detect any such heroes, that it is not worthy of its heroic epoch.

Let us now see whether this new movement has already produced any typical works.

One of the works which is regarded as a typical expression of the method of Socialist Realism is Sholokhov's *The Upturned Soil* which has already been mentioned in the chapter on the Five-Year Plan literature. Among the Five-Year Plan works it stands out owing to its greater inner freedom and objectivity. It satisfies the requirements of Socialist Realism inasmuch as it gives a picture of the Socialist reality drawn on a vast scale, and shows us a whole sector of Soviet Russian life. Sholokhov is also successful in creating striking typical figures. Davydov, a Communist worker who combats the small-bourgeois instincts and tendencies of the Cossacks; Nagulnov who represents the Left wing excesses within the Communist Party and is ultimately excluded from it; Ostrovnov, a thrifty farmer who in joining the collective farm and even becoming its manager pursues his own personal and class ends—are all typical figures. But there is little of socialistic heroism in the novel;. it portrays no heroes. Perhaps the author meant Davydov to be the embodiment of revolutionary heroic qualities, but the Davydov of the novel displays very little heroism. In general, it is very difficult to say why Sholokhov's

Upturned Soil should be regarded as a work of a Socialist Realist and not of a realist *tout court* ; or what there is in its method to distinguish it from some of the earlier works of Soviet literature handling the realities of Soviet life in a spirit of Realism.

The same applies to another novel which has been assiduously trumpeted as a great achievement of Socialist Realism—Bruno Yasensky's *A Man Changes His Skin*. Yasensky is a curious instance of a non-Russian writer writing in Russian. He is a German-Polish Communist who settled in Russia a few years ago. His previous works were, I think, written in French, the best known of them being a revolutionary Utopia *I Burn Paris*. There are at present in Soviet Russia several foreign Communists who have become Soviet writers : besides Yasensky one can name two Magyars, Illesz and Gidaszy. The Bolsheviks are naturally proud of this proof of the international character of their literature. *A Man Changes His Skin* also belongs in a way to the Five-Year Plan literature. Its action takes place in Tadjikistan in Central Asia. Its principal character is a young American engineer Clarke, and its subject the gradual transformation of Clarke from a typical bourgeois into a revolutionary Communist. The novel is set against the background of Socialist construction in Central Asia.

Among the recent works that are much discussed in the Soviet Press, Avdeyenko's *I Love* and Yakov Ilyin's *The Great Conveyer* are typical of the tendency towards a genre standing half-way between fiction and non-fiction. Both are industrial novels, describing their authors' actual experience at the real industrial undertakings, and thus containing a strong personal element. *I Love* is the autobiography of a Magnitogorsk workman full of Socialist enthusiasm and joy of life. In *The Great Conveyer* a contrast is drawn between the Socialist and bourgeois industrial methods. Though not exactly belonging to the " literature of the fact ", which prevailed under the Five-Year Plan, both these works are artistically un-organized and if they are to be taken as typical of Socialist Realism, they reveal a rather dangerous tendency to obliterate the line between art and life (to a certain extent this tendency is felt even in Sholokhov's *Upturned Soil*).

The Statutes of the Union of Soviet Writers stipulate that Socialist Realism must tend not only to describe the realities of the new world, but also to *reform* men, to educate them towards Socialism. Several among the recent works of Soviet literature deal with this " reform-ing " aspect of Communism. The two most notable are Zoshchenko's *Story of One Life* and Pogodin's play *The Aristocrats*. Both have for their subject the con-struction of the White Sea (Stalin's) Canal, built with the labour of criminals and political prisoners under the supervision of the O.G.P.U. Both describe the moral (and political) regeneration wrought by this work in the hearts of men engaged in it. Zoshchenko has chosen for his hero an ordinary criminal. The Soviet critics see in his newest work a further step in the direction of por-traying a positive character (the first hint of it was seen by them in the hero of *The Restored Youth*—see Chapter IV) and a renunciation of Zoshchenko's customary satirical method and attitude. Pogodin gives in his play, produced with great success in January 1935 by Okhlop-kov's Realistic Theatre, a wider picture and draws a greater number of regenerated characters, the principal among them being a gangster and an engineer formerly engaged in wrecking activities. Both Zoshchenko and Pogodin paint their O.G.P.U. men in sentimentally idealized colours.

Kataev's novel *Forward, Oh Time !* which has already been analysed in Chapter VII, is also often regarded by the Soviet critics as an instance of Socialist Realism. It is a novel of the second period of the Five-Year Plan literature, different in many a way from the novels of its first period (Pilnyak, Leonov, Gladkov, Shaginyan). Here too, of course, there is a portrayal of Socialist reality. There is even a peculiar Socialist mass heroism. But there are neither real heroes nor real types in Kataev's novel. His Realism is a-psychological. In its method his novel differs from the majority of the realistic works of the latest period of Soviet literature, and in any case it is difficult to trace it back to the classics of traditional Realism whom Gorky and other exponents of Socialist Realism set up as masters and models to the younger Soviet writers. It rather bears traces of Western European and American influences. About two years ago curious discussions were going on in Soviet literary circles as to whether Soviet literature should learn from the Russian classics or watch over the latest developments of the European and American literature and keep step with them. This referred, of course, to the questions of form and literary method. The nationalistic view was advocated chiefly by the conservative Realists from among the proletarian writers (Fadeyev, Sholokhov, and others), while some of the young " bourgeois " individualists (Olesha, Kaverin, and Kataev) came forward as Westerners and " Modernists " and called upon Soviet literature to learn from Proust, Joyce and Dos Passos. These three names are usually mentioned in connection with Western European influences in contemporary Russian literature. But one can hardly speak of any serious influence exercised by Joyce or Proust. The only writer who had elements in common with Joyce was Andrey Bely, but in his case it was a question not of influence but of treading on the same unexplored ground. Bely arrived independently at many of the things which the Western

European reader is accustomed to associate with Joyce. As regards Proust, his influence is felt to a certain extent in the prose of Boris Pasternak, and to a still lesser extent, perhaps, in the work of Yury Olesha. But the great majority of Soviet Russian literature is quite free from it. More real is the influence exercised on contemporary Russian literature by John Dos Passos. His novels are being translated into Russian, his plays staged in Moscow. What attracts the young Soviet writers is his cinematographic technique of the novel with its multitude of characters, its rapidly shifting scenes, its close-ups, as well as his revolutionary mentality and his attempts to create a type of novel in which individual destinies are dissolved in the mass and in a wide current of time. Jules Romains, to whose *Unanimisme* Dos Passos's technique can be partly traced back, had a less direct influence on the Soviet novel. Dos Passos's influence is especially felt in the construction of Kataev's *Forward, Oh Time !* Some traces of it can also be found in the novels of Kaverin, although in the case of this young " Westernizing " Romanticist it is complicated by several other and totally different influences—of Hoffmann, Poe and others. Kaverin's toying with the plot has some affinity with André Gide's method in *Les Faux Monnayeurs*—a novel which makes an important landmark in modern European literature and has not been without influence on several of Gide's contemporaries in different countries. A similar tendency can be discerned in Leonov's *Thief* (Firsov's novel within Leonov's). Gide is very popular with the Soviet official literary circles, especially since he has proclaimed his faith in the Soviet social experiment, but the bulk of his literary work, with its undercurrent of Protestant individualism, remains ideologically alien to the dominant tendencies in Soviet literature.

If it is possible to speak at present of any serious

Western European influences in Russian literature, it is rather the influence of the classics of European Realism, especially of Balzac, in whom of late the Soviet critics and writers have been taking great interest. It is Balzac's social psychology and physiology that appeal to the adepts of Socialist Realism. The " Classics-*versus*-Joyce " controversy was revived at the Pan-Soviet Literary Congress by Karl Radek in his paper on " International Literature." While admitting the value of studying Joyce, Radek said that he would rather see the young Soviet writers follow in the path of Pushkin and Tolstoy than emulate Joyce in whom the decadence of bourgeois society has produced its *fine fleur*.

EPILOGUE: 1935·1943

I. SOCIALIST REALISM IN THEORY AND PRACTICE

1. *The Theory*

IN 1934 Socialist Realism was proclaimed *the* doctrine and method of art, in all its forms, in the Soviet Union. Innumerable attempts were at once made to define the meaning of this rather vague formula, attempts that have hardly been more successful and definitive of late (and the subject still crops up now and again) than they were at first (see pp. 238-251). A number of works, especially novels and plays, have also been produced since 1935 which are officially recognized to be in keeping with the requirements of Socialist Realism. We shall see presently what some of them are and what Socialist Realism means in practice. But before we do so, it might be worth while looking at the main tendencies represented by Socialist Realism as it emerges from the writings of Soviet authors and their interpretation by Soviet critics who play a great part in laying down the rules of art in the Soviet Union.

The primary impulse of Socialist Realism was of a negative, rather than positive, nature. It was a reaction against certain existing tendencies and practices (or malpractices). It was, in fact, a two-pronged reaction. It was born of the reform which swept away " proletarian " literary and artistic organizations and attempted to raise the general level of Soviet artistic production which had fallen very low during the First Five-Year Plan. In the eyes of its sponsors it was aimed at achieving an all-round improvement in Soviet literature (I am at present confining myself to literature—the effect of Socialist Realism in other fields of art will be made clear from what follows).

K
253

EPILOGUE : 1935–1943

To improve the language and style which had become slipshod and sullied, to do away with the barrenness which resulted from the uniformity of themes and the one-sidedness of their treatment, to reinstate *man* in the place which belonged to him—such were the tasks which the champions of Socialist Realism set themselves. It is in my opinion the last of these objects—the re-affirmation of the value of the human being—which is the most important and gives us the clue to Socialist Realism by lending it a certain positive content. Perhaps it would even be better to speak of Socialist Humanism, rather than of Socialist Realism—the phrase would have more meaning and would enable us to draw a clearer distinction (as far as literature and the theatre are concerned in any case) between the period from 1924 to 1928 (also predominantly realistic, as I have tried to make clear in this book) and the period after 1934. It is this heightened interest in man, and especially the *new* man, the Socialist man, which characterizes the tendency now prevailing in Soviet art. This shift of stress coincided with some important changes in the life and outlook of the Soviet Union in the period between 1933 and 1939.[1] At the first Pan-Soviet Congress of Writers (see pp. 234 and ff.) this element of humanism in the new outlook was unmistakably stressed by several Soviet authors.

Inasmuch as Socialist Realism aimed theoretically at raising the level of literary production, while at the same time enlarging the scope of the artist, it showed itself in its progressive aspect. But closely connected with this

---

[1] By the majority of foreign observers these changes have been directly associated with the realization of the imminent threat of Nazi aggression. One of these changes was a complete reversal of the official Soviet policy towards the family. Not only the individual but also the family was reinstated in its rights. Family bonds of unity were encouraged and furthered as a prefigurement of the wider national unity. Everything that contributed towards greater unity in the face of ultimate aggression on the part of the dreaded enemy was welcomed and supported. (Cp. especially Bernard Pares's *Russia* in the Penguin edition.)

aspect was another which I would describe as reactionary. For Socialist Realism was at the same time a reaction against what was described, rather meaninglessly, as "bourgeois Formalism" by which was really meant all experimentation with form and technique for their own sake. Art in the most revolutionary State in the world run by the most advanced political party (the facts which naturally led in the first stages of the revolution in Russia to an alliance between what one can conveniently describe as "Left Wing" elements in art with the ruling class and party)—this revolutionary art had suddenly turned Conservative and began to look askance at all revolutionary experiments, dubbing them as "bourgeois Formalism". It was on this banana peel of "bourgeois Formalism" that poor Shostakovich tripped up in 1935 and fell in disgrace from which he had to work his way out. This he succeeded in doing in his Fifth Symphony.[1] His Seventh (or Leningrad) Symphony, which would probably be described as an instance of Socialist Realism in music (whatever that may mean), has completely vindicated him as a true Soviet artist. This persecution of "bourgeois Formalism", often coupled with "Romanticism",[2] involved also such acknowledged leaders of the Soviet theatre as Meyerhold and Tairov, with whose names have been associated some of its most daring and interesting experiments, if not achievements. Tairov has since managed to work his way back into the fold, while Meyerhold, though not actually "liquidated", as was at one time rumoured, is still under a cloud or, rather, "on probation".

In fine arts Socialist Realism has led to a frank revival of rather stiff and lifeless "Academicism".

· · · · ·

[1] See an interesting article on Shostakovich by Gerald Abraham in *Horizon*, September 1942.
[2] Cp. Joseph McLeod's *The New Soviet Theatre* (London, Allen & Unwin, 1943), *passim*.

EPILOGUE : 1935–1943

The question of the artist's freedom is inevitably raised whenever one approaches the literature of a totalitarian country such as the U.S.S.R. I have dealt with it briefly in a Postscriptum to the Introduction to this book with reference to Max Eastman's *Artists in Uniform*. Mr. Eastman, of course, is fundamentally right in his contention that artists have to wear " uniform " in the Soviet Union, and are under compulsion to " toe the line "—the general line of the Soviet Government whatever this line may be at any given moment. The point is that the line itself changes, that it may be now broader now narrower, and thus allow of greater or lesser degree of freedom for the artist both in the choice of his theme and in its treatment. The whole history of literature in Russia since the Revolution is an illustration of this point. To which may be added that of late, in the years preceding the present war, the " line " of the Soviet Government has not been entirely of its own choosing : in part it has been imposed on it by outside events, in part it has been shaped in response to, or in anticipation of, certain undercurrents of implicit public opinion. It is only thus that one can account for the new patriotic trends in the U.S.S.R. which even in their form of expression are in sharp contradiction with the whole tradition of the Communist Party. Although the name of Lenin is still constantly invoked and conjured up, it is difficult for anyone who is familiar with his views and writings to imagine him subscribing to much of what is now being said or written in the Soviet Union. The very phraseology of new Soviet patriotism sounds so un-Lenin-like.

Under Socialist Realism the writer has, of course, a greater scope than he had during the first Five-Year Plan period. Vague though Socialist Realism is, its very conception calls for more latitude and greater objectivity,

256

especially with regard to the past. But, on the other hand, it imposes in its turn certain limitations on the artist, and to say that there is more freedom for the artist now than there was in 1921 or between 1924 and 1928 would be wrong. Unseen censorship is all the time at work in the Soviet Union, combined with a certain prophylactic self-discipline on the part of the artists themselves. Certain subjects and certain works are still taboo. The principle *audiatur et altera pars* simply does not exist. To imagine that under Socialist Realism it would be possible to lift the ban on Zamayatin's *We*, or to publish a work permeated with religious spirit, is impossible, although under the new dispensation, and especially since the war, when the Church has been drawn into the movement for national unity, it would be perhaps just as injudicious for a Soviet author to indulge in anti-religious propaganda. A case is known of a well-known Communist author who was given a showdown for failing to present in due light the positive effects of Russia's conversion to Christianity. Marx's authority, if I am not mistaken, was invoked.

Take also patriotism. Between 1929 and 1932, or even earlier, throughout the first period of the Revolution when its internationalist aspect was to the fore, there was no harm in being unpatriotic and it was even considered good form to scorn the past. Now a Soviet writer would run a great risk if he were to fail on the score of patriotism. And patriotism no longer means pride in the " conquests of the Revolution ", but also pride in Russia's past, in her military glory, in her territorial expansion, in her historical achievements. All this shows how radically the " general line " can change. Still, the necessity to toe it remains. But there is no denying that with the broadening of the line itself, with the general attitude becoming more tolerant, literature gains.

Harmful restrictions on the artist's freedom are but one

aspect of the picture, however. Mr. W. H. Chamberlin hits the nail, when in his *Russia's Iron Age* he draws the following contrast between old and new censorship :

" The Tsarist censorship was purely negative and did not affect an author who was content to leave political themes alone. There was no effort in pre-war days to force novelists to sing hymns of praise to the Tsarist political and economic system ; the few authors who did write what might be called monarchist propaganda found few readers and are now entirely forgotten. Very different is the situation to-day. Not only is open criticism of the existing régime, of course, forbidden but the author is expected to strike a positive note, to show that all is working out for the best in the Soviet world. If he does not, the stigma of class enemy may be affixed to him."

This " positive " censorship has an even more damaging effect on literature. If you think that Trotsky had merited of the Revolution in its initial stages, you must not say so. But that is not enough. You are expected not only to abstain from giving Trotsky his due, but also to portray him as a traitor even in those early days when he was laying down the foundations of the Red Army. You are expected to say that it was Trotsky who bungled the whole campaign during the Civil War and that but for Stalin it would have been wellnigh lost (such is, after all, the real *raison d'être* of Alexey Tolstoy's novel *Bread* which deals with the defence of Tsaritsyn).

Socialist Realism may aim at the truth, but as the well-known Soviet writer Gladkov put it in 1934, " it demands not general truth, but a specific truth, our Communist truth. The writer of our days is not a cold observer ; he is filled with fire and passion. He is an austere, absolutely truthful painter, but also a fiery tribune."

Nor is the truth of Socialist Realism the whole truth. I do not know whether Ernest Hemingway's remarkable novel of the Spanish Civil War (*For Whom the Bell Tolls*) has been translated in the Soviet Union and what Soviet critics have said of it if so, but I feel safe in affirming that here is a book which could not have been written by a Soviet author. No one doubts Mr. Hemingway's sympathy with the Spanish Republican cause or his abhorrence of Fascism, but one could not ask for a better illustration than is supplied by this book of the fundamental difference between Socialist Realism and Realism *tout court*.[1] What Soviet author could have allowed himself such a tale of the execution of Fascists as the one told by Pilar to Robert Jordan ? And is it not rather significant that apart from the *reportage* of Mikhail Koltsov (incidentally, where is now this incisive but talented Soviet journalist ?) and Ilya Ehrenburg, the Civil War in Spain, in which the Soviet Union played such an outstanding part, has not found a worthy reflection in Soviet literature ? In Konstantin Simonov's play *Paren iz nashego goroda* (*A Lad from Our Town*) it is only part of the picture.

Here is another case in point. One may agree or disagree with Ehrenburg's picture of France on the eve of the war (in *The Fall of Paris*) and with his novelist's analysis of the causes which led to France's collapse. It fits in with the requirements of Socialist Realism, and apart from a certain fundamental bias gives a sufficiently *nuancé* picture, avoiding the over-simplified black-and-white pattern. But the completeness of its realism is

---

[1] When the above was already written I happened to come across an interesting review of Hemingway's work by Arturo Barea published in *Horizon* (May 1941, vol. III, No. 17). Barea writes from the point of view of a Spaniard and disagrees entirely with most of Hemingway's critics. He comes, in fact, to the conclusion that Hemingway has failed " to render the reality of the Spanish War in imaginative writing ". Barea ascribes this failure to " the fact that he (Hemingway) was always a spectator who wanted to be an actor, and who wanted to write as if he had been an actor. Yet it is not enough to look on : to write truthfully you must live, and you must feel what you are living." The truth of this last statement seems to me open to question, but Barea's opinion of Hemingway's novel is worth recording.

vitiated by the omission of such an important element
of the whole as the Soviet-German pact of 1939 and the
effect it had on France, and on French Communists in
particular. The whole subject of that pact and of Soviet-
German relations between August 1939 and June 1941
seems taboo in Soviet literature.

But apart from these sins of omission, Socialist Realism
is also guilty of sins of commission, of deliberate creation
of myths. Filmgoers in this country were able to see
some time ago the film called *The Defence of Tsaritsyn*.
Whatever its merits or demerits as a film, only those who
are sufficiently familiar with the history of the Revolution
were able to detect in it a subtle tampering with facts,
a tendency to represent the struggle for and around
Tsaritsyn as mainly, if not exclusively, a struggle with
the Germans, the "Whites" being their duped tools.
The fact that the main body of the Whites—the
Volunteer Army of Generals Denikin and Alexeyev—
never made common cause with the Germans but regarded their struggle as part of the general war between
the Allies and Germany on the side of the Allies, is conveniently glossed over in this film and in all present-day
Soviet comments on the subject. There are similar
elements of legend in Pogodin's play about Lenin (*The
Man with the Gun*) which is often taken to be a good
specimen of Socialist Realism.[1] The Soviet régime is in
fact busy creating its own mythology. It has its own
" myth " of Stalin and its own " myth " of Lenin. The
figure of .Lenin, which soon after his death acquired
mythological dimensions, has of late been endowed with
new mythical elements to suit the new trends and requirements. The myth of Lenin as a great Russian patriot is
being assiduously propagated by the Soviet press and on

[1] See a detailed and enthusiastic account of this play in Joseph McLeod's
The New Soviet Theatre.

the wireless, and a becoming veil is thrown over his activities during the last war. At times one is almost tempted to re-baptize Socialist Realism and call it " Socialist Idealism "—such an important part in it is played by " idealization " and " myth-making ".

.   .   .   .   .

In 1939, when it was seen that the " reforms " of 1932 and the adoption of " Socialist Realism " had not brought about the expected revival of literature (as compared with the period 1924-28, literature certainly showed less vitality, variety and spontaneity), it was decided to resort to a novel measure designed to encourage it. Official annual prizes—called " Stalin Prizes "—for the best works in the domains of novel, drama, poetry and criticism were founded by the Soviet Government, the first prize amounting to a handsome sum of 100,000 roubles. Since then these prizes have been regularly awarded every year. Among their recipients to date are some of the leading Soviet authors, including Sholokhov, Alexey Tolstoy, Leonov, Ehrenburg (for his *Fall of Paris*), Korniychuk, Simonov, Virta, and Tikhonov (for his poem about Kirov).

2. The Practice

A. Some Older Writers

I will now examine the work, since the introduction of Socialist Realism, of some of the better-known Soviet writers whose earlier literary output has been discussed in this book, as well as of some new-comers to Soviet literature.

(a) Leonov

Leonid Leonov's *Doroga na Okean* (*The Road to the Ocean*) is certainly an interesting work. As usual with Leonov, it is extremely complicated and unwieldy in

261

structure, with numerous intersecting lines of narrative and a great number of characters bound to each other by complex ties. Its usual structural complexities are still further enhanced by a curious superimposition of three temporal planes in the narrative : the present, the past and the future. There are, in fact, three independent narratives as it were, running parallel to each other. In one which unrolls in the present—about 1934 or 1935— the background for the action is provided by the life, political and otherwise, of the Volga-Revizan railway of which Kurilov, the novel's principal character, is the political director. The railway, however, is only a background and in the general economy of the novel its life and the problems it faces do not play a very important part. The main interest is psychological and lies in complex human relationships. Kurilov takes a notable place in Leonov's portrait gallery, this being the author's first attempt to put a real Communist in the centre of the picture, to make him the pivot round which the story turns and all other relationships are built up. Kurilov is an active Communist with a distinguished party and Civil War record, with a past that obliges and a responsible position in the present. Communist critics have reproached Leonov for toning down the political " aspect " of his hero, for dwelling on his " human, all too human " feelings and failings. It is no accident perhaps that Leonov shows us Kurilov under this " human " angle, at grips with an incurable disease and gradually realizing, as death approaches, how little personal enjoyment he took from life. Hence his mild platonic " affairs ", his interest in other people's lives, his unexpected tolerance for one of his bitterest class enemies, his brother-in-law Omelichev whom he discovers in the employ of his railway. Kurilov ends by dying after an unsuccessful operation performed on him by the famous surgeon Ilya

EPILOGUE : 1935-1943

Protoklitov, the husband of Liza, a small actress whose whole life and outlook are transfigured after meeting Kurilov. Ilya has a brother, Gleb, who, next to Kurilov, is the most important character in the book and whose presence in it is one of its mainsprings. Gleb is a former White officer, an active enemy of the Communists. By clever deceit he worms his way into the Communist Party and secures for himself an important post under Kurilov. In Kurilov he sees a danger to his plans and by a series of clever moves tries to forestall him. Afterwards he goes very near to suggesting to his brother Ilya the idea of a surgical murder. Gleb's undoing comes during a periodical purge in the Communist nucleus of his railway depot. Despite his clever tissue of lies, despite an artistically faked proletarian autobiography (Leonov is here at his best), his efforts are of no avail : at the last moment his own brother unmasks him. Although some of Leonov's best writing and deepest psychological insight went to the making of Gleb, the ultimate mainspring of his activities remains obscure. Is it sheer ambition, a desire to succeed ? Or is he sincerely trying to make up for his past and turn over a new leaf ? Nor do we learn of his ultimate fate.

So much for the present plane of the story. Parallel to it runs the story of the past, concerned with the past of the same railway, its construction with the concomitant interplay of private interests, of unsavoury speculation, etc. The author introduces a young Communist journalist, a friend of Kurilov's, Peresypkin by name, who unearths this past story of the Revizan railway from forgotten archives and oral legends. The link which connects the past story with the present is a certain Pokhvisnev who happens to be the uncle of Liza Protoklitova. But this story of the past, told with many unsavoury details, in that Dostoevskian vein of which Leonov

263

is so fond, seems hardly an essential element' of the whole.

Superimposed on those two stories, which jostle and interfere with each other, making the reader at times lose his bearings, is a third story—a Utopian picture of the future world, of Ocean, "the mother of the cities of the future" (situated apparently somewhere in the Far East), to which the author himself travels in company with Kurilov and Peresypkin, and which is presented simultaneously as a projection of the author's and Kurilov's mind and as a reality of the future. A great deal of this story is given in long footnotes, sometimes occupying whole pages—a most irritating device! The greater part of it is devoted to the *military* events of the future, to the wars between the Federated Soviet Republics and the remaining non-sovietized world. Soviet critics have reproached Leonov for having thus circumscribed his vision and failed to visualize the *man* of the future and the kind of life he is going to live. This aspect of the problem is only hinted at here and there. In fact Leonov has shirked the most difficult part of his Utopian venture. He has also failed in achieving an organic blend between his Utopia and the rest of the novel, the footnote device being a clear evidence of his failure. But though taken as a whole Leonov's novel is rather a failure, it is an interesting and at times even a brilliant failure.

Recently Leonov has been deserting the novel for drama. Apart from an adaptation of some of his novels for the stage, he wrote during the last six or seven years several original plays—*Gorod Untilovsk* (*The Town of Untilovsk*), *Polovchanskie Sady* (*The Polovchan Orchards*), *Metel* (*The Blizzard*), and others. His latest dramatic work is a war play in four acts called *Nashestvie* (*Invasion*), for which he was awarded one of the Stalin Prizes for 1942. A detailed analysis of it is given below in Section III.

(b) *Fedin*

Konstantin Fedin's only major work since 1934 is the novel *Pokhishchenie Evropy* (*The Rape of Europe*), the first volume of which was briefly mentioned in Chapter III of this book (see pp. 40–42). The second volume appeared in 1935. Fedin's object in the first volume was to show the decaying bourgeois Europe as seen by a keen Russian observer, a Communist journalist, Rogov, who has some traits in common with two of Fedin's earlier heroes, Startsov and Nikita Karev, and probably reflects something of the author's own personality. The difference, however, is that he is a Communist and is not faced with the problem of reconciling himself to the Revolution. But in the first volume we see him engrossed almost entirely in personal affairs and easily succumbing to the charms of bourgeois women. In Fedin's (or Rogov's) approach to Europe there is something of Dostoevsky's attitude *à rebours* : Europe also appears to him as a kind of cemetery full of sacred but dead things, the source of all life being in Communist Russia.

The capitalist world is personified chiefly in the van Rossums, a family of Dutch timber merchants who had vast interests in Russia before the Revolution and obtained from the Soviet Government a concession for their former forests. Philip van Rossum, the younger brother, who is responsible for the firm's dealings with Soviet Russia, stands for the modern progressive spirit in business ; knowing Russia and the Russians well, he likes the country and has no prejudice against the new regime. In this he finds himself more or less opposed to his elder brother and partner, Lodevijk, who dislikes the idea of trading with " those godless Bolsheviks " and looks askance at the extension of the firm's business in Russia, especially as the affairs of the concession run far from smoothly, and there are growing signs of the Soviet Government's unwillingness to continue it on the old basis. But Lodevijk's health is failing (he dies soon after) and Philip has his own way. The third representative of the van Rossum family is Philip's and Lodevijk's nephew, Frans, who is the firm's agent in Russia and is married to a Russian lady with a somewhat romantic past : dissatisfied (though without any underlying political grounds) with her drab life in Soviet Russia, Klavdia Andreyevna escaped across the Finnish border and became virtually an *émigré*, adopting the career of a cabaret dancer. It is in one of the Riga cabarets that Frans van Rossum meets her and falls in love with her. He takes her back to Russia as his wife. At the time Rogov arrives in Holland she is there on a visit to Philip. It is now Rogov's turn to fall in love with her— they go back to Russia as lovers.

A different type of capitalist mentality to Philip's is represented by Sir Justus Elderling-Geyser, in whom the Soviet critics perceived an intentional likeness to Sir Henry Deterding ; it is true that although Fedin took pains to camouflage his name, that of " Shell " appears in the novel *en toutes lettres*. But whereas the van Rossums are portrayed as three-dimensional human figures, Elderling-Geyser resembles a flat cartoon of a capitalist " shark ". There are also some episodic figures of German and Swiss industrialists, of social-democratic German town councillors, and a rather colourful hunchbacked exponent of Nazism, slightly reminiscent of Goebbels.

There is little incident and little movement in the first part of the novel. Much of it is taken up by descriptions— some of them very good, such as the urban landscapes of Bergen and Amsterdam, executed in the Dutch manner ; by long conversations between Rogov and Philip, and Rogov and Klavdia, on the subject of Europe and Russia ;

by Rogov's own meditations ; and by several interpolated episodes, such as the rising of the German unemployed, intended to show the process of decay in Europe. There is about the whole novel that static quality which was already felt in Fedin's *Brothers*. But here it is still more accentuated.

The second volume, if anything, is still more slow-moving. The action is transferred here to Russia and passes in Soroka on the Murmansk coast, in Leningrad, and in Moscow.

At the end of the first volume Philip van Rossum sails for the North of Russia to discuss and settle the affairs of his concession. The second volume opens with his arrival in Soroka. The scenes of the official welcome to van Rossum and to foreign sailors, of the modest " banquet " in the local club, are well done, but do not advance the story. There is also a very good description of a Northern Russian forest as a setting to Philip's hunting expedition with some local sportsmen to one of the White Sea islands.

The main lines of the narrative are leisurely pursued in the second volume. We see Philip and Frans fighting a losing battle over the concession, which is finally annulled : the Soviets are now strong enough to dictate their terms, and Philip has to content himself with the rôle of a timber broker on behalf of Soviet Russia. His business defeat is compensated by his " conquest " of Klavdia whom, after Frans's death in a motor accident (or suicide ?), he takes back with him to Holland. The main defect of the novel is the lack of unity of design as between its two parts—easily accountable if we take into consideration that the theme which was to form the core of the first volume had in the meantime lost its actuality and acuity. The second volume degenerated consequently into a series of scenes with no backbone to them. In the first volume this backbone is formed by the satirical picture of decaying Europe, but there is no corresponding counter-picture of Russia in the second. There is in it some good character drawing ; but as a novel it does not come to life and is definitely inferior to Fedin's earlier novels, especially to *Cities and Years*, which remains his best. The attractive mythological title seems rather far-fetched. In the first volume it could be related to Rogov's " abduction " of Klavdia, but this is undone in the second volume where Klavdia is in turn " abducted " by Philip. At the same time, though Philip van Rossum is thwarted in his plans and returns from Russia disillusioned, there is hardly any question as yet of an ideological or political " rape of Europe ".

Fedin's only work since *The Rape of Europe* known to me is his short novel *Sanatoriy " Arktur "* (*Sanatorium " Arcturus "*). It is not a very significant work, and although in subject slightly reminiscent of Thomas Mann's *Magic Mountain*, cannot be compared with that great work. The action is set in Davos in a sanatorium for tubercular patients. The principal character is a young Russian who is recovering from tuberculosis. He is one of Fedin's favourite " reasoning observers ". There are also some lightly drawn portraits of other people with whom he comes in contact during his stay in Davos—the doctor who runs the sanatorium in the teeth of great financial difficulties which make him resort to all kinds of makeshifts in attracting patients and in the end bring about his suicide ; his young Jewish assistant who falls in love with the hero, the latter, who is at first attracted by another girl, in the end responding to her love ; a conventional English couple ; a girl in the last stage of tuberculosis who dies in the sanatorium after attempting to run away from it ; another doctor, serious-minded, generous, conscientious ; a rich and eccentric Hungarian lady whose ailments are more or less imaginary ; the servants of the sanatorium ; and a few other episodic figures. There is very little action—Fedin's static quality finds food in this picture of semi-real existence on the confines of death. It is a soft pastel picture and the author succeeds very well in rendering the peculiar atmosphere of a Davos sanatorium.

(c) *Kataev*

Kataev's *Beleyet parus odinoky* (*Lone White Sail*) is one of the best works of this author. There is an element of pleasant freshness about it. Its autobiographical background is obvious. The action is set in Odessa where Kataev himself grew up and where his father was a teacher. The principal characters in the book are two boys : one, Petya Bachey, the son of an Odessa teacher ; the other, Gavrik, a little fisherman. The action takes place in 1905, against the background of the first Russian Revolution. We catch glimpses of the *Potemkin* mutiny, of a Jewish pogrom, of street fighting and strikes in Odessa. One of the characters in the book, with whose destiny Petya's life becomes accidentally entangled and who supplies some of its most dramatic moments and episodes, is Rodion Zhukov, a sailor from the *Potemkin*, who returns secretly from Rumania, is chased by the police in the steppes of Bessarabia, hides himself in a coach in which Petya, his father and his little brother are returning from their summer holidays, boards in Akkerman the same steamer, is found out by a plain-clothes policeman, jumps overboard (providing Petya with some unforgettable and exciting experiences) and is picked up by a fishing boat in which are Petya's friend, little Gavrik, and his grandfather. They live in a shack on the seashore. Zhukov is brought there, delirious with fever, but soon his whereabouts are discovered by the police, and with the help of Gavrik's brother, Terenty, a railway fitter and a member of the Bolshevik party, he escapes through the catacombs. For a long time he lives in hiding, engaged in clandestine revolutionary activities ; then he is arrested, but once more escapes with the help of Terenty, Gavrik and Petya, this time sailing for abroad in Gavrik's grandfather's boat.

The interest and the charm of the book do not lie, however, in the adventures of Rodion Zhukov, about whom Kataev had already written a story before, but in the fresh and delightful presentation of the two boys—one belonging to the middle class, or rather the intelligentsia, the other a little Odessa street Arab—and in their half-childish, half-grown-up adventures and experiences, the grown-up element being introduced, especially in Petya's case, by the Revolution which suddenly encroaches upon their everyday life. Here and there the author forgets that he is showing us the 1905 Revolution through the eyes of nine-year-old boys, and there are passages—for example about religion and the Church—which must jar on readers' ears whatever their views ; but these are few, and against them can be set such wholly delightful pages as the opening description of Petya's last day on a seaside farm in Bessarabia ; or Petya's school entrance examinations when he is deeply disappointed by not being allowed to recite to the end his favourite poem of Lermontov about the " lone white sail " ; or the street game of " buttons ", of which Gavrik is a recognized champion, and how this involves Petya in a petty theft, lies and other misdeeds ; or the wanderings of the two boys about Odessa in the days of the Revolution, when Petya unwittingly carries in his school satchel cartridges which he believes to be Gavrik's spoils at " buttons ". These and other scenes have about them an accent of freshness and spontaneity and show a real and deep insight into children's psychology. The novel was turned by Kataev himself into a very successful play for the Children's Theatre in Moscow and later made into a film.[1]

(d) *Kaverin*

The element of personal life, the stressing of which was demanded by Socialist Realism, played a large part in two novels of Veniamin Kaverin which he has written since his *Anonymous Artist* (see pp. 50-55). The problem of the individual's integration in society had always interested Kaverin, but this time he is more frankly interested in the individuals themselves and in their personal problems. *Ispolnenie zhelaniy (The Fulfilment of Desires)*, a fairly long novel published originally in two volumes, has for its hero Trubachevsky, a young student of literature who makes a literary discovery. The " social " element is introduced by a friend of his, Kartashikhin, a proletarian by origin, who is contrasted with Trubachevsky as a more useful and purposeful member of society. Another character, Novodvorov, introduces simultaneously political and detective interest, being a secret agent of some anti-Soviet *émigré* organization. An old professor of literature for whom Trubachevsky works, his son (also a social enemy), and his daughter who is in love with Kartashikhin, are other chief characters in the novel. It is much more straightforward and simple in outline than *Anonymous Artist*—there is no " toying with the plot " of which Kaverin used to be so fond and which now might easily lead to a charge of " bourgeois Formalism ". On the other hand, there is some fine character drawing, and one of the attractions of the novel is that it depicts certain less familiar aspects of Soviet life, Kaverin being one of the few Soviet authors who stick to the intelligentsia *milieu*. The message of the novel is not very obvious, unless it is

[1] The film was shown in London before the war.

to be sought in the ultimate winning back to community of Trubachevsky, who for a time goes astray.

Kaverin's latest novel *Dva kapitana* (*Two Captains*) is a charming story woven round the Arctic explorings of a Russian captain. Though again there is no daring toying with the plot, the construction of the novel shows certain original devices. There is a mild atmosphere of mystery about this novel and an element of pleasant freshness and novelty as compared with the general run of Soviet novels, some of the inevitable ingredients of which have by now become rather insipid. Kaverin's " Western European " literary upbringing, his interest in the plot, in " adventure ", are certainly refreshing. Reading *Dva kapitana* one is somehow reminded of Arthur Ransome's adventure stories for children. It is almost a book for children which can be read and enjoyed by grown-ups.[1]

(e) *Alexey Tolstoy*

Alexey Tolstoy's great historical novel about Peter the Great remains unfinished. He is engaged now on another historical theme—a play about Ivan the Terrible in accordance with a new interpretation of this remarkable and colourful personage of Russian history (see more about this in Section II).

Tolstoy's work since 1935 includes his novel *Khleb* (*Bread*), the subject of which is the defence of Tsaritsyn (Stalingrad) by Stalin and Voroshilov and the exposition of Trotsky's treacherous conduct. He has also completed his vast epic of Russian life on the eve of, and during, the Revolution, begun when he was still an *émigré* (the first part of it appeared in an *émigré* review in Paris). Entitled *Khozhdenie po mukam* (*The Way Through Hell*), it is a large-scale canvas of Russia during the last war and the

---

[1] In my book I have not even broached the subject of children's literature in Soviet Russia. It is vast, and much of it is delightful, both in prose and in verse.

Revolution. The central figures in it are Ivan Telegin and his fiancée and later wife Dasha, two typical members of the Russian pre-revolutionary intelligentsia, ·who gradually come to see the truth of the Revolution and to place themselves in its service. In some parts of this long novel Tolstoy the keen observer, as distinct from Tolstoy the reasoner, is at his best. Tolstoy's strongest point is his powerful vitality, which springs from the Russian soil. In this he is somewhat akin to his great namesake. But he lacks the latter's analytical power. As a well-known Soviet critic, Kirpotin, puts it : " All Tolstoy's best works have been born . . . of his love for his country. Only when he uses his genius on the problems affecting Russia and the Russian people does he create to the full of his capacity."

It is significant that in the same article Kirpotin compliments Tolstoy on having rid himself of the elements of modernist, " Left " (inverted commas are Kirpotin's) style, which can be found in his pre-revolutionary work, and on learning from the great Russian classics—Pushkin and Tolstoy, Gogol and Lermontov, and Gorky.

For the whole of his *The Way Through Hell* Tolstoy was awarded one of the Stalin Prizes for 1942.

(f) *Ehrenburg*

The only work in Soviet literature dealing with the present war outside Russia seems to be Ilya Ehrenburg's *Padenie Parizha (The Fall of Paris)*, recently translated into English. It was written before Hitler's invasion of Russia and gives a picture of France between 1935 and 1940, analysing, in the form of a novel and through a variety of characters representing various strata of French society, the causes of France's collapse. It is thus primarily a social-political novel. Ehrenburg has always been a journalist and the journalistic approach is strongly felt in his novels. He is quick to respond to topical themes. A man of no stable convictions, he has a versatile, keen and observant mind. He knows his France, where he has lived on and off for years, and he loves the country and its people. He lived in Paris through the tragic days of the debacle and was able to see much for himself. He understands the French, and his character studies of French politicians of various shades, industrialists, intellectuals and workers, are on the whole true to life. The general picture is, of course, coloured by a definite bias. It may be roughly described as the conviction that the salvation of France lay in its working class, or even perhaps in the Communist Party. One may agree with this or not, but such is the author's standpoint, and most of the characters are there to illustrate and prove it. Michaud and Denise Tessat (who rallies to the people, forsaking her own class and family), Pierre Dubois and Agnès who are of the middle class but also come to be with the people, are those who represent true France. To them are opposed most of the politicians (those of the Front Populaire are shown in an even more unpleasant light than some of the Right Wing ones like Ducamp in whom there is a healthy core of deep-seated French patriotism), industrialists or unhinged young intellectuals like Lucien Tessat who moves from one extreme to another and from a Left Wing intellectual Communist becomes a Fascist and admirer of Franco. One of the most interesting characters in the book is Dessère, a rich industrialist, a class enemy with the redeeming features of common sense and genuine attachment to his country. He perceives the futility of the policy pursued by the ruling classes which are adding grist to Hitler's mills ; he is aware of the rottenness which deeply affects the very heart of France. Unlike his fellow politicians and industry captains he is a good Frenchman at heart. For a time

274

he finds some belated personal solace, if not happiness, in his love for Jeannette, a young but frustrated actress, but in the end is driven to inevitable suicide. Jeannette, Lucien and Pierre are killed, Agnès is shot by the Germans for harbouring some de Gaulle supporters. Denise and Michaud, who love each other, survive and, firm in their loyalty to Communism, look forward to coming battles and to the better future which will be forged in them. Their deep-rooted faith in the distant land of Socialism is made much of by the author, but, as already pointed out, Ehrenburg's whole conception is vitiated by the discreet drawing of a veil over the Soviet-German pact and the havoc it caused in the ranks of French Communists. Many Frenchmen will perhaps resent Ehrenburg's picture of France in pre-war years as rotten almost to the core. But those who love their Paris, whether Frenchmen or not, will be grateful to the author for the finely suggested Parisian atmosphere and an affectionate portrayal of many sides of French life and character.

During the period under survey Ehrenburg also published a novel from Soviet life — *Ne perevodya dykhaniya* (*Without Taking Breath*). It is set in the extreme North of Russia, and its dominant note is the joy of new creative life.

(g) *Others*

Except for the last instalments of his *Quiet Don*, which show no falling off of his creative power, and form a worthy sequel to this work of *grande haleine* (if not of absolute greatness), nothing significant has come since 1935 from the pen of Mikhail Sholokhov. For the last part of *Quiet Don* Sholckhov was awarded a Stalin Prize. Since the war he has been writing war stories and sketches.

Two other well-known Soviet writers—Babel and Olesha

—seem to have completely disappeared from the.literary stage. Olesha's disappearance is one of those disquieting mysteries with which Soviet life at times presents us (where is, for instance, Osip Mandelstam, one of the most interesting surviving representatives of pre-revolutionary poetry ? There have been some rumours that he was sent to a concentration camp after the murder of Kirov in 1934). Babel's " come-back " to literature, hinted at after the " reforms " of 1932, has not materialized. His meteoric literary career seems to be over. It is, of course, possible that his creative source has just dried up. This is less likely in the case of Olesha, and it looked in 1935 as though, with the advent of new " Socialist Humanism ", he might come into his own. But little has been heard of him since his *Strict Youth*, and since the war his name has been absent from the main Soviet publications. Another prominent Soviet writer to be definitely confined to the limbo of disgrace has been Boris Pilnyak.

The collaboration between Ilya Ilf and Evgeny Petrov, the joint authors of those two delightful picaresque novels, *Twelve Chairs* and *The Little Golden Calf*, was broken by Ilf's death in 1940. Petrov also died in 1942 in the neighbourhood of Sevastopol, during the siege. Before Ilf's death they published a volume of their American travel impressions, called *Odnoetazhnaya America* (*One-storied America*)—a witty satirical picture of some of the less familiar aspects of American life. Their book of stories (*Tonya*) is rather uneven. Many of the stories are topical *feuilletons* or anecdotes dealing with various shortcomings in Soviet life and organization. The title story, which is considerably longer than the rest, has an American background and describes the first steps of a young Soviet couple in unfamiliar American surroundings. There is a touch of satire in it, but it is much less successful than in their "documentary" *One-storied America*. Much more witty and amusing is another satirical story, also aimed at America, where Columbus is shown rediscovering modern America.

.   .   .   .   .

Socialist Realism has found an abundant reflection in recent Soviet drama where it has ousted both the romantic tendencies and the one-sided, "black-and-white" pattern of topical drama, so popular during the Five-Year Plan period. It is doubtful, however, whether Socialist Realism has led to the creation of a real Soviet repertory. This problem still remains unsolved, and the Soviet theatre is still in search of its author. Some people would say perhaps that it has found such an author in Nikolay Pogodin, one of the most prolific among the younger Soviet dramatists, whose plays *Chelovek s ruzhyem* (*The Man with the Gun*) and *Kremlevskie kuranty* (*The Kremlin Chimes*) have had a great success. I am not sufficiently familiar with Pogodin's latest developments to be able to say whether in him the Soviet theatre has found its Ostrovsky, Chekhov or Ibsen. Joseph McLeod in his *New Soviet Theatre* [1] calls Pogodin "one of the great names in Soviet Dramaturgy".

B. *The New-comers*

(a) *Herman*

When and how Yury Herman made his literary début I do not know, but his first major work was the novel *Nashi znakomye* (*Our Friends*) which appeared in 1936. It was an immediate success, partly because it satisfied a widespread demand for pictures of everyday life and

---

[1] Mr. McLeod's book is full of uncritical enthusiasm and has some unfortunate factual errors. But it contains a wealth of information otherwise inaccessible to non-Russian readers.

ordinary people. Its very title is apparently designed to
convey the idea that people in the book are such as any
reader can meet in everyday life in the Soviet Union.
Almost throughout the book, which is long, somewhat
old-fashioned in construction and tries to be very " true
to life ", the author succeeds in maintaining an accent of
quiet, unobtrusive veracity, and only towards the end
does he run the risk of sliding into a pit of sentimental
idealization. The writing is not very careful, at times
even slipshod. *Nashi znakomye* is a story of an attractive
Soviet girl, Antonina Stàroselskaya, a dreamer in search
of a meaning of life which she finally finds in social work
and in a marriage (her third, the first two having been
failures) to a Cheka official who twice crosses her path
before she really gets to know him.

The story begins in 1925, during the Nep period (there
is a clearly detectable undercurrent of hostility in the
author's portrayal of Nep conditions) with Antonina, a
sixteen-year-old girl, being left all alone in life after the
death of her father, an accountant in some Soviet institution. She gives up school, sells her father's belongings
and starts looking for work. In the course of this search,
at one of the labour exchanges, she makes the acquaintance
of a famous and popular actor and falls in love with him—
dreamily and romantically, in a youthful way. After a
performance for which he gives Antonina and a friend
of hers free tickets, he takes them to supper in a luxurious
restaurant, and this constitutes the climax of Antonina's
romance, for the next day the actor goes away, leaving
Antonina to her dreams of him. She meets him years
later when she is already married for the second time,
only to discover that, contrary to what she had felt, she
no longer loves him. After the interlude with the actor
she drifts, gradually and more or less against her will, into
marriage with Skvortsov, a sailor in the Soviet merchant

fleet whom she had met on the day of her father's funeral. Skvortsov is engaged in smuggling activities and Antonina becomes his unwilling accomplice. When Skvortsov is caught by the G.P.U., Antonina is summoned and questioned by Altus whom she had casually met before and with whom she is later to find her happiness. Skvortsov is sentenced to three years of hard labour, but Antonina is let off. She finds work as a hairdresser's assistant, but continues to lead the same half-dreamy, half-real existence, hardly conscious of its purpose and vaguely feeling that some such purpose must be found. A neighbour of the Skvortsovs, Pal Palych Shvyryatykh, a former waiter, maître-d'hôtel and director of restaurants under the old régime, now in charge of one of the Soviet canteens, takes an interest in Antonina, is fascinated by her quiet charm and falls in love with her. An oldish man, who has lost in the Revolution not only his actual fortune but also his dream of becoming a landowner and retiring to the country, he is at bottom not bad and full of gentle and genuine solicitude for Antonina and for Fedya, her son by her marriage with Skvortsov. In his friendship Antonina finds an escape from her solitude. Skvortsov, whom Antonina had divorced in the meantime, returns after having served his term of hard labour and Antonina has not the heart and the will to refuse him. For a time they live together ; then Skvortsov is run over by a car. Just as she had drifted into marriage with Skvortsov—because there seemed to be nothing else to do—so now she drifts into marriage with Pal Palych. Outwardly their marriage is happy at first. Pal Palych is full of love and tenderness for Antonina, while she, though not loving him, owes him a debt of gratitude. In her innermost self she is, however, still dissatisfied with life and tormented by vague yearnings. This brings about a stupid affair with one of Pal Palych's former customers, a representative of the old bourgeoisie. It culminates in a repulsive scene during which Pal Palych beats up his rival almost to death, while Antonina realizes that her behaviour was stupid and undignified. She makes up with Pal Palych and relapses into the old smooth groove. They plan a journey to the Crimea, when suddenly this frail structure of Antonina's existence is upset by an unexpected visit from Tatyana, former caretaker of the house where Antonina used to live. She is also Skvortsov's former lover, but now is running a stockbreeding farm somewhere in the country. For a few days Tatyana, the new and changed Tatyana, a useful member of society, stays with Antonina, and after seeing her off Antonina decides to break with Pal Palych. Instead she goes to her new friend Zhenya Sidorova and her husband (who works on the same housing estate as Pal Palych)—and turns over a new leaf. This escape from Pal Palych and the atmosphere of quiet smugness concludes the first two parts of the novel. The third tells of Antonina's regeneration through study and work and of the ultimate happiness she finds in her marriage with Altus. The dreamer becomes a socially useful member of community without losing her charm. This theme of regeneration of socially hostile or indifferent elements became, after 1934, one of the favourite themes of Soviet literature. Yury Herman seems to be particularly attracted by it : in one way or another he has made use of it in several of his shorter stories. These are rather uneven in quality, which makes it not very easy to arrive at a final assessment of Herman's literary value. Some of his stories are not only slipshod and clumsy in construction, but strike a cheaply sentimental note. There is a certain amount of sentimentality in *Nashi znakomye*, too. But the quiet and unassuming veracity of its general tone, the old-fashioned slowness of its tempo, the attractiveness of its heroine and the humanity even of its "negative" characters (of Pal Palych, for instance), lend it a certain charm of its own. Of Herman's other stories the most interesting is a longish short story called *Alexey Zhmakin*. Its hero is an escaped criminal, tracked by an energetic and virtuous G.P.U. official who is, however, bent on "reforming" his quarry rather than on bringing him to bay. Both the character of Zhmakin and the situations in this story are rather unusual; there is an atmosphere of tension, and the interest is sustained throughout. The virtuous G.P.U. official (Lapshin) appears also in another story where he himself is the principal character, but being rather wooden and stilted the whole story lacks the interest which Herman succeeds in arousing with his Zhmakin.

(b) *Virta*

Another new-comer to the first rank of Soviet literature since 1935 is Nikolay Virta, whose name figured a year or two ago among the winners of Stalin literary prizes.

His actual beginnings, just as those of Herman, are not known to me. He made his name with the novel called *Odinochestvo (Solitude)* which was conceived as the first part of a trilogy. Unlike Herman's *Nashi znakomye*, this novel has a very definite social-political theme. Its subject is the famous large-scale peasant rising led by Antonov in the province of Tambov in the very first stages of the Revolution, which caused much worry to the Soviet Government and for a time seemed likely to become a serious threat to the very existence of the new régime. The main character of the novel is Antonov's right-hand man Storozhev, a well-to-do peasant. The interesting subject, the variety and wealth of characters involved, the skilful handling of the material, made *Solitude* one of the literary events of its year.

The trilogy planned by Virta has not yet been completed but its second volume appeared in 1939 under the title of *Zakonomernost* (*Lawfulness*). It is closely connected with *Solitude*. The hero of the former, Storozhev, does not make a personal appearance but hovers in the background and is an important factor in the story. The same part of Russia is the scene of action, but at a much later period. There are frequent references to Antonov and his movement, and the survivals of " Antonovism " among the peasants and the hidden anti-Soviet elements in the intelligentsia and the Soviet " bureaucracy " linked up with the old Social-Revolutionary party, are stressed. At the beginning of the novel we are introduced into the household of Nikita Kagarde, a teacher and one of Antonov's former lieutenants, and are told his story. His son Lev, who is shown to us as a boy and then as a young man, is the hero of the novel. An ambitious youth, who inherits his father's hostile attitude to the Soviet régime, he becomes the centre of a wreckers' organization in the small provincial town of Verkhnerechensk. Intelligent, unscrupulous, with a gift and a craving for leadership, he succeeds not only in drawing into his net some of the anti-Soviet elements in the Soviet institutions, but also in corrupting some of the best elements among the youth of the town who, dissatisfied with the drab reality, are on the lookout both for ideals and for adventures. Kagarde supplies them with both. Most of these young people ultimately find their way back into the fold and are shown as innocent victims of Kagarde's charms and cunning. Lev himself, unmasked and held at bay, disappears in the nick of time from the town. He goes to Moscow where for a time he changes his methods and tactics without giving up his fundamental anti-Soviet aims. He thinks himself safe, while all the time in fact he is being closely watched by the vigilant organs of political security. He meets his end while on his way to a meeting with

Storozhev on the Polish frontier : Storozhev, who had been living in Poland all this time, is supposed to cross over into Russia as soon as a signal is given for a general anti-Soviet uprising.

Virta's novel was, as far as I know, the first important Soviet book which dealt with the background of the wreckers' and Trotskyists' trials. It is very interesting inasmuch as it shows the complexity of the characters involved in anti-Soviet activities, and especially the variety and complexity of their underlying motives. It is true that Virta does his best to show Lev Kagarde in all his repulsiveness, but some of his original victims, willing and unwilling, are very attract ve. The picture given by Virta is, of course, far from be ng complete and some of the most interesting psycholog.cal riddles presented by the famous " trials " are left unsolved. Certain aspects of the whole affair are not touched upon.

The moral of the tale, as seen by the author, is given in the Epilogue which has for its motto a line from Sophocles : " That which is coming . . ." Here are some passages from it :

" The last full stop has been put, and perusing what I have written I relive the events which shook Verkhne-rechensk in the years which preceded the Great Offensive. Everything comes back to life before my eyes. Men who took part in those events pass in a long file. Every one of them is either dear or loathsome to me. Pondering over them, I recall the years long gone by, our youth, searchings, the quiet streets of our town through which lay our hard road pitted with many obstacles.

" We have come out on the right road and we know where it leads us. Everything is behind and everything is ahead, everything is known, everything is understood, time has lifted its veils.

" The Bogdanovs, murderers and hirelings of murderers, have been caught and brought to book from their stinking underworld, and the world started back in horror from this abyss of baseness. Their repugnant road is ended—they died the death of mad dogs. But have all of them been caught and brought to trial before the people ?

"We must learn to distinguish between enemies and friends, learn to search and to find, to love and to hate. Let us be prepared—storms are still ahead of us. And if honest eyes, after reading all that has been written here, are opened wider, hearts will beat faster and reason will tell them : Do you realize who they are, into what abyss they wanted to precipitate our life ? Is that not the most precious reward of my work ? "

The Epilogue explains the title of the book : it refers to the lawful course of the Revolution and the lawfulness of its Nemesis.

Perhaps Virta's novel is the best specimen of what is expected of a Socialist Realist, for it combines edifying purpose with a sufficiently detached portrayal of realities.

(c) *Ostrovsky and Makarenko*

Mention should also be made of two authors who found no place in the body of this book and whose works have become very popular since its publication. One of them is Nikolay Ostrovsky, a Communist of true blood who during the last few years of his life was blind and bedridden and became almost an institution in one of the health resorts in the Caucasus, where numerous people made special pilgrimages to see him. His autobiographical novel *Kak zakalyalas stal* (*The Tempering of Steel*) dealt with the formation of character of a young active Communist under the Revolution, his childhood, his part in the Civil War and the subsequent reconstruction. The hero of the novel—Pavel Korchagin—became one of the most popular characters in Soviet fiction. Ostrovsky's novel belongs to the genre of " near-documentary " fiction.

Still nearer to the document are the two books of
A. Makarenko which enjoyed enormous success — *Peda-
gogicheskaya poema* (*Educational Epic*) and *Kniga dlya
roditeley* (*Book for Parents*). Both deal with educational
themes, the former describing in great detail and very
vividly the famous experiment of the Soviet " Borstal ",
the Gorky colony for difficult boys and waifs and strays
of the Revolution.

(d) Pavlenko

At the 1934 Congress of Soviet Writers great stress was
laid on the necessity of creating special " national defence
literature " (*oboronnaya literatura*) in view of the growing
threat to the security of the Soviet Union. Several works
were written to meet the demand for this " defence
literature " on which the sailor-author Vsevolod Vishnevsky particularly insisted. A good and typical example of
it is P. Pavlenko's *Na vostoke* (*In the East*).

It has no individual hero in the literary sense, while
in a different sense nearly all its numerous characters,
drawn lightly with a few strokes, are represented as heroes
in their respective walks of life (with the obvious exception
of the enemies of the U.S.S.R.). Its underlying idea —
an idea on which Socialist Realism lays stress—is that
small and seemingly inconspicuous doings are just as
" heroic " under the circumstances as the most startling
exploits. The real hero of Pavlenko's book is the Soviet
Far East with its spirit of enterprise, daring and enthusiasm. Men of the Soviet Union are shown here on
the remote fringe of the vast Soviet state, blazing new
trails and building a new life. The book has a definite
propaganda object and value, inasmuch as it portrays
the work of reconstruction and the military preparations
on the Soviet Far Eastern frontier in anticipation of a
Japanese aggression. To many people in those days the

menace of Japanese aggression seemed more immediate and real than the menace of Nazi Germany.

The first two parts of the novel (which starts in 1932) deal chiefly with peaceful activities, with the construction of new towns in Siberian forests, the working out of new and daring projects by the younger Soviet generation which the author characterizes in the following words :

> " And so they came out in hundreds of thousands and in millions in order to keep pace with the Revolution and not to lag a step behind it. Their fathers had burnt out estates, had defended scores of fronts, had lost their wives and become disused to their children, and the sons were building towns and creating stable families, were becoming used to sleeping eight hours and eating three times a day."

It is a picture of the Revolution settling down to peaceful activity after a hectic period of struggle and destruction. A whole galaxy of builders, explorers, collective farm managers, military commanders, Ogpu officials, etc., passes before our eyes, while we also get glimpses of the frontier skirmishes and of the Chinese and Korean guerrilla leaders, as well as of the Japanese and White Guard spies who cross the frontier from Manchukuo. In fact the peaceful construction is but one side of the picture. Gradually military activities and military preparations come to the forefront. Part IV of the novel, the action of which is set at some future though not very distant date (" the year 193 ..") describes the war between the U.S.S.R. and Japan, started by the latter and won by the former : Tokio is bombed and destroyed from the air, the Japanese fleet is defeated by Soviet submarines and the Japanese attack on land fails, thanks to some mysterious and deadly electrical weapon invented by the Soviets ; the rising of the Japanese workers and the insurrection in China combine to make the military defeat of Japan complete and final. The last part of the book describes the feverish building of a new town, called Sen-Katayama after the well-known Japanese revolutionary, which is to house 70,000 Japanese, Chinese, Korean and Manchu war prisoners as well as its Russian builders, and which is to symbolize the triumph of international brotherhood. One of the episodes in this last part of the book is the trial in Sen-Katayama of the chief villain of the novel, the old and astute Japanese arch-spy Murusima, but strangely enough the outcome of the trial is not mentioned.

Pavlenko's book, which partakes both of a chronicle and of a military Utopia, gives some very interesting glimpses of Soviet life and activities in the Far East, but it shows traces of hasty writing, and the episodes dealing with the Japanese and White Guard spying activities smack of cheap thriller and are unconvincing despite the attempt to give them a ring of authenticity.

It is interesting to note that the attitude of Pavlenko does not support the view that as early as 1936 internationalism had given way to nationalism in the U.S.S.R. Pavlenko seems to have little use for Russian (or even Soviet) patriotism. Although he does take a patriotic pride in Soviet achievements he lays more stress on the old Bolshevik idea of world revolution and the coming collapse of the old capitalist world. England is taken to symbolize this old world :

"Whole nations were dying before one's eyes. Political systems established in the course of centuries crumbled to pieces. England was tossing in agony and the young nations, her labourers, stood by with their mouths agape with joy and happiness. With England a whole epoch in the history of mankind was passing away. If it were possible to impersonate political régimes, we would have seen a decrepit gentleman posing as a diplomat and educator who after his death turned out to be only a secondhand dealer and usurer.

And as always happens in the life of men, no sooner had this enterprising merchant died than a hungry shoeblack emerged and on the strength of a certain similarity in their biographies claimed to be the historical successor of the deceased."

The " hungry shoeblack " claiming, according to Pavlenko, British succession, is Japan. When one of the characters of the novel says : " There are a million Communists in Europe—the war will be to the end ", he expresses the internationalist idea underlying Pavlenko's book.

(e) Shpanov—a Literary Curiosity

Be it only à titre de curiosité it is worth mentioning a book which appeared just a few months before the conclusion of the Soviet-German pact (it was signed for the press in May 1939). It is by a hitherto completely unknown author, Nikolay Shpanov, and is called *Pervy udar* (*The First Blow*). In the same volume are also included some short stories of little literary distinction or general interest. The subject of *The First Blow* (it is a longish short story of some 120 pages) is the first twenty-four hours of the coming war between the U.S.S.R. and Germany. All the characters are members of the Red Army air force, bomber and fighter pilots and navigators, paratroops, etc. The interest is centred almost exclusively on the air war, which is shown as being of paramount importance. Within the very few hours of the outbreak of the war a Soviet bomber force undertakes a long-distance raid and bombs the industrial targets in Nuremberg, causing great havoc there, and after returning safely to its base is preparing for another raid. The author gives us some interesting glimpses into the life of the Soviet air force and draws, somewhat superficially, a number of characters of its members. There is a slight love interest in the story, but it is of little moment. Shpanov's forecast of the character of the coming war

288

proved quite wrong in the light of subsequent events. Equally wrong was his estimate of the international situation in which the war broke out. This is dealt with in a preliminary chapter. Shpanov was right only in foreseeing the Nazi aggression against Russia. But at the time this was a generally held opinion in the Soviet Union. According to Shpanov, Russia had to withstand the aggression alone, although there is a hint at the end of the introduction that at the last moment France, under the pressure of the Popular Front movement, was about to throw in her weight on Russia's side. Great Britain, on the contrary, is shown as taking a position of neutrality, rather benevolent to Germany. Poland comes in on Germany's side as her half-willing ally. The prophecy, as far as the immediate future was concerned, completely miscarried : three months after the publication of Shpanov's book the Soviet Union concluded a pact with Hitler, Poland was attacked by Germany and England and France at once declared war on the Nazis. An interesting point about Shpanov's book is that he does not mince words ; although some of the names of German generals are fictitious, Germany herself as the attacking party is named *en toutes lettres*, and the description of the first Soviet raid is full of factual topographical detail.

What happened to Shpanov's book after the conclusion of the Soviet-German pact, whether it was withdrawn from circulation, I do not know, but most probably it was. Since then Shpanov's name has now and then appeared under some recent war stories and sketches. His work is, however, of little intrinsic value ; its only interest lies in the curious light it throws on the famous saying : *Habent sua fata libelli. . . .*

. . . . .

The following Soviet authors mentioned in this book have died since 1935 : Mikhail Bulgakov, Ilya Ilf, Gorky,

Afinogenov (killed in 1941 during an air raid on Moscow), Evgeny Petrov (killed in 1942 in Sevastopol, where he had come to report the siege for Soviet and American newspapers), Nikolay Ostrovsky, Makarenko, Chapygin, Romanov, and Zamyatin (died in 1937 in Paris). Since the publication of the second edition of this book the following have also died : Yury Tynyanov and Alexey Tolstoy.

II. THE NEW PATRIOTIC TREND
1. *The New Outlook*

Only the blind can fail to see the profound change which has come recently over the official Soviet outlook. It does not matter, after all, whether it is a change of " ideology ", or merely of " phraseology ", due to sheer political opportunism, for here one is inevitably reminded of Goethe's *Sorcerer's Apprentice* :

> Die ich rief, die Geister,
> Werd' ich nun nicht los.

Intelligent foreign observers who know and understand old Russia and the Soviet Union differ in appraising the new spirit of patriotism which during the last six or seven years has seized hold of the Soviet people and its rulers. For some, as for instance for Sir Bernard Pares, it has been a sign of a welcome and healthy return to certain basic Russian traditions, a rediscovery by new Russia of her lost soul, of her true national self. Others, like Mr. Louis Fisher, have seen in it—quite rightly from their point of view—a danger signal, a portent showing that Soviet Russia was becoming fundamentally more " re-actionary " than some of the " capitalist " states formerly denounced by her as mainstays of reaction. Only the vast and credulous majority of " Left Wing " admirers of the Soviet Union (especially in this country), who are ready to accept with their mouths agape everything " Soviet ", do not even stop to think over the meaning of the recent changes.

Epilogue : 1935–1943

I am not concerned here, however, with the political effects or implications of this significant change, the beginning of which can be traced back to 1937, but only with its reflection in literature. This is to be sought above all in the historical novel. From Chapter IX my readers will have learnt that the historical novel had long before 1937 a special appeal to Soviet authors. But the recent swing-over to patriotism has affected both the choice of subject and its treatment. Formerly, historical novelists in Soviet Russia were interested primarily in all revolutionary epochs, in social and political movements. Hence the novels dealing with the Cossack rebellion of Stenka Razin, with the peasant risings during various epochs, with the dissemination of revolutionary ideas in the eighteenth century (Olga Forsh's *Radishchev*), with the French Revolution itself, with the Decembrists (Tynyanov's *Kyukhlya*). Even Alexey Tolstoy's *Peter the First* was concerned above all with the revolutionary aspect of Peter's reign. Had Tolstoy been writing it now the patriotic note would certainly have been sounded at a much fuller blast. For now the centre of interest has shifted to epochs of Russian national struggle and to national rather than revolutionary heroes. Some of the revolutionary idols still have, of course, their place in the official shrine of Communist Russia, but their images have been hastily repainted and adjusted. No longer are they mere revolutionaries, they are also " true Russian patriots ". The very word " Russia ", seldom used during the first twenty years of the Revolution, is again on everybody's lips. There are some war articles of Ehrenburg in which the word " Soviet " (let alone Communist) is not used at all, but the words " Russia " and " Russian " occur in almost every line. The pride of place in the official Soviet shrine has been given to entirely new and unexpected images. They include Dmitry Donskoy and St.

Alexander Nevsky, two great national heroes of early Russian history of whom it can be safely said that little was known or heard of them outside Russia before this war. Now their names have become familiar to everybody in the countries which are fighting Hitlerite Germany. They also include the more familiar names of two famous Russian generals, Suvorov and Kutuzov, and the two great patriots of the so-called Time of Troubles (early seventeenth century), Minin and Pozharsky. This latter case is particularly interesting and significant as an illustration of the profundity of the change of outlook. For Minin and Pozharsky, who incidentally symbolize the alliance between the people and the nobility in a movement of national unity, not only removed the danger of Russia's subjection to foreign domination, but also saved Russia from a social revolution and paved the way for the election of the Romanov dynasty. Ten years ago a man like Ivan Bolotnikov, who during the same period represented the forces of social unrest and anarchy, had a much greater appeal and interest to Soviet authors and readers than Minin or Prince Pozharsky. Both friends and enemies of Bolshevism saw in Bolotnikov's " ideas " and methods some points of affinity with Bolshevism. To-day we do not hear of any Red Army tanks or planes being named after Bolotnikov, but everybody could read some time ago of the exploits of a tank called "Pozharsky", and the name of Minin is constantly evoked as the name of a great Russian patriot. As to Dmitry Donskoy, Alexander Nevsky, Suvorov and Kutuzov, everybody knows that decorations bearing their names have been added to the highest military awards in the Red Army. To these names one might add, with certain reservations, the names of at least two Tsars—Peter the Great and Ivan the Terrible. Both of them have a certain claim for recognition on the part of the Soviet Union for their

" revolutionary " methods and acts. Peter the Great has often been regarded as a revolutionary from above. As to Ivan the Terrible, he was the Tsar who did not stop at using most cruel methods in crushing the Boyar oligarchy. But it is the national and constructive aspect of these two Tsars that is particularly stressed now—Ivan's struggle for the Baltic and expansion towards the East, and Peter's successful continuation of Ivan's task and success in raising Russia to the status of a great European power.

There has been some controversy as to whether this new patriotism in Russia can be described as *Russian* nationalism. Mr. Louis Fisher seems to think so. Others maintain that it is certainly not exclusively Russian and embraces all the multi-national population of the Union. I think that the latter view is more correct, but that at the same time it is wrong to speak of " Soviet " patriotism, such as it was understood earlier (a good expression of this Soviet patriotism is Pavlenko's novel *In the East*, but it is a stage already past—cp. above, pp. 285 and ff.). What we see now is Russian *Imperial* patriotism, for the Soviet Union is an empire all but in name. It is only fair to note, however, that the Russian people is not at present treated as *primus inter pares*, but as the leading and superior nationality. The treatment of nationalities in the Soviet Union may have changed for the better, but the old Russian patriotism at its best was the same kind of *Imperial* patriotism embracing all the numerous nationalities. That is why it was often to be met with in people of non-Russian nationality.

There is no need to dwell on all the various manifestations of this rehabilitation of the national Russian traditions in the U.S.S.R. The press and the radio bring every day fresh and striking examples of this tendency. Not only the military glories of Russia, associated with the names of Suvorov and Kutuzov, but also the achievements of the Russian State are now receiving a completely new treatment at the hands of Soviet historians, authors, and politicians.[1]

An interesting example of the "revaluation of all values" now going on in the Soviet Union is to be found in an article on Dostoevsky by a well-known Soviet critic, V. Ermilov.[2] The title itself is significant : " A great Russian writer—F. M. Dostoevsky." Of course, there was never any question of ostracizing Dostoevsky in the U.S.S.R., or even of denying him greatness as a writer, but he was seldom or never quoted among the great Russian classics from whom young Soviet writers were advised to learn. There was also a clear tendency to disregard completely Dostoevsky as a thinker and teacher (the two aspects of his which pre-revolutionary and *émigré* Russian students of Dostoevsky—Shestov, Berdyaev, Bulgakov, Rozanov, Ivanov and others— brought to the fore), and to treat him as a purely literary phenomenon. Dostoevsky's *Besy* (*The Demons*) was certainly regarded as a dangerous book, as a lampoon on Russian revolutionary intelligentsia, and at one time at least it was banned from public libraries in the Soviet Union.

Now Ermilov re-discovers Dostoevsky not as a writer, as a master of original style or of skilful plot, but as a national and moral teacher, as a preacher of Humanism, and thus an essentially " anti-fascist " writer. Dostoevsky's well-known hatred of Prussianism is made much of, and he is represented not as a precursor of Nietzsche, but as a denouncer of Nietzschean morality *avant la lettre*, as a prophet, in fact, who foresaw the advent of inhuman Nazism (some rather unkind blows are dealt by Ermilov *en passant* to the late Leo Shestov). Even Dostoevsky's

---

[1] In a recent introduction to Pushkin's *Bronze Horseman*, broadcast on Moscow wireless, it was stated that St. Petersburg was " a magnificent embodiment of Russian military glory and Russian statecraft."

[2] *Literatura i iskusstvo*, 5th September 1942.

Besy is now treated as a prophecy, not of the Revolution of course, but of the "political gangsters" of Nazism. It is true that Ermilov accompanies his article with a number of reservations, that he leaves out of account Dostoevsky's religious conception, that he notes Dostoevsky's "contradictions" (of which, of course, he had many). But the significant conclusion of the article is that the new Soviet man has much to find in and learn from Dostoevsky, and this not as a novelist but as a teacher of true humanism.[1]

2. *Recent Historical Novels and Plays*

In literature the new patriotic spirit has provoked a large crop of historical novels dealing with the critical moments in the national life of Russia and with Russian national heroes.

One of the earliest periods in Russian history to attract the attention of Soviet authors is the struggle against the Tartars with its climax in the famous Kulikovo battle in which Dmitry Donskoy defeated the Tartars of Khan Mamay and thus paved the way for Russia's final liberation from the Mongol yoke. Dmitry Donskoy is the central figure in the historical novel of that name by Sergey Borodin (real name—Amir Sargidzhian). St. Sergius of Radonezh, one of the great figures in Russian Church history and himself an ardent patriot, also plays an important part in the novel. But the real hero of the book is the Russian people of whom Borodin shows us many varied representatives and who appear also in mass scenes. For this novel Borodin was awarded one of the

[1] In May 1943 the State Museum of Literature in Moscow announced that it was preparing for publication a volume entitled *Dostoevsky on the Germans*, where Dostoevsky's unfavourable judgments on the Germans as a nation were to be collected from his articles, diaries, and letters (including some unpublished ones). It is significant that in announcing the forthcoming publication the official Soviet News Agency described *The Demons* as one of Dostoevsky's greatest novels. Hitherto *The Demons* was regarded in the Soviet Union as the quintessence of Dostoevsky's "reactionaryism".

Stalin Prizes for 1941. His short Life of Dmitry Donskoy
has been printed and circulated in hundreds of thousands,
if not millions, of copies.

The struggle with the Tartars on a vaster plane, and
seen also from the other side, is the subject of a historical
trilogy by V. Yan (Yanchevetsky), another Stalin Prize
laureate. Two parts of it have appeared so far—*Chingis-
Khan* (*Ghenghiz-Khan*) and *Baty* (*Batu*). It is a colourful
work for which the author has drawn on various historical
sources, both Russian and Oriental. He also makes large
use of Russian folklore.

The reign of Ivan the Terrible, and especially Ivan's
Livonian wars which he fought to secure for Russia an
outlet to the Baltic, is the subject of the first part of
another trilogy—*Ivan Grozny* (*Ivan the Terrible*), by
Vl. Kostylev. Ivan the Terrible is also the hero of a play
on which Alexey Tolstoy is engaged at present. In this
connection it is interesting to note that Tolstoy's namesake
and distant relation, the poet Alexey Tolstoy (1817–1875),
who wrote a dramatic trilogy dealing with the period of
Ivan and his successors (*The Death of Ivan the Terrible,
Tsar Fedor* and *Tsar Boris*), a novel situated in the same
period (*Prince Serebryany*) and the famous ballad *Vasily
Shibanov*, which gives a striking portrait of Ivan, not only
stuck to the traditional view of the latter as first of all a
cruel and perverse despot, but viewed the whole period
as one of the worst pages in Russian history. He idealized
Kievan Russia, and for him Muscovite Russia represented
a sad falling off of moral and political standards. His
twentieth-century successors are taking quite a different
view. In accordance with the more modern and objective
interpretation (dating back to before the Revolution), they
treat the cruel Tsar as a great statesman and a far-sighted
Russian patriot.

The war of 1812 against Napoleon is a source of much

inspiration to Soviet writers and artists. Here perhaps the existence of Tolstoy's unique masterpiece puts the present-day authors off any attempt to tackle the subject on a large scale. But there is no scarcity of works dealing with individual figures or episodes. One of the most popular is the play *Fieldmarshal Kutuzov*, by the well-known playwright, Vladimir Solovyev. A stage version of the war scenes in Tolstoy's *War and Peace* was produced last year in Moscow. Several other plays have been inspired by the same epoch, while two young writers, I. Bakhterev and A. Razumovsky, wrote a play about Suvorov (*Fieldmarshal Suvorov*) which will be familiar to many people in this country who saw the film version.

The most ambitious undertaking in recent historical fiction is, however, S. Sergeyev-Tsensky's three-volume epic of the Crimean War—*Sevastopolskaya strada* (*The Ordeal of Sevastopol*). The author has set himself an almost Tolstoyan task of giving a whole picture of Russia in 1854-55 against the general historical background of contemporary Europe, of doing for the Crimean War what Tolstoy did for the Napoleonic Wars of 1805-1812. The result is a volume of some 1500 pages. There is in it, of course, more war than peace, because, unlike the period covered by Tolstoy, the whole of the period chosen by Sergeyev-Tsensky was taken up by the war. We see Sevastopol preparing for the attack, the scuttling of the Russian fleet in the bay, the battles of Alma and Inkermann, the siege of the city, the Charge of the Light Brigade, the St. Petersburg, London and Paris background—with Nicholas I, Queen Victoria and Napoleon the Little all making their appearance on the scene ; the despatch of the first Russian Red Cross nurses to the front, and so on— in fact the whole variegated panorama of the war passes before our eyes. The author has drawn excellent portraits of Admiral Kornilov, the great hero of the early siege ;

of Menshikov, the Russian commander-in-chief; of several Russian, British and French generals ; of Pirogov, the famous Russian surgeon and educationist. Some of the battle scenes are extremely well done. The description of the scuttling of the fleet is particularly good. Interlocked with the narrative of the historical events are one or two personal stories, in the course of which the author takes us to the " rear ", to an estate in the Kursk province and shows us some provincial characters. *The Ordeal of Sevastopol* is one of the best historical novels to come from the Soviet Union, and in spite of its inordinate length would be well worth translating into English. It was written before the siege of Sevastopol by the Germans and is free from undue reading of actuality into the past, although one of the author's tasks is obviously to show the enduring qualities of the Russian soldier, those qualities which he has displayed in all wars, including the present. The novel is not free from a certain anti-English bias which the author might have wished to eliminate had he been writing later.

Sergeyev-Tsensky has since written another interesting historical novel, this time choosing a subject much nearer to us in time. It is called *Brusilovsky proryv* (*Brusilov's Break-through*) and deals with the 1916 offensive of the Russian armies on the south-western front and its entire background. The first instalment of this novel (it will be in two parts) appeared in the review *Novy Mir* for 1942. The opening chapter shows us several ordinary officers discussing in a railway carriage on the way to the front Russia's military and political situation in early spring of 1916 and future prospects. Sergeyev-Tsensky has succeeded very well in conveying the atmosphere of " patriotic anxiety " which characterized all Russian conversations in those days. This scene in the railway carriage might almost have been a verbatim shorthand report of an actual conversation. Later we get the first glimpse of General Brusilov who is apparently to play an important part in the novel, though not the part of its hero. The latter is reserved, one feels, for the average Russian soldier and officer. Brusilov has just been appointed Commander-in-Chief of the south-western front. We see him with the old General Ivanov whom he has replaced, and then in an audience with the Emperor. The first instalment of the novel ends with the arrival of two young officers, who are apparently to play an important part in the action, at the front. We are introduced to a number of officers, of whom one, bearing a German name, looks very much like a potential fifth columnist.

Sergeyev-Tsensky's novel is another instance of the revised approach to the past, even the recent past.

III. LITERATURE AND THE WAR

As behoves a totalitarian country, literature in the Soviet Union has since June 1941 become part of a total war effort. It is one of the war weapons, and not an unimportant one at that. War is at present practically the only concern and the only subject of every Soviet author. Many of them are with the armies or near the front. Others, although not at the front, are doing some war work and writing about nothing but war or subjects having some bearing on it (patriotic historical novels, biographies of national heroes, etc.).

The place and function of literature during the war have been stated clearly and succinctly by the official organ of the Union of Soviet Writers and of the official Committee on Art :

"What is of paramount importance to-day as never before is the *activizing* function of art which possesses the invaluable faculty of inspiring men to fight, of helping them in the struggle.

"The expression 'military theme' is inaccurate. What we want is not military, but *militant* literature.

EPILOGUE : 1935-1943

We want not an ordinary ' military ' art but a *fighting*
art (*voyuyushcheye iskusstvo*).

" Only that art is enduring and beautiful which takes
an active part in the life of its epoch. In our days to
take part in life is to take part in the war." [1]

In another leading article the same official newspaper
wrote :

" Always bound up closely with the life of the people,
Soviet art since the outbreak of the war has entered
upon a new phase of its development. Henceforth it
was called upon to serve one single object—the cause
of victory over the enemy. It was meant to become a
weapon in the hands of the soldier who has risen to
defend his country. It had to rear the fighting spirit of
the people, to strengthen the force of patriotism, to fan
hatred for German-Fascist invaders, to call for revenge.
It was to show the moral greatness of the Soviet people,
their tenacity, their faith in the coming victory." [2]

The war output of Soviet literature is enormous and it
is not easy at this stage to survey it critically. Much
of it is of ephemeral nature and belongs to that literature
of which Ehrenburg has said : " A writer must know
how to write not only for the centuries. He should know
also how to write for the one short second if the fate of
his people is to be decided in this second." This vast
literature comprises novels, plays, poems, sketches,
reportage, patriotic articles, and historical works linking
up the present war with the past traditions. In the list
of war authors one meets with many familiar names,
though some strike one by their absence.

Naturally enough the bulk of this war literature consists
of short works—stories and front-line sketches. There
are collections by Sholokhov (his short story called *Hate*,
told in the form of a talk with a Red Army officer, is very
effective, but it is rather a sketch than a story), by Evgeny

[1] *Literatura i iskusstvo* (formerly *Literaturnaya Gazeta*), 19th September 1942.
[2] *Literatura i iskusstvo*, 17th October 1942.

Petrov (who reported the fighting on the Moscow front for Russian and American newspapers), by Kataev (*Voennye rasskazy*), by Ehrenburg (*Voyna*), by Vladimir Stavsky (some very good documentary *reportage* from the Moscow front), by Boris Gorbatov (*Rodina*), by Konstantin Simonov and many others. A place apart belongs to a volume of short stories by Nikolay Tikhonov (*Cherty sovetskogo cheloveka*), describing Leningrad during the siege. A Soviet critic has described it as the first elements of a Leningrad Iliad. In one of Tikhonov's stories—*Vstrecha (An Encounter)*—a character, an old history teacher, asks a chance acquaintance in the street: "Do you know where you live? You live in Ilion. I don't know of a city the legend of which would be as sublime as the legend of Troy, and only our city to-day, don't you think so, has not only matched Ilion but even excelled her in heroism." The other answers: "Perhaps you are right, but in our Troy there will be no Trojan horse. There won't be—never!"

A story by Yury Herman, with an English title (*Be Happy!*), has among its characters several British airmen in the North of Russia. It is told in the form of a diary of a Soviet girl attached to the aerodrome used by the British as their base. The R.A.F. pilots are drawn with great sympathy.

One of the features of many of these stories and sketches is their documentary or near-documentary character; another—the stress which the best lay on the unheroic simplicity of the war heroes and on their plain human feelings, that "sacred simplicity" (to use Tikhonov's words in one of his poems) which "is simpler than any complicated truths". In many of these stories the note of hatred is sounded of course.

"The war has taught our artists to speak the language of wrath and hatred—"

wrote *Literatura i iskusstvo* on 25th July 1942.

Collections of patriotic articles by Alexey Tolstoy and Ilya Ehrenburg have enjoyed enormous success. Many of them are passionate lyrical professions of faith in Russia, others are topical echoes of the war. Tolstoy is more Russian, more national. Ehrenburg, whose culture is more cosmopolitan, strikes a European note parallel with the Russian patriotic one. Russia is fighting not only for her freedom, independence and honour, but also for European civilization—such is one of Ehrenburg's *leitmotifs*.

Both Tolstoy and Ehrenburg seem to enjoy greater popularity as war authors than any other contemporary Soviet Russian writer. It is interesting therefore to note that both of them took a patriotic attitude during the last war when the political leaders and founders of the Soviet Union were in the "defeatist" camp. Both for a time took sides with the so-called "White" or anti-Bolshevik movement, guided also in those days by their patriotic understanding of the moment. Apparently the new patriotic mentality has come to them easier and more naturally than to some of the more orthodox writers of the post-revolutionary generation.

Of the longer prose works dealing with the war the Soviet press has been full of praise for Vasily Grossman's *Narod bessmerten* (*The People is Deathless*) which I have not been able to read. A long novel dealing with the "home front" is Arkady Perventsev's *Ispytanie* (*The Trial*). In the centre of it are a Soviet aircraft factory and a group of its personnel and their families. It is a good picture of Soviet life behind the front line during the first stages of the war. Its hero is Bogdan Dubenko, a Ukrainian, genial and energetic. He is chief engineer of the factory and we see him at work, in war councils and in the midst of his family. The centre of interest of the narrative is in the factory's evacuation to the Urals.

Perventsev is not quite a newcomer to Soviet literature. His earlier novel (*Kochubey*) was a colourful tale of the civil war in the Kuban.

Playwrights have been even more active than novelists, and have produced a number of patriotic war plays. One of the most popular, according to all accounts, is Simonov's *Russkie lyudi* (*The Russians*), of which the heroine is a girl scout. The play was written by Simonov at the front. It has been staged with great success by a number of central and provincial theatres and also given at the front.

Another play by Simonov (*Paren iz nashego goroda*— *A Lad from Our Town*), although not actually a war play, shows a type of young man whose like are to be found to-day in the Red Army. Its hero, Sergey Lukonin, is a tank driver before the war and takes part in the Spanish Civil War.

Alexander Korniychuk,[1] the Ukrainian dramatist who apparently writes in Russian, has written two war plays. One of them is called *Partizany v stepyakh Ukrainy* (*Guerrillas in the Steppes of the Ukraine*) and is a war sequel to his peace-time play *In the Steppes of the Ukraine* —about collective farming; the other is called *Front* (*The Front*).

The play about guerrillas is rather weak, both its situations and its characters being somewhat stilted. The best among the characters are those in whom there is a relieving touch of humour—Galushka and the two old peasants who remind one of some of Gogol's characters. One of them is shown dying a simple, senseless, and yet tragic, death.

The Front has become one of the most widely discussed sensations of the theatrical season of 1942, not so much as a drama as because of the problem which Korniychuk

---

[1] His name has now been Russianized and is spelt " Korneychuk."

has raised in it. He shows two different types of Red Army commanders. One is embodied in Ivan Gorlov, an old soldier of the Revolution who still thinks in the antiquated terms of the Civil War and pooh-poohs the modern conception of technical warfare. Gorlov has personal courage, he has a distinguished revolutionary past, but he does not fit in with the new requirements, and he surrounds himself with men who also do not rise to the occasion. This entourage of Gorlov on his staff is deliberately portrayed by Korniychuk in satirical, grotesque tones. Even their names, in the good old tradition of eighteenth-century satirical comedies, are expressive of their character.

To Gorlov is opposed another Red Army general, Ognev, a much younger man. Gorlov is inclined to look at him from above, because he was a mere child when Gorlov was already fighting in Budenny's army. But Ognev has a much better understanding of what is required in this war, and in the end he takes the place of Gorlov who is dismissed. Korniychuk intensifies the dramatic conflict by introducing two other Gorlovs into the play—Ivan's son and brother. Both of them are opposed to old Gorlov and are instrumental in bringing his downfall. Gorlov's son, who dies a hero's death during a reconnaissance, is a great admirer of Ognev.

Korniychuk has been praised by the Soviet press for fearlessly tackling a problem of first-rate importance for the Red Army. This play is another instance of that process of " revaluation of all values " which is going on in the U.S.S.R.

The heroic behaviour of Soviet citizens remaining behind the German lines is the subject of Fedin's play *Ispytanie* (*The Ordeal*) which I have not read. The same theme is treated in an interesting way in another play which seems to me to be one of the best so far produced

by Soviet dramatists.   It is Leonid Leonov's *Nashestvie*
(*Invasion*) for which he was this year awarded a Stalin
Prize.   It was written in 1942 in Chistopol, far from the
turmoil of the war, on the Kama, the great and majestic
tributary of-the Volga.   At the moment when these lines
are being written, the Maly Theatre of Moscow, the home
of classical Russian drama, is preparing its production.

The play is full of dramatic tension, of poignant scenes.
The action is set in a small Russian town lying along the
road of the German advance on Moscow in 1941.   The
play begins at the moment when the Germans are about
to enter the town.   Preparations for its evacuation are
already under way.

In Act One we are introduced to the household of
Dr. Ivan Talanov, an oldish and rather typical Russian
country doctor who enjoys both respect and affection
of his patients and of the entire population of the town.
In pre-revolutionary Russia there were a great many
such zemstvo doctors.   There are still many of them left.
There is nothing to indicate that he is a Communist ;
rather everything points to his not being one.   The
household consists of his wife Anna, of whom we learn
that she was a talented pianist but gave up her career for
the sake of her family ; of their daughter Olga, a young
school teacher ; of Demidyevna, the old nurse, sharp-
tongued but kind-hearted, who is regarded as a member
of the family ;   and of Demidyevna's granddaughter
Aniska, who has just escaped from a near-by village
occupied by the Germans.   We are also introduced to
the invisible presence of another member of the Talanov
family—the son Fedor whose portrait as a small boy in
sailor suit dominates the Talanovs' modest living-room.
Fedor is the first link in the chain binding a personal
drama with the tragedy of the people.   Some years ago
he had shot a woman he loved.   He is now undergoing

his sentence but for some time has not given any news of himself. When the curtain goes up, we see Anna Talanova writing a letter to Fedor. A certain Koko-ryshkin, an insignificant and unprepossessing individual with ingratiating manners, comes to see Dr. Talanov on business. Then appears Olga with the great news : she has just seen Fedor outside. Soon he appears himself—the dramatic return of the prodigal son. Broken physically and morally, he adopts a cynical pose behind which one feels the tragedy of a man who has lost himself and his place in life, who is capable of some desperate action, good or evil, but is trying to hide the despair of his emptied soul under this cynical bravado. Act One contains two more dramatic entries. Soon after the arrival of Dr. Talanov, who takes the presence of his son almost for granted and soon proceeds to examine him professionally, comes Andrey Kolesnikov, chairman of the local executive committee. The object of his visit is to offer Talanov two places in his car to enable him to leave the town before the Germans enter it. Fedor is hidden behind a screen. Talanov refuses Kolesnikov's offer. It transpires that Kolesnikov himself does not propose to go away for good. He has other plans. One can guess what they are—he will lead the local guerrillas. It is also possible to guess that Kolesnikov and Olga are in love.

After a time Kolesnikov notices Fedor's coat. Fedor steps out. There is a strange scene between the two. Fedor guesses at once the real object of Kolesnikov's staying behind and offers to join his guerrilla detachment :

"Wouldn't you like to accept one such . . . reformed character ? It is true he has no solid references, but—he will carry out anything. And he is not afraid of death : for three years he slept in its arms."

After a minute of awkward general silence Fedor adds : "It doesn't suit your book ? " Kolesnikov replies that

he is not staying in the town, and wishes Fedor to find
his " place in life ".

In the meantime there has been a usual air raid.
Explosions are heard. One of the windows is blasted in,
the light goes out. When a lamp is lit, the inmates of
the room notice a stranger sitting on a chair by the door.
He looks like an old, half-crazy tramp, but turns out in
the end to be Nikolay Fayunin, described in the list of
dramatis personæ as " of the dead ". He is a former rich
flax manufacturer of the town and the owner of the house
where the Talanovs live. Kokoryshkin, " the rising star ",
immediately throws off his mask : " Welcome to you,
sir. . . . So it has come to be ? " Fayunin goes to the
telephone and calls the militia. There is no answer—
the municipal authorities have fled. " Lord, bless· our
new era ", says Fayunin, and to the accompaniment of
machine-gun rattle in the street, he adds : " Lord, now
lettest Thou Thy servant depart in peace, according to
Thy word : for mine eyes have seen . . ."

The Act ends with the window and the black-out frame
being broken from the outside, and helmeted German
soldiers peering in.

The Second Act is divided into two scenes. It opens
in the same room, but the room has changed—it looks
drab and poky. Instead of Fedor's portrait there is a
gap in the wall. Through the middle window one can
see the church with its belfry cut off. Fayunin is now
mayor of the town. Olga pretends to go to school (of
which only a shell remains), but is really working for the
guerrillas. Every day some Germans are killed by
unknown persons and a note pinned to the body with
the words " *Dobro pozhalovat* "—" Welcome to you ".
This phrase runs through the play, becomes its symbolical
leitmotif, gradually acquiring fuller and wider significance.
It is first used by Fedor to Kolesnikov. Kokoryshkin

greets Fayunin with it. Then it acquires new and sinister
significance for the Germans who are haunted by it.
The Germans know that the " avengers " are led by a
certain Andrey : a reward is offered for his head. Fayunin
suspects that Talanov knows the secret and tries to play
up to him.

In the same scene the German Commandant Wibbel,
accompanied by Kunz, his aide-de-camp, and Mosalsky,
" a former Russian " (that is, an *émigré*), comes to inspect
Talanov's flat, which it is proposed to requisition for the
German army. Fayunin skilfully puts him off the idea
by suggesting that the place is infested with mice. Instead
he will use the apartment himself, leaving one room to
the Talanovs.

The scene ends on a highly dramatic note : Aniska
is brought in and attended to by Talanov—she has been
raped by Kunz and several German soldiers. Demidyevna
is distracted with grief.

Scene Two of Act One shows the Talanovs pressed into
one small room. Preparations are going on in Fayunin's
part of the apartment where Kokoryshkin is fussing about.
When the scene opens, Talanov is reading, his wife doing
the washing up. Aniska lies semi-delirious behind a
chintz curtain. Olga comes in, followed by Kolesnikov,
who has been wounded in the arm. Talanov dresses his
wound. A knock is heard on the door. It is Fedor.
Kolesnikov hides behind the screen. Fedor has not slept
for forty-eight hours and gives the impression of being
drunk. His behaviour is somewhat different from the
first night, but equally strange. He asks his father for
a medicine which would burn his inside. Talanov
considers this request and then answers : " All right,
I'll give you a medicine than which nothing can be stronger
in this world. Drink it at a gulp, if you can." He draws
aside the gay chintz curtain behind which Aniska lies,

and tells briefly her sad tale. A brief scene ensues between
Fedor, Aniska, and Demidyevna. The profound effect
it makes on Fedor is just hinted at. Before going Fedor
asks his father to kiss him " in advance and for everything
at once ". Then he discovers Kolesnikov's presence.
When Olga tries to explain it away Fedor brushes aside
her explanations, and the following dialogue takes place :

" FEDOR (*ironically*) : I see no point in concealing the
fact that such a famous man has come to consult the
doctor. (*Looking straight into* KOLESNIKOV'S *face*) :
They have set a substantial prize on you, citizen
Kolesnikov.
" KOLESNIKOV : I am aware of it, citizen Talanov.
" FEDOR : But it isn't enough for one like you. I
would have given ten times more. (*In a ringing and
challenging tone*) : Try to unravel my mental processes,
old man. I am now going to leave the house. That is,
before I am driven out. Won't you give me some
errand ? Can't I pass some message to your people ?
" KOLESNIKOV : Well, you see . . . I have no messages
to give. And there is no one to pass it on to.
" FEDOR : So, I see. . . ."

After a display of intentional buffoonery Fedor goes
out. Once more Kolesnikov is on the point of departing
when two other buffoons enter : Fayunin, and behind
him Kokoryshkin carrying a tray with wine glasses—an
improvised housewarming celebration. " I am sorry,
I see you have visitors ", says Fayunin. Without a
moment's hesitation Anna steps forward and says :
" Visitors and a joy, Nikolay Sergeyevich. Our son has
just come back to us." " He crossed the front line ",
Talanov caps her lie. While Olga formally introduces
them : " Please meet. Fedor Talanov. And this is our
Mayor, Fayunin." At a stroke, a new and tense situation
is created. They exchange ceremonious bows. Kokoryshkin pretends not to notice anything. He knows, of

309

course, who Kolesnikov is. They all take glasses.
Kokoryshkin's hands holding the tray tremble. Fayunin
tells him to take a glass and " congratulate the young man
on his return ". Kokoryshkin chooses a glass and blurts
out : " *Welcome to you*, Fedor Ivanovich." Everybody is
embarrassed. Kokoryshkin seems to realize his slip.
"Forget those words—you'll get into a soup", Olga
tells him.

Act Three takes place in Fayunin's room—the same
room which the Talanovs occupied at the beginning of
the play, but redecorated and adapted to suit the taste
of its new possessor. Fayunin is celebrating his nameday
and expecting guests of honour : Wibbel the Commandant, Spurre from the Gestapo and other Germans.
The Act begins with a conversation between Fayunin
and Kokoryshkin, the latter hinting that in return for
advancement (money does not attract him, he wants
power) he might be able to discover the identity of the
mysterious guerrilla leader who by his " welcome " notes
has terrorized the Germans. Fayunin refuses to promise
anything. In the meantime the first guests assemble—
a procession of puppets. Then comes Spurre preceded by
Mosalsky—another puppet or robot (" he walks as though
on wheels "). Kokoryshkin approaches him with a
beaming face and once more the ill-starred formula
escapes him : " Welcome to you, welcome. . . ." This
has the effect of a bombshell. Spurre, who thinks Kokoryshkin is the elusive Kolesnikov himself, seizes him by
the collar and leads him to the door. A muffled shot is
heard outside.

The feast begins. At a given moment it is interrupted
by Mosalsky, who gets up to make a speech on behalf of
Wibbel. " At this moment we are expecting a telephone
message of colossal importance ", says Mosalsky. Spurre
goes to the telephone. Mosalsky continues :

"The rusty padlock which for a thousand years has been hanging on the gates to the East has been broken. Gentlemen, Moscow has been taken."

Fayunin makes surreptitiously a sign of the cross. Relief or sorrow ?—it can be either. All the guests raise their glasses to drink the toast. The telephone bell rings. Spurre takes up the receiver. But instead of the glad tidings of the capture of Moscow, he hears that Wibbel and several other officers have been murdered. The murderer has been caught and will be presently brought in. A scene of confusion, followed by tense expectation. The puppet-like guests melt away, but the Talanovs arrive, belated and unsuspecting. Fayunin tells them the news. Soon the murderer is brought in. It is Fedor. He is questioned by Mosalsky and gives his name as Andrey Kolesnikov. " Your occupation ? " asks Mosalsky. " I am Russian. Defending my country ", answers Fedor. Both Talanovs, when questioned, confirm that he is really Kolesnikov. The mother finds enough courage to say that she had not seen him for ten years but seems to recognize him. The father casually observes that they have met at official meetings. Fayunin knows the truth, but for reasons known only to himself keeps his counsel. His game is not quite clear. Fedor is led away to be interrogated. A despatch rider arrives with an urgent message : things are going badly for the Germans on the Moscow front. Spurre orders the interrogation to be put off till next day. Fayunin is finally left alone when suddenly real Kolesnikov comes in. Fayunin at first keeps up the pretence of believing that he is Fedor. He tells him how when the Russians were retreating he was standing at the roadside.

"Suddenly a young lad in a soldier's coat jumped down to me, embraced me, burned me with his hot breath. 'Don't be sad, gran'dad', he said. 'The Russians will come back. They always come back.' . . . What do you think, will the lad keep his word ? "

Kolesnikov gives an evasive answer. Suddenly Fayunin opens his cards and makes it clear that he knows who Kolesnikov is. He offers to let him out. Has his deep-rooted Russian feeling got the better of him ? Is he afraid of the Russians returning as promised by the lad in soldier's coat and does he want to secure Kolesnikov's protection in advance ? He almost says as much. Then all of a sudden he advises Kolesnikov to " save Olga from the noose ". Kolesnikov's reaction to this is somewhat unexpected. He seems to see through Fayunin and at the same time to foresee the future, and says :

" Yes, your young lad will come back, Nikolay Sergeich. Your bullet is ready for you in the cartridge. Traitors are not taken prisoner. . . . I thought at first that you wanted to quench your injuries in the Russian conflagration. A proud man will pay three times with his death for the right to take revenge. But you have forgiven everything. You don't exist, Fayunin. The whirlwind of war has lifted you up like a cloud of stinking dust. You think you are the master of the town, but it's I who am it. Here I stand before you, unarmed, your prisoner. . . . And yet you are afraid of me. A coward even when he is strong relies primarily on his enemy's mercy. Now I am going, and you daren't even shout to the German sentry and tell him to shoot me in the back. Dead, we are even more terrible, Fayunin."

He goes. Fayunin rushes to the telephone, talks to Spurre, asks him to send men, and mutters to himself : " You'll come back for her, sonny. The night is long—don't hurry with your answer "—and the curtain falls, somewhat mysteriously, on Act Three.

In Act Four we see the basement of a warehouse converted into a prison. The presence of gallows in the yard outside is delicately revealed. Olga ; two of Kolesnikov's assistants, Tatarov and Egorov ; the thirteen-year-old Pashka from Aniska's village and his old grand-

father, and a few others, are awaiting their execution.
There is also a would-be madman—he is the man who
had been spying on Kolesnikov outside Talanov's house.
A little later Fedor is brought in from interrogation,
during which he was beaten up. The atmosphere of
impending doom is subtly suggested. Against it Olga's,
Tatarov's and Egorov's heroism stands out. They hold
a conference, discuss whether Fedor can be accepted into
their detachment, ask him to explain his behaviour. He
recalls Aniska.

" TATAROV : You did not become Kolesnikov out of
spite ? You did not think : ' Well, if you don't accept
me alive, you'll have to accept me dead. You can look
from my father's window at me swinging on the swings
for you.' If so we have no use for people like that.

" OLGA : Explain, Fedor, to them why you assumed
another man's name.

" FEDOR : I thought (*and in his smile there is something
of the boy on the broken photo*) . . . that they would be
still more terrified when Kolesnikov, already dead,
would swoop on them again. I am sure, he is not
asleep now, not asleep. . . .

(*Silence.*)

I have handed you my life . . . and I am not asking
you for a receipt."

Egorov then proposes to vote Fedor's admission, to
which the old man, Proshka's grandfather, simply
remarks : " One doesn't ask to be received as a hero . . .
one enlists off one's own bat." The matter is settled—
Fedor is accepted as " a new Kolesnikov ". Egorov
embraces him. At this moment Spurre, Mosalsky and
some soldiers come in. Fedor, Tatarov and Egorov
volunteer to be the first three. They are led away to be
hanged. Before the turn of the others comes, Proshka,
who has climbed on some boxes to see what is happening
outside, sights Russian paratroops coming down. The

barred window of the prison is broken and several men
dash in, Kolesnikov at their head. Among them is the
lad in a soldier's coat who had promised Fayunin that
the Russians would come back. Fayunin himself is
discovered in the next door basement (what was he doing
there is not clear—hiding ?). The following scene takes
place between the lad and Fayunin :

> " LAD : You seem to have thrived on the crust I
> gave you, gran'dad.
> (FAYUNIN *does not speak.* TALANOV *and his wife
> come down the stairs.*)
> " LAD (*touching* FAYUNIN's *shoulder*) : There is even
> no room for us here to rejoice, gran'dad. (*There is an
> iron sound in his caress.*) Let's go out into the open,
> and embrace each other there. (*They go out.*) "

The play ends with a brief dialogue between Olga and
her mother :

> " OLGA : Mother, your eyes are dry. It won't do,
> you must cry for Fedor, mother. He went away and
> has now come back. He is standing next to you, he is
> again yours, mother.
> " ANNA : He's come back, he's mine, he is with us."

On this note of triumph of spirit over death the play ends.
I have given this disproportionately long analysis of
Invasion in order to show how Leonov handles his difficult
theme, for it seems that this play promises well to be the
great event of the present theatrical season in Russia.
It has the makings of a great play, although it does not
perhaps quite reach the mark. The fact that the play
has been awarded a Stalin Prize shows that it is regarded
as worthy of Socialist Realism. It is in fact " realistic "
enough and its " Socialism " is vouched for by the general
tendency, by the elevating and edifying effect it must
have, even by the introduction of the element of " Stalin
myth " in the prison scene, in the dialogue between

Proshka and his grandfather. But what a difference between this play and Korniychuk's *Guerrillas in the Steppes of the Ukraine*. Korniychuk's play is conventional and pedestrian. In spite of its dramatic theme, it leaves one cold. Leonov hovers dangerously on the borderline of melodrama (many of his situations are in fact melodramatic), he makes too much use of coincidences, but he is saved from skidding by the subtle symbolism of his play, by his gentle turning of some of the most dangerous corners.

Let us have a look at Leonov's characters. Some of them will be familiar to readers of Leonov's novels. Fedor, for instance, is a distant relation of Mitka Vekshin in *The Thief* or of Veniamin in *River Sot*, a man with no place in life, with a burnt-out soul, a man lost but not beyond recall. The impact of the war brings about his spiritual salvation, even though physically he was, and is, doomed. Fayunin and Kokoryshkin have also their ancestors in Leonov's novels. Fayunin is a social enemy, no doubt. He is, after all, mean and despicable ; his final fate—hinted at in the parting words of the Lad in Soldier's Coat—is inevitable and deserved. But all the time one feels that Leonov is at pains to hint at some redeeming feature in his make-up. Is it to be sought in his instinctive ineradicable Russianness ? He is playing the Germans' game, he is serving his German masters, but —one feels it—there is no love lost between them. There is almost a warmth of feeling in his voice when he tells Kolesnikov about his meeting with the Young Lad. There is even a note of admiration in his reference to Mme Talanova as an " iron old woman " after the dramatic scene in which Fedor poses as Kolesnikov, knowing that he is courting death.

Of the " positive " characters which are always very

difficult to draw, the Talanovs are Leonov's greatest success. They are the " unheroic heroes " of this war ; they are not even Communists, but ordinary Russian people, such as are to be met in real life, or in the works of nearly all great Russian writers.

Olga is also very delicately drawn, without any emotional overtones, and appears as a quiet, strong-minded, purposeful girl, one of those modern Russian girls of whom one hears so much now. Even in the portrait of Kolesnikov, Leonov has managed to avoid " hagiographic " approach, though he is more conventional than the others.

The Germans in the play are deliberately contrasted with the other characters and are shown as mechanical puppets, not human beings.

A play must ultimately be judged on the stage and not in reading. Leonov rightly leaves some scope both for the actors (this applies especially to Fayunin and to Fedor) and to an intelligent and intuitive producer on whom it will greatly depend what use to make of Leonov's subtle touches of symbolism which form an undercurrent of the play. *Invasion* is certainly one of Leonov's successes and one of the best works in Soviet war literature. In the hands of an intelligent director it will probably make a very good film.

There is only one play I know of which has for its subject the war outside Russia. It is *Den zhivykh* (*The Day of the Living*), a romantic and symbolic drama about Czechoslovakia by Mme Alexandra Burshtein. I have not read the play, but an article in *Literatura i iskusstvo* (25th July 1942) gives some idea of its argument and structure.

The first act takes place in 1938 in the days of Munich, the second and third in 1941. The principal character is Kašparek, an old radio news announcer. During the tragic days of 1938 he is sure that his country will oppose

Hitler, that there will be a war and that it will be a lucky war. He hurries to the studio, not wishing to yield to anyone the honour of being the first to announce Czechoslovakia's decision to resist. Instead, he is given to read a bulletin announcing the capitulation. He cannot stand it and loses consciousness.

Three years pass between the first and the second acts. Kašparek is still working as announcer for the Prague radio, but now, guarded by storm-troopers, he has to read out German lies. Actually he knows more than the people and is sure of Germany's final defeat, but he does not know what to do with his knowledge. Then he meets Portniažka, a legendary character, a kind of Czech Till Ulenspigel, who inspires Kašparek to a heroic deed. During the next news bulletin he starts reading, instead of the official bulletin, his own good news. Before he can finish, he is shot in the back. His granddaughter Libuša inherits his dream of freedom and his hatred for the invaders. She helps Tonda, Portniažka's assistant, who later goes to Russia. Other characters in the play are Professor Vodička, Ružena who also works for the radio, a churchyard caretaker, an engine-driver, a policeman, a woman innkeeper. In the second part of the play the greater part of the action is set in the cemetery over which hover the shades of Jan Hus and Jan Žižka. It is here that we see Vodička appear : he grows out of a grave mound which suddenly turns out to be " a very queer old man wearing an old-fashioned frock-coat and carrying a fat umbrella ". Afterwards Vodička is seen writing anti-Nazi leaflets. A secret anti-Nazi printing press is housed in one of the vaults.

Den zhivykh is a symbolic drama voicing the faith in the rebirth of the Czech nation. Its romantic symbolism strikes an unusual note in the present-day Soviet drama. There is in it a strong element of fantasy. The demarcation line between the dead and the living is apparently deliberately obliterated. The underlying idea expressed in the title is that to-day it does not matter who is dead and who is alive, both the dead and the living are working for to-morrow, and to-morrow will be the " day of the living ".

IV. SOME RECENT POETRY

What would have been before the Revolution or in its early stages a literary event—a new book of poems by Anna Akhmatova—passed without much notice in 1940. Published when the ties between this country and the Soviet Union were at their slenderest, this book, called *Iva* (*Willow Tree*) and comprising in addition to a small number of new poems a selection from Akhmatova's earlier books, has unfortunately not reached England. Judging by criticisms which appeared in the Soviet press, Akhmatova has remained true to her individualist self, and her poetic voice sounded in 1940 as a voice from the past.

Poetry in the Soviet Union has of late shown no signs of revival, although a number of new poets are busy writing verse. One of the features common to many of them is a desire to appeal to large masses, to be simple and unsophisticated. Many of the younger Soviet poets write popular songs, and this tendency towards the song has especially increased since the war.

Among these younger poets one of the most popular is Konstantin Simonov, who is also a playwright and storyteller. In his poetry the motifs of love and tenderness are blended with the expression of vigour and purposefulness of the new man. Simonov has written a great deal of war poetry. In one of his typical poems he says :

" The gallant ones have but immortality—For the gallant there is no death.—If you do not want death, be gallant—Therein lies the whole secret."

One of Simonov's war poems—*Zhdi menya* (*Wait for Me*)—addressed by a man at the front to his beloved—enjoys extraordinary popularity. A not very good English translation of it has appeared in one of the numbers of *International Literature* (published in Moscow).

Another very popular poet is Alexey Surkov. His first book of verse appeared in 1930. Since then he has published five more—the last (*December before Moscow*) in 1942. Surkov's poetry is also simple and song-like. He is the author of two widely popular Red Army songs— *The Red Cavalry Song* and *The Song of the Bold*. Many of his war poems have a distinct lyrical accent. Here are four characteristic lines from one of his war poems included in his latest book :

> You are now far, far away,
> Snow and blizzard are between us.
> It is not easy for me to reach you,
> But it's only four paces to death.

Hatred in the name of love is one of the motifs of his war poetry, and one of the sections in his *December before Moscow* is entitled " I Sing Hate ".

Poets like Evgeny Dolmatovsky and Stepan Shchipachev seem to be also very popular with the Soviet man in the street. There is a certain naïve and pleasant simplicity in their poems—no bombast—but one would hardly call it distinguished poetry.

Still more popular are the catchy songs of Lebedev-Kumach, one of which has become the signature tune of Moscow Radio.

One of the quite recent new-comers to Soviet poetry is Caesar Solodar, but it is still difficult to detect in his poetry a poetic individuality.

Of the earlier and more distinguished poets, Boris Pasternak apparently has published nothing but translations since his *Second Birth* (see p. 171). His translations include a new and very interesting version of *Hamlet*, which is to be used by the Moscow Art Theatre in their new production, and a new translation of *Romeo and Juliet* completed last year. Pasternak is also engaged on a volume of prose memoirs dealing with the Revolution of 1905, through which he lived as a boy in Moscow. I have not seen or heard of any of Pasternak's war poems.

Nikolay Tikhonov has since 1935 written a book of poems entitled *Ten druga* (*The Shadow of a Friend*) which embodies his European impressions (Belgium, Austria, France, England). In some of them we see Tikhonov at his best. The title is rather significantly borrowed from Batyushkov, a Russian classical poet of early nineteenth century. Tikhonov's longer poem, *Kirov s nami* (*Kirov is with Us*), earned him a Stalin Prize. Tikhonov, who throughout the siege of Leningrad remained in the city which he has come to represent in Soviet literature (there is more of the Leningrad tradition in him than in any other Soviet poet), has been busy writing stories, sketches and poems about the war. One of his longer war poems is an epic of the twenty-eight heroes of the Panfilov division. Another war poem—*Moscow and Leningrad*—was broadcast some time ago by Moscow Radio. Written at the time when Leningrad was besieged and Moscow under threat, it is full of noble and sustained patriotic eloquence.

The war has given new accents to the poetry of Ilya Selvinsky, one of the original "Constructivists" (see pp. 174-75). His poem *Rossii* (*To Russia*), printed in the review *Oktyabr*, although marred by a few rather weak lines and even one or two whole stanzas, shows genuine lyrical force and freshness of expression. There is nothing in it of Selvinsky's "Constructivist" experimenting—it is simple and straightforward, but genuine in its patriotic emotion where tenderness and pride are combined.

BIBLIOGRAPHY

There is no general survey of Soviet Russian literature in any language. Russian works on post-revolutionary literature cover only, as a rule, the first ten years. The principal among those which treat the subject systematically and in its full scope are the following:

GORBACHEV: *Sovremennaya russkaya literatura* (L., 1928).

LEZHNEV and GORBOV: *Literatura revolyutsionnogo desyatiletya* (Kharkov, 1929).

KOGAN: *Literatura velikogo desyatiletya* (L., 1927).

Studies of the most important individual writers will also be found in:

VORONSKY: *Literaturnye tipy* (M., 1927).

POLONSKY: *Ocherki sovremennoy literatury* (M., 1930).

SLONIM: *Portrety sovetskikh pisateley* (Paris, 1932),

and in Italian in:

LO GATTO: *La Letteratura sovietista* (Roma, 1928).

Literature in inter-relation to politics and Government policy in literary matters are treated in Polonsky's *Ocherki literaturnogo dvizhenya revolyutsionnoy epokhi* (M. & L., 1929).

The same problems are dealt with in Max Eastman's *Artists in Uniform, A Study of Literature and Bureaucratism* (George Allen & Unwin, London, 1934). The author, Trotsky's friend, biographer and admirer, and himself a Communist, attacks most violently the policy of bureaucratization of literature pursued by Stalin's Government. Though not quite consistent, it gives a valuable account of the methods of the Communist Party and Government in literary matters up to 1932 and contains some very interesting documents.

Chapters on post-revolutionary literary output within their respective chronological limits will be found in the following foreign histories of modern Russian literature :

MIRSKY, D. S. : *Contemporary Russian Literature: 1881–1925*, George Routledge & Sons, London, 1926.

POZNER, WLADIMIR : *Panorama de la littérature russe*, Kra, Paris, 1929.

SAKULIN, P. : *Die russische Literatur*, Akademische Verlagsgesellschaft Athenaion, Potsdam, 1927.

ARSENIEW, N. VON : *Die russische Literatur der Neuzeit und Gegenwart in ihren geistigen Zusammenhängen*, Dioskuren-Verlag, Mainz, 1929.

HOFMANN, M., LOZINSKY, G. and MOTCHOULSKY, C. : *Histoire de la littérature russe*, Payot, Paris, 1934.

The following *anthologies* contain specimens of post-revolutionary fiction :

COURNOS, JOHN : *Short Stories out of Soviet Russia*, Dent, London and Toronto, 1929, re-issued 1932 (quoted further as Cournos).

GRAHAM, STEPHEN : *Russian Great Short Stories*, Benn, London, 1929.

KONOVALOV, S. : *Bonfire: Stories out of Soviet Russia*, Benn, London, 1932 (quoted further as *Bonfire*).

SLONIM, MARC and REAVEY, GEORGE : *Soviet Literature: An Anthology*, Wishart & Co., London, 1933 (quoted further as Slonim).

POZNER, W. : *Anthologie de la prose russe contemporaine*, Kra, Paris, 1929.

Principal translations, classified in accordance with the subject-matter of each chapter of this book, are given below under two headings : (1) English, and (2) French. Here and there English and French works on the authors and subjects concerned are also indicated, but these references have no claim to completeness, especially where periodicals are concerned. For general French literature on Soviet Russia the reader can consult the bibliography of V. VICTOROFF - TOPOROFF (*Rossica et Sovietica*, Paris, 1932). Cf. also : VL. BOUTCHIK : (*Bibliographie des œuvres littéraires russes traduits en français*, Orobitg, Paris, 1935). In English there is so far no such bibliography, but it is certainly badly needed.

Translations of post-revolutionary Russian fiction into German are very numerous—more numerous than in any other language—but for technical reasons, with one or two exceptions, these have not been included in this bibliography.

CHAPTER I

BELY : There are no English translations of Bely except a fragment from *Kotik Letaev* in Slonim and some poems. Nor has Bely been translated into French. His earlier novels—*Petersburg* and *The Silver Dove*— exist in German translations. On Bely consult Mirsky, *Contemporary Russian Literature*, especially pp. 225–235 ; Pozner : *Panorama*, pp. 173–184, and the present writer's obituary notice in *The Slavonic Review* for July 1934.

GORKY : (1) *Decadence*, trans. Veronica Scott Gatty, Cassell & Co., London, 1927 ; *Bystander*, trans. B. G. Guerney, Cape, London ; Cape & Harrison Smith, New York, 1930 ; *The Magnet*, trans. Alexander Bakshy, Cape, London, 1931 ; *Other Fires*, trans. A. Bakshy, D. Appleton & Co., New York and London, 1933 ; *Reminiscences of Leonid Andreyev*, trans. Katherine Mansfield and S. S. Koteliansky, Heinemann, London, 1931 ; *On Guard for the Soviet Union*, Martin Lawrence, London, 1931 ; *Days with Lenin*, Martin Lawrence, London, 1933.

(2) *Ma vie d'enfant, Mémoires autobiographiques*, trad. Serge Persky, Paris, 1921 ; *En gagnant mon pain, Mémoires autobiographiques*, trad. Serge Persky, Paris, 1923 ; *Souvenirs de ma vie littéraire*, trad. M. Dumesnil de Gramont, Paris, 1923 ; *Lenin et le paysan russe*, trad. M. Dumesnil de Gramont, Paris, 1925 ; *Un premier amour*, Kra, Paris, 1925 ; *Notes et souvenirs*, trad. Dumesnil de Gramont, Paris, 1927 ; *Les cafards*, Calmann-Lévy, Paris, 1928 ; *Les Artamonov*, trad. Dumesnil de Gramont, Calmann-Lévy, Paris, 1929 ; *Eux et nous*, Editions Sociales Internationales, Paris, 1932 ; *Vie de Klime Samguine*, trad. Dumesnil de Gramont, Rieder, Paris, 1932.

On Gorky see Alexander Kaun : *Maxim Gorky*

and his Russia, Cape, London, 1932 (it deals, however, rather with the biographical and political aspects
of Gorky than with the literary).

ALEXEY N. TOLSTOY : (1) *The Affair of the Basseynaya
Street; A White Night* (both in Cournos) ; *Vasily
Suchkov* (in *Bonfire*) ; *Imperial Majesty* (first volume
of *Peter the First*), trans. H. Chrouschoff Matheson,
Elkin Mathews & Marrot, London, 1932.

(2) *Ibicus, ou les aventures de Nevzorov*, trad. B.
Cauvet Duhamel, Ed. Montaigne, Paris, 1926 ; *Le
Chemin des tourments*, trad. Dumesnil de Gramont,
Rieder, Paris, 1930.

EHRENBURG : (1) *The Love of Jeanne Ney*, trans. Helen
Chrouschoff Matheson, Peter Davies, London, 1929 ;
A Street in Moscow, trans. Sonia Volochova, Grayson
& Grayson, London, 1933 ; *Out of Chaos*, trans.
Alexander Bakshy, Holt, New York, 1934 (this is a
translation of *The Second Day*).

(2) *Un évènement bien curieux* (in *Scènes de la
Revolution Russe*, trad. Serge Leskov, La Renaissance
du Livre, Paris, 1923); *Rapace*, trad. Uzlac, Cahiers
Libres, Paris, 1927 ; *Rapace*, trad. G. Aucouturier,
Gallimard, Paris, 1931 ; *La vie de Gracchus Babeuf*
trad. Madeleine Etard, Paris, 1929 ; *La ruelle de
Moscou*, Les Revues, Paris, 1930 ; *IO CV.*, Les
Revues, Paris, 1930 ; *Europe, société anonyme*, Ed. du
Tambourin, Paris, 1932 ; *Le deuxième jour de la création*,
trad. M. Etard, Gallimard, Paris, 1933 ; *Duhamel,
Gide, Malraux, Morand, Romains et Unamuno vus
par un écrivain de l'U.R.S.S.*, Gallimard, Paris, 1934.

VERESAEV : (1) *The Deadlock*, trans. Nina Vissotsky and
Camilla Coventry, Faber & Gwyer, London, 1927 ;
The Sisters, Hutchinson, London, 1934.

SERGEYEV-TSENSKY : (1) *The Man You Couldn't Kill* (in
Cournos) ; *Womenite Farm*, trans. N. B. Jopson (in
the *Slavonic Review*, vol. xii, No. 34, July 1933).

(2) *Transfiguration*, Rieder, Paris, 1930.

PRISHVIN : (1) *A Werewolf of the Steppe* (in Cournos).

ZAMYATIN : (1) *We*, trans. J. Zilboorg, Dutton, New York,
1925 ; *The Cave*, trans. D. S. Mirsky (in the *Slavonic*

Review, No. 4, 1923 ; reprinted in *Bonfire*); *Mamay* (in Slonim).

(2) *Nous autres*, trad. B. Cauvet Duhamel, Galmard, Paris, 1929.

CHAPTER II

BABEL : (1) *Red Cavalry*, trans. John Harland, Knopf, London, 1929 ; *Gedali* and *Dolgushov's Death* (in *Bonfire* ; the latter also in Cournos) ; *The Letter* and *Salt* (in Cournos) ; *The Story of my Dovecot*, trans. D. S. Mirsky (in the *Slavonic Review*, No. 28, June, 1931) ; *The End of Saint Ipaty* and *The Awakening* (in Slonim).

(2) *Cavalerie rouge*, trad. Maurice Parijanine, Rieder, Paris, 1930.

VSEVOLOD IVANOV : (1) *The Child* (in *The Nation and Athenaeum*, June 27 and July 4, 1925 ; also in Cournos) ; *When I was a Fakir* (in Cournos) ; *Unfrozen Water* (in *Bonfire*) ; *The Desert of T·ib-Koy* (in Slonim).

(2) *Le train blindé numéro 1469*, trad. Siderski, Gallimard, Paris, 1930 ; *L'Enfant*, trad. André Pierre, 1924 (in *Oeuvres Libres*, No. 34).

CHAPTER III

FEDIN : (1) *The Orchard* (in *Bonfire*).

(2) *Transvaal, Les moujiks*, trad. V. Parnac, Ed. Montaigne, Paris, 1927 ; *Les Cités et les Années*, trad. Mme. Ergaz, Paris, 1930.

LEONOV : (1) *The Thief*, trans. Hubert Butler, Secker, London, 1931 ; *Sot*, trans. Ivor Montagu and Sergei Nalbandov, Putnam, London and New York, 1931 ; *Ivan's Misadventure* (in Cournos) ; *The Knave of Diamonds*, trans. N. B. Jopson (in the *Slavonic Review*, vol. xi, No. 32, January, 1933) ; some extracts in *Bonfire*.

KAVERIN : Except for an extract from *The Anonymous Artist* and a sketch entitled *The Return of the Kirghiz* (from *Prologue*), both in Slonim, there are no English translations.

LAVRENEV : (2) *Le Quarante et unième*, trad. André Pierre et Marc Slonim, 1930 (in *Oeuvres Libres*, No. 107) ; *Le Vent*, trad. F. Lortholary, 1932 (*ibid.*, No. 128).

CHAPTER IV

SEYFULLINA : (1) *The Lawbreakers* (in Slonim).

(2) *Virineya*, trad. Hélène Iswolsky, Gallimard, Paris, 1927.

ROMANOV : (1) *Without Cherry Blossom*, trans. L. Zarine, Benn, London, 1930 ; *Three Pairs of Silk Stockings*, trans. L. Zarine, Benn, London, 1931 ; *The New Commandment*, trans. Valentine Snow, Benn, London ; Scribner & Sons, New York, 1933 ; *On the Volga* (short stories), trans. Ann Gretton, Benn, London, 1934.

(2) *Amours russes, trois paires de bas de soie*, trad. Nad Cyon, Ed. de France, Paris, 1933 ; *Le Camarade Kisliakov*, trad. Mme. Andreiewa, Babu, Paris, 1933.

LIDIN : (1) *The Apostate*, trans. Helen Chrouschoff Matheson, Cape, London, 1931 ; *Harps* (in *Bonfire*); *Glaciers* (in Cournos).

KATAEV : (1) *The Embezzlers*, trans. L. Zarine, Benn, London, 1929 ; *Forward, Oh Time!* trans. Charles Malamuth, Gollancz, London, 1934 (American edition under the title *Time, Forward!* Farrar & Rinehart, New York, 1933); *The Golden Pen* (in Slonim).

(2) *Rastratchiki*, trad. André Beucler, Gallimard, Paris, 1928 ; *Ils ont mangé la grenouille*, trad. A. Beucler, Gallimard, Paris, 1934.

ZOSHCHENKO : (1) Zoshchenko's stories have appeared in reviews and magazines ; here are some translations I was able to trace : *Fine Lady* (*The New Statesman and Nation*, August 27, 1932); *Pelageya* (*ibid.*, September 17, 1932) ; *Dog's Nose* (*ibid.*, October 15, 1932); *Joys of Civilization* and *Doubting Thomas* (*The Slavonic Review*, vol. vii, No. 21, March 1929) ; *A Hasty Affair*, *A Story of Adventure*, *The Night of Horror*, *A Damp Business* (all in *Bonfire*); *A Mistake* (in Slonim).

(2) *La Vie joyeuse*, trad. Siderski, Gallimard, Paris, 1930.

ILF and PETROV : (1) *Diamonds to Sit On*, trans. Elizabeth Hill and Doris Mudie, Methuen & Co., London, 1930 ; *The Little Golden Calf*, trans. Charles Malamuth, Grayson & Grayson, London ; Farrar & Rinehart, New York, 1932.

(2) *Douze chaises*, Albin Michel, Paris, 1929 ; *Un millionnaire au pays des Soviets*, trad. V. Llona et P. Stavrov, Albin Michel, Paris, 1934.

OGNEV : (1) *The Diary of a Communist Schoolboy*, trans. Alexander Werth, Gollancz, London, 1928 ; *The Diary of a Communist Undergraduate*, trans. A. Werth, Gollancz, London, 1929.

(2) *Le journal de Kostia Riabtsov*, trad. et adapté H. Pernot, Calmann-Lévy, Paris, 1929.

ZAYAITSKY : (1) *The Forgotten Night* (in *Bonfire*).

NIKITIN : (2) *La capitale de l'Oural* (in *Scènes de la Révolution Russe*, trad. Serge Leskov, La Renaissance du Livre, Paris, 1923).

CHAPTER V

GLADKOV : (1) *Cement*, trans. A. S. Arthur and C. Ashleigh, Martin Lawrence, London, 1929.

(2) *Le Ciment*, trad. Victor-Serge, Editions Sociales Internationales, Paris, 1928.

PANFEROV : (1) *Brusski*, trans. Z. Mitrov and J. Tabrisky, Martin Lawrence, London, 1930.

(2) *La Communauté des Gueux*, Editions Sociales Internationales, 1re partie, trad. Marie Borissov et Z. Lvovsky, Paris, 1931 ; 2e partie, trad. Z. Lvovsky et Lydie Silbert, Paris, 1932.

LIBEDINSKY : (1) *A Week*, trans. Arthur Ransome, Allen & Unwin, London, 1923 ; *A Letter* (in *Bonfire*).

(2) *La Semaine*, Editions Sociales Internationales, Paris, 1927.

FADEYEV : (1) *The Nineteen*, trans. R. D. Charques, Martin Lawrence, London, 1929.

(2) *La Défaite*, Editions Sociales Internationales, Paris, 1928.

SHOLOKHOV : (1) *And Quiet Flows the Don*, trans. Stephen Garry, Putnam, London and New York, 1934.

(2) *Sur le Don paisible*, trad. V. Soukhomline and S. Campaux, Payot, Paris, 1930–31 ; *Les Défricheurs*, trad. D. Ergaz, Gallimard, Paris, 1933 ; *Terres défrichées*, trad. avec autor. de l'auteur par Alice Orane et Georges Roux, " Horizons," Paris, 1933.

TARASOV-RODIONOV : (1) *Chocolate*, trans. Charles Malamuth, Heinemann, London ; Doubleday, Doran & Co., New York, 1933.

(2) *La Révolution de février* 1917, trad. Marc Semenoff, Gallimard, Paris.

NEVEROV : (1) *Tashkent*, trans. Reginald Merton and W. G. Walton, Gollancz, London, 1930.

(2) *Tachkent, ville d'abondance*, trad. Brice Parain, Gallimard, Paris.

SERAFIMOVICH : (2) *Le torrent de fer*, Editions Sociales Internationales, Paris, 1929.

FURMANOV : (1) *Chapayev*, Martin Lawrence, London, 1935.

(2) *Tchapaïev*, trad. A. Oranovskaia et A. Roudnikov, Editions Sociales Internationales, Paris, 1933.

SEMENOV : (1) *The Birth of a Slave* (in *Bonfire*) ; an extract from *Natalia Tarpova* (in Slonim).

(2) *La faim*, trad. Brice Parain, Ed. Montaigne, Paris, 1927.

VESELY : (1) An extract from *Russia Washed in Blood* (in *Bonfire*).

DEMIDOV : (2) *Le Tourbillon*, trad. N. V. Troukhanova-Ignatieff, Editions Sociales Internationales, Paris, 1929.

CHAPTER VI

OLESHA : (1) *The Cherry Stone* (in Slonim) ; an extract from *Envy* (in *Bonfire*).

CHAPTER VII

(1) PILNYAK : *The Volga Flows to the Caspian Sea*, Peter Davies, London, 1932 ; LEONOV : *Sot* (see above under Chapter III) ; KATAEV : *Forward, Oh Time!* (see above under Chapter IV).

(2) PILNYAK : *La Volga se jette dans la Mer Caspienne*,

trad. G. Aucouturier, Ed. du Carrefour, Paris, 1931;
PILNYAK : *La Septième République, Le Tadjikistan*,
trad. Michel Matveev et Pierre Morhange, Rieder,
Paris, 1933 ; SHAGINYAN : *Hydrocentrale*, Editions
Sociales Internationales, Paris, 1933.

CHAPTER VIII

(1) ZAMYATIN : *We* (see above under Chapter I) ; BULGAKOV :
Days of the Turbins (a play) in *Six Soviet Plays*, edited
by Eugene Lyons, Gollancz, London, 1935.

(2) ZAMYATIN : *Nous autres* (see above under Chapter I).

EASTMAN's *Artists in Uniform* deals in detail with the
" cases " of Pilnyak and Zamyatin, together with the
documents bearing thereupon (Chapters VIII and XI,
pp. 82 and 104).

An American book with a rather misleading title—
Popular Poetry in Soviet Russia, by G. Z. PATRICK (University of California Press, Berkeley, 1929)—gives an account
of the post-revolutionary " peasant " poetry and contains
specimens of the poetical work of KLYUEV, KLYCHKOV and
other poets often branded as " kulak." The author shows
himself in great sympathy with the main motifs of early
Soviet peasant poetry.

CHAPTER IX

(1) A. N. TOLSTOY : *Imperial Majesty* (see above under
Chapter I) ; GUL : *General B.O.*, trans. L. Zarine,
Benn, London, 1930 ; VINOGRADOV : *The Black
Consul*, trans. Emile Burns, Gollancz, London, 1935.

(2) TARASOV-RODIONOV : *La Révolution de février* 1917
(see above under Chapter V) ; GUL : *Lanceurs de
bombes, Azef*, trad. N. Guterman, Gallimard, Paris,
1931 ; CHAPYGIN : *Stenka Razine*, Payot, Paris, 1930.

Cf. also D. S. MIRSKY's article *Der russische
historische Roman der Gegenwart* in *Slavische Rund-
schau*, 1932, No. 1.

CHAPTER X

(1) The following poets are represented in Messrs. Reavey's and Slonim's Anthology: Mayakovsky, Esenin, Pasternak, Tikhonov, Selvinsky, Bezymensky, Ushakov. The translations are far from satisfactory. Translations from Esenin and Mayakovsky have also appeared in other (earlier) anthologies and in some magazines.

The story of Esenin's and Mayakovsky's suicides is told in EASTMAN's *Artists in Uniform*.

G. Z. PATRICK's *Popular Poetry in Soviet Russia* (see above, under Chapter VIII) gives an account of the proletarian poets and contains translations from Alexandrovsky, Bezymensky, Gerasimov and others.

(2) MAYAKOVSKY: *Le nuage dans le pantalon*, Les Revues, Paris, 1930; ESENIN: *Requiem*, Gallimard, 1930.

Cf. BENJAMIN GORELY: *Les Poètes dans la Révolution Russe*, Gallimard, Paris, 1934.

CHAPTER XI

A brief account of the Soviet theatre, inevitably coloured with official optimism, is to be found in the book of P. A. MARKOV, *The Soviet Theatre* (Gollancz, London, 1934). In French there is a good book by NINA GOURFINKEL, *Le théatre russe contemporain* (La Renaissance du Livre, Paris, 1931). There have also been numerous articles, both English and French, in general and special reviews and magazines. A collection of six Soviet plays has quite recently been published by Victor Gollancz (*Six Soviet Plays*, edited by EUGENE LYONS, with an Introduction by Elmer Rice, London, 1935).

(1) LUNACHARSKY: *Three Plays* (*Faust and the City*, *Vasilisa the Wise*, *The Magi*), trans. L. A. Magnus and K. Walter, Routledge, London, 1923; KATAEV: *Squaring the Circle*, trans. and adapted N. Goold-Verschoyle, Wishart & Co., London, 1934 (another version in *Six Soviet Plays*); IVANOV: *Armoured Train* 14-69, trans. Gibson-Cowan and

BIBLIOGRAPHY

A. T. K. Grant, Martin Lawrence, London, 1933 ;
TRETYAKOV : *Roar China!* trans. F. Polianovska and
Barbara Nixon, Martin Lawrence, London, 1931 ;
MAYAKOVSKY : *Mystery-Bouffe*, trans. George Rapall
Noyes and Alexander Kaun (in " Masterpieces of
the Russian Drama," D. Appleton & Co., New
York and London, 1933) ; BULGAKOV : *Days of the
Turbins* (in *Six Soviet Plays*) ; POGODIN : *Tempo*
(*ibid.*) ; GLEBOV : *Inga* (*ibid.*) ; AFINOGENOV : *Fear*
(*ibid.*) ; KIRSHON : *Bread* (*ibid.*).

(2) LAVRENEV : *La Rupture*, trad. A. Roudnikov
et A. Oranovskaia, Bureau d'éditions, Paris, 1931.

CHAPTER XII

The following articles deal chiefly with the views of
the Formalist school :

A. VOZNESENSKY : *Problem of Method in the Study
of Literature in Russia* (*The Slavonic Review*, vol. vi,
No. 16, June, 1927).

B. TOMASHEVSKY : *La nouvelle école d'histoire littéraire en Russie* (*Revue des Etudes Slaves*, t. 8, fasc.
3 and 4, 1928).

N. GOURFINKEL : *Les nouvelles méthodes d'histoire
littéraire en Russie* (*Le Monde Slave*, février, 1929).

In EASTMAN one finds the views of VORONSKY and
POLONSKY and the story of their " persecution " at the
hands of the proletarian extremists set forth in Chapters
XIII and XIV (pp. 149–161). In a Supplement Eastman
gives a translation of POLONSKY's essay, *Lenin's Views of
Art and Culture* (pp. 217–252).

CHAPTER XIII

The only non-Russian book, known to me, dealing with
the problems discussed in this Chapter is the already
mentioned MAX EASTMAN's *Artists in Uniform* (see above,
p. 253).

Cf. also : TROTSKY : *Literature and Revolution*, trans.
by Rose Strunsky, International Publishers, New York ;

BIBLIOGRAPHY

Allen & Unwin, London, 1925; SLONIM's Introduction
to *Soviet Literature* (Wishart, London, 1933) and the
section on Criticism in the latter.

CHAPTER XIV

(1) AVDEYENKO: *I Love*, trans. Anthony Wixley, Martin
Lawrence, London, 1935.

(2) SHOLOKHOV: *Les Défricheurs; Terres défrichées* (see
above under Chapter V)—these are two versions of
the *Upturned Soil*; AVDEYENKO: *J'aime*, trad. Alice
Orane et Georges Roux, " Horizons," Paris, 1933.
There are two German translations of Sholokhov's
Upturned Soil—both published in Zurich under the title
Neuland unter dem Pflug. The English translation is in
preparation.
Cf. D. S. MIRSKY's essay on " Soviet Russian Novel "
in *Tendencies of the Modern Novel* (Allen & Unwin,
London, 1934; also in *The Fortnightly Review* for June,
1934).

The following translations from authors not dealt with
in the present work have come under my notice:

(1) SHISHKOV: *Children of Darkness*, Gollancz,
London, 1931; VOINOVA: *Glittering Stones*, Heine-
mann, London, 1933; YAKOVLEV: *The Chinese Vase*;
CHETVERIKOV: *Corpses*; FIBIKH: *The Execution*
(all in *Bonfire*); ZOZULYA: *A Tale about Ak and
Humanity* and *The Mother* (in Cournos); GLEB
ALEKSEYEV: *Other Eyes* (ibid.); GABRILOVICH: *The
Year* 1930 (in Slonim).

(2) CHPILEVSKY: *Copains*, Les Revues, Paris,
1930; VERA INBER: *La place au soleil*, Ed. des
Portiques, Paris, 1932.

SUPPLEMENTARY BIBLIOGRAPHY

The list of books below is divided into two parts. The first contains bibliographies and works about the Soviet Union in the English language published since 1935 (or earlier, if for some reason omitted from the Bibliography attached to the first edition of my book). No attempt has been made to give anything like a complete list of books on the U.S.S.R. Those works only are included which either bear directly on the problems of literature, art, and culture in general, or are of general interest from the point of view of latest developments and changes in the Soviet outlook. For any further reference the reader must turn to Mr. Grierson's excellent bibliography (see below).

Part Two lists English translations of works of Soviet literature. Here I tried to be as full as possible, but I did not include translations which appeared in the United States or in the U.S.S.R. I am aware also that there must be gaps in my list of English publications.

1. BIBLIOGRAPHIES AND GENERAL WORKS.

(A) *Bibliographies*

GRIERSON, PHILIP : *Books on Soviet Russia.* 1917–1942. *A Bibliography and a Guide to Reading.* Methuen, 1943, 368 pp.

In spite of certain inevitable omissions and a few errors or misprints, this is a most valuable work, being the first attempt at compiling an extensive bibliography of English books about Russia since the Revolution. Books are conveniently classified under numerous headings, and most of the entries are accompanied by a note on their character and point of view. Some important works in languages other·than English are also included.

MARTIANOV, N. N.: *Books available in English by Russians and on Russia, published in the United States.* Privately printed. New York, 1935, 48 pp. (2nd edn., 1936, 54 pp.; 3rd edn., 1939, 52 pp.).

POSTNIKOV, S. P.: *Bibliografiya russkoy revolyutsii i grazhdanskoy voyny (1917–1921). Iz kataloga biblioteki Russkogo Zagranichnogo Arkhiva.* Ed. by Jan Slavik. Prague, 1938, 460 pp.

A very useful bibliography based on the catalogue of the Russian Historical Archives in Prague. Includes a number of non-Russian works, but has no pretence at completeness, being in fact only a catalogue. Covers only the 1917–1921 period.

Russia. A Select Reading List. Bristol Public Libraries, 1942, 27 pp.

A list of books on Russia available in the public libraries of Bristol.

YAKOBSON, S., and EPSTEIN, F.: "A List of Books in English on Russia, published in 1935." *Slavonic and East European Review,* XV, 1936–1937, pp. 482–490.

(B) *General Works and Works on Art and Literature*

Art in the U.S.S.R. Ed. by C. G. Holme. (Special Autumn number of *The Studio.*) *The Studio,* 1935, 138 pp.

Some valuable illustrations.

BASILY, N. DE: *Russia under Soviet Rule. Twenty Years of Bolshevik Experiment,* Allen & Unwin, 1938, 508 pp.

Mr. Grierson says that it is "the most thorough survey of Soviet history and achievements yet made by an *émigré*; . . . a most valuable book."

BORKENAU, F.: *The Communist International,* Faber & Faber, 1938, 442 pp.

CHAMBERLIN, W. H.: *Russia's Iron Age,* Duckworth, 1935, 400 pp.

The best foreign work on the Five-Year Plan Period.

Confessions of an Individualist, Duckworth, 1940, 336 pp.

Throws an interesting light on the author's gradual disillusionment in the Soviet régime.

CHESTERTON, Mrs. C. : *Sickle or Swastika?* Stanley Paul, 1938, 268 pp.
> A considerable part of this book is devoted to the first Congress of Soviet writers.

CONOLLY, VIOLET : *Soviet Tempo. A Journal of Travel in Russia*, Sheed & Ward, 1938, 189 pp.

CROSS, SAMUEL : " Notes on Soviet Literary Criticism : (i) The Criteria of Socialist Realism. (ii) Schematization in Soviet Literary Criticism." *The Slavonic Year-Book*, being Volume XX of *The Slavonic and East European Review*, George Banta, Menasha, Wisc., 1941, pp. 323–329.

DANA, H. W. L. : *Handbook on Soviet Drama : Lists of theatres, plays, operas, ballets, films, and books and articles about them*, New York, American-Russian Institute, 1938, 158 pp.

DAVIES, J. E. : *Mission to Moscow*, Gollancz, 1942, 415 pp.

DICKINSON, T. H. : *The Theatre in a Changing Europe*, Putnam, 1938, 492 pp. (articles on Russian Theatre by J. Gregor and H. W. L. Dana).

GIDE, ANDRÉ : *Back from the U.S.S.R.*, trans. from the French by D. Bussy, Sheed & Ward, 1937, 121 pp.
> *Afterthoughts. A Sequel to " Back from the U.S.S.R."*, Sheed & Ward, 1938, 142 pp.

HINDUS, MAURICE : *Russia Fights On*, Collins, 1942, 255 pp.

HOUGHTON, NORRIS : *Moscow Rehearsals. An account of methods of production in the Soviet Theatre*, Allen & Unwin, 1938, 313 pp.
> A thorough study of recent developments in the Soviet Theatre.

ISWOLSKY, HELEN : *Soviet Man—Now*, trans. from the French, Sheed & Ward, 1936, 86 pp.

JAMES, C. L. R. : *World Revolution 1917–1936. The Rise and Fall of the Communist International*, Secker & Warburg, 1937, 429 pp.

JOHNSON, HEWLETT : *The Socialist Sixth of the World*, Gollancz, 1939, 384 pp.

KAUN, ALEXANDER : " Russian Poetic Trends on the Eve of and the Morning After 1917." *The Slavonic Year-Book*, being Volume XX of *The Slavonic and East European Review*, 1941, pp. 55–84.

LAVRIN, JANKO : *An Introduction to the Russian Novel,* Methuen, 1942, 216 pp.

An excellent concise book on the main trends of Russian fiction. The last three chapters deal briefly with post-revolutionary literature.

Literature of the Peoples of the U.S.S.R., The, Moscow, VOKS, 1934, 205 pp.

LONDON, KURT : *The Seven Soviet Arts,* Faber & Faber, 1937, 381 pp.

LYONS, EUGENE : *Assignment in Utopia,* Harrap, 1938, 658 pp.

Modern Moscow, Hurst & Blackett, 1935, 286 pp.

Chapters XI, XV, XX and XXI throw an interesting light on the cultural aspect of the Soviet Union during a certain period.

McLEOD, JOSEPH : *The New Soviet Theatre,* Allen & Unwin, 1943, 242 pp.

The latest book on Soviet theatre, supplementing N. Houghton's work. Uncritically enthusiastic, but contains valuable information, not easily accessible to foreign readers.

MAYNARD, JOHN : *Russia in Flux before October,* Gollancz, 1941, 301 pp.

Russian Peasant and other Studies, Gollancz, 1942, 512 pp.

A valuable analysis of recent trends of development. Much wider than its title would suggest.

MUGGERIDGE, MALCOLM : *Winter in Moscow,* Eyre & Spottiswoode, 1934, 252 pp.

PARES, BERNARD : *Russia,* Penguin Books, 1941 (2nd and 3rd edns. revised, also 1941), 256 pp.

An excellent compact survey of Russia, in both its everlasting and topical aspects, by the foremost British student of things Russian. More than half of the book is devoted to post-revolutionary Russia. The author takes a sympathetic attitude towards the latest phase of developments.

Playtime in Russia. By various authors. Ed by H. Griffith, Methuen, 1935, 249 pp.

Problems of Soviet Literature. Reports and Speeches at the First Writers' Congress. Ed. by H. G. Scott, 1935, 279 pp.
Speeches by Zhdanov, Gorky, Bukharin, Radek and Stetsky.

Russia and the West (Changing World Series, No. 1), Oxford, 1942, 23 pp.

SEGAL, LOUIS: *The Real Russia*, Evans Bros., 1943, 159 pp.
Superficial and uncritical.

SOUVARINE, B. : *Stalin. A Critical Survey of Bolshevism*, trans. from the French by C. L. R. James, Secker & Warburg, 1939, 690 pp.
The most serious Life of Stalin written from a hostile point of view.

Soviet Comes of Age, The. By 28 of the foremost citizens of the U.S.S.R. Foreword by S. and B. Webb, Hodge, 1938, 337 pp.

STEPUN, F. : *The Russian Soul and Revolution*, trans. E. Huntress, Scribners, 1936, 184 pp.

TERRELL, R. : *Soviet Understanding*, Heinemann, 1937, 284 pp.

TROTSKY, LEON : *The Revolution Betrayed*, trans. Max Eastman, Secker & Warburg, 1937, 312 pp.

U.S.S.R. Handbook, Gollancz, 1936, 643 pp.

VOIGT, F. A. : *Unto Caesar*, Constable, 1938, 359 pp.
Not a book on Russia specially, but one of the best existing studies of Totalitarianism and its " philosophy ".

WEBB, SIDNEY and BEATRICE : *Soviet Communism : a New Civilisation*, 2 vols., Longmans Green, 1935, 1174 pp. (2nd edn., 1937 ; 3rd edn., 1941).

WERTH, ALEXANDER : *Moscow in '41*, Hamish Hamilton, 1942, 268 pp.

WILLIAMS, A. R. : *The Soviets*, New York, Harcourt, 1937, 554 pp.
Contains a large and useful bibliography.
The Russians, The Land, the People and Why They Fight, Harrap, 1943, 248 pp.

SUPPLEMENTARY BIBLIOGRAPHY

2. TRANSLATIONS

AFINOGENOV, A. : *Distant Point*, trans. and adapted by Hubert Griffith, The Pushkin Press, 1941, 95 pp.

BABEL, I. : *Benia Krik. A Film Novel*, trans. I. Montagu and S. S. Nalbandov, Collet, 1935, 96 pp.

CHUMANDRIN, M. : *White Star*, Lawrence, 1933, 80 pp. (printed in the U.S.S.R.).

EHRENBURG, ILYA : *The Fall of Paris*, trans. G. Shelley, Hutchinson, 1942, 382 pp.

GAIDAR, A. : *Timur and His Comrades*, trans. Musia Renbourn, Pilot Press, 1942, 86 pp.

A charming story for children.

GORKY, M. : *Culture and the People*, Lawrence & Wishart, 1939, 224 pp.

Essays on cultural subjects.

The Specter, trans. A. Bakshy, New York, Appleton-Century Co., 1938, 680 pp.

The last volume of the *Klim Samgin* tetralogy.

A Book of Short Stories, ed. A. Yarmolinsky and Baroness M. Budberg, Foreword by Aldous Huxley, Cape, 1939, 403 pp.

HERMAN, Y. : *Antonina*, trans. S. Garry, Routledge, 1937, vi+470 pp.

A translation of *Nashi znakomye*.

Alexei the Gangster, trans. S. Garry, Routledge, 1940, 288 pp.

A translation of *Zhmakin* and *Lapshin*.

ILF, I., and PETROV, E. : *The Little Golden Calf*, trans. C. Malamuth, Introduction by A. Lunacharsky, Grayson & Grayson, 1932, 384 pp.

ILYENKOV, V. : *Driving Axle. A Novel of Socialist Construction*, Lawrence, 1933, 455 pp.

KASSIL, LEV : *The Story of Alesha Ryazan and Uncle White-Sea*, Lawrence, 1935, 48 pp.

One of the best writers for children.

KATAEV, V. : *Lonely White Sail, or Peace is where the Tempests Blow*, trans. C. Malamuth, Allen & Unwin, 1937, 341 pp.

KAVERIN, V. : *The Larger View*, trans. E. L. Swan, Collins, 1938, 484 pp.

A translation of *Ispolnenie zhelaniy*.

338

Leonov, L. : *Tuatamur*, trans. I. Montagu and S. Nal-
bandov, Collet, 1935, 50 pp.
> *Skutarevsky,* trans. A. Brown, Lovat Dickson, 1936,
> 431 pp.
Makarenko, A. : *Road to Life*, trans. S. Garry, Nott,
1936, 287 pp.
> A translation of *Pedagogicheskaya poema*.
Matveyev, V. : *Commissar of the Gold Express. An
Episode in the Civil War*, Lawrence, 1933, 212 pp.
> *Bitter Draught*, trans. D. Flower, Collins, 1935, 297 pp.
> The originals of these two works are unknown to me.
Mayakovsky and His Poetry : Compiled by H. Marshall,
Pilot Press, no date [1941 ?], 149 pp.
> Contains an Introduction and numerous transla-
> tions from Mayakovsky, mostly by the compiler.
> Also two essays on Mayakovsky.
Olesha, Y. : *Envy*, trans. Anthony Wolfe, Hogarth Press,
1936, 275 pp.
Panferov, F. : *And Then the Harvest*, trans. S. Garry,
Putnam, 1939, 457 pp.
> A sequel to *Bruski*.
Pavlenko, P. : *Red Planes Fly East*, trans. S. Garry,
Routledge, 1938, 523 pp.
> A translation of *Na vostoke*.
Perventsev, A. : *Cossack Commander*, trans. S. Garry,
Routledge, 1939, 331 pp.
> A translation of *Kochubey*.
Prishvin, M. : *Jen Sheng : the Root of Life*, trans.
G. Walton and P. Gibbons, Foreword by J. S.
Huxley, Melrose, 1936, 157 pp.
Romanov, P. : *Diary of a Soviet Marriage*, trans. J.
Furnivall and R. Parmenter, Introduction by J.
Lavrin, Nutt, 1936, 143 pp.
Serafimovich, A. : *The Iron Flood*, Lawrence, 1935, 246 pp.
Shiryaev, P. : *Taglioni's Grandson. The Story of a Russian
Horse*, trans. A. Fremantle, Putnam, 1937, 291 pp.
Sholokhov, M. : *The Don Flows Home to the Sea*, trans.
S. Garry, Putnam, 1940, 868 pp.
> Continuation of *Quiet Don*.
> *Virgin Soil Upturned*, trans. S. Garry, Putnam,
> 1935, 496 pp.

TOLSTOY, A. : *Darkness and Dawn*, trans. E. Bone and
E. Burns, Gollancz, 1935, 584 pp.
Part of *The Path of Sufferings*.
Peter the Great, trans. E. Bone and E. Burns,
Gollancz, 1936, 463 pp.
The Death Box, trans. B. G. Guerney, Methuen,
1936, 357 pp.
Bread, trans. S. Garry, Gollancz, 1937, 447 pp.
TYNYANOV, Y. : *Death and Diplomacy in Persia*, trans.
A. Brown, Boriswood, 1938, 359 pp.
A translation of *Smert Vazir-Mukhtara*.
VORONSKY, A. : *Waters of Life and Death*, trans. L. Zarine,
Allen & Unwin, 1936, 343 pp.
Autobiography of a well-known Soviet critic.
ZOSHCHENKO, M. : *The Woman who could not Read, and
Other Tales*, trans. E. Fen, Methuen, 1940, 153 pp.
The Wonderful Dog, and Other Tales, trans. E. Fen,
Methuen, 1942, 180 pp.
Soviet stories, poems and plays are also to be found in
the following collections :
Azure Cities : Stories of New Russia, trans. J. J. Robbins,
ed. J. Kunitz, Modern Books, 1929, 320 pp.
(Contains A. Tolstoy, *Azure Cities* ; V. Ivanov,
The Baby ; Neverov, *Marya the Bolshevik* ; Shishkov,
Cranes ; Volkov, *The Miracle* ; Romanov, *Black
Fritters* ; Seifullina, *The Old Woman* ; Pilnyak, *The
Law of the Wolf* ; Babel, *The Letter* ; Zoshchenko,
Gold Teeth ; Lyashko, *The Song of the Chains* ;
Shaginyan, *Three Looms* ; Lidin, *Youth*.)
Soviet Short Stories : (" Life and Literature in the Soviet
Union "), ed. I. Montagu and H. Marshall, Pilot
Press, 1942, 154 pp.
(Contains Y. Olesha, *The Cherry Stone* ; A.
Platonov, *The Third Son* ; I. Ehrenburg, *New Short
Stories* ; V. Ardov, *Happy Ending* ; V. Lidin,
Hamlet ; Y. Tynyanov, *Second Lieutenant Also* ;
A. Isbach, *The Parcel* ; T. Kerash, *Trial by Elders* ;
M. Zoshchenko, *Dawn of the New Day* ; K. Paustov-
sky, *The Sailmaker*.)
Modern Russian Stories : Selected and translated by
Elisaveta Fen, Methuen, 1943, 254 pp.
(Contains A. Tolstoy, *The Viper* ; M. Zoshchenko,

What the Nightingale Sang Of; K. Fedin, *The Chronicle of Narovchat*; A. Neverov, *Andron the Good-for-Nothing*; B. Pilnyak, *A Year of Their Life*; L. Leonov, *Three Tales*; P. Romanov, *Sex Problems*; I. Babel, *The Birth of a King*.)

Russian Short Stories, Faber & Faber, no date [1943 ?].

(Reprints of earlier translations. Present-day writers represented are I. Babel, V. Ivanov, V. Kataev, L. Leonov, M. Prishvin, S. Sergeyev-Tsensky.)

Soviet Anthology : Selected and edited by John Rodker, Cape, 1943, 231 pp.

(Contains stories by I. Babel, D. Bergelson, R. Freierman, M. Gorky, V. Grossman, V. Kaverin, V. Kataev, L. Lench, K. Paustovsky, P. Pavlenko, B. Pilnyak, A. Raskin and M. Slobodskoy, N. Tikhonov, N. Virta, M. Volosov, L. Weisenberg, and M. Zoshchenko. The majority translated by Alec Brown or Stephen Garry.)

Four Soviet Plays : ed. Ben Blake, Lawrence & Wishart, 1937, 427 pp.

(Contains Gorky, *Yegor Bulychev and Others*; Vishnevsky, *An Optimistic Tragedy*; Pogodin, *The Aristocrats*; Kocherga, *Masters of Time*.[1] The *Aristocrats* is translated by H. G. Scott and R. S. Carr, the others by A. Wixley.)

Soviet Literature Art Music : ed. by M. Grindea, Practical Press Ltd., 1942, 48 pp.

(This is a queer little booklet, comprising original matter and reprints. Many of the latter are unacknowledged. Mostly translations of poems and short essays ; some of them in French and Spanish. There is a brief essay by Herbert Marshall on " Various Aspects of Soviet Culture ".)

Modern Poems from Russia, trans. Gerard Shelley, Allen & Unwin, 1942, 93 pp.

Includes some present-day poets. Translations are far from good, and the comments inadequate.

Many war stories and sketches are to be found in English translation (rather poor) in *International Literature*, a magazine published in Moscow.

---

[1] This is a translation of *The Watchmaker and the Hen* (see pp. 199-200).

INDEX

Note on Transliteration.—The system of transliteration of Russian names adopted in this book is practically the same as the one used by D. S. Mirsky in his two books. It follows the system, approved by the British Academy, save for the following main deviations : (1) whenever a double " e " occurs in Russian, a " y " has been inserted (*e.g.* Fadeyev for Fadeev) ; (2) soft signs, when they are final or occur between two consonants, have been left out (*e.g.* Gorky for Gor'ky, Gul for Gul'), whilst between a consonant and a vowel they have been rendered by a " y " (*e.g.* Grigoryev) ; (3) in names of foreign origin the original spelling has been retained (*e.g.* Ehrenburg, Eichenbaum, Mandelstam, and not : Erenburg, Eikhenbaum, Mandelshtam). Some of the names occurring only in French bibliographical references are given in the Index in their French form (*e.g.* Chpilevsky for Shpilevsky, Motchoulsky for Mochulsky, etc.).

In the Index that follows the stress is indicated throughout, so that it can serve as a guide in this respect. The stressing of the names throughout the text, however desirable it may have been, would have been technically difficult to carry out. A special note is to be made of the endings " -*ev* " and " -*yev* " which, when accented, are always pronounced " *yof* " (*e.g.* Ognèv = Ognyòf) ; the same applies sometimes to the stressed " e " in the middle of a name (*e.g.* Budènny = Budyònny).

Abraham, Gerald, 255
Acmeism (poetical school), xiv, 173, 175, 185
Æschylus, 197
Afinogènov, 190, 192, 290, 331, 338
Akhmàtova, xiv, 2, 215, 318
Akìmov, 187
Aldànov, 156
Alexander Nevsky, 292
Alexandròvsky, 79, 330
Alexèyev, Gleb, 264
Alexèyev, General, 98, 260
All-Russian Writers' Association, 227
Amaglobèli, 197
Anderson, H. C., 42
Andrèyev, 255
Antònov, 281, 282
Àrdov, 340
Aròsev, 101
Arsèniev, 322
Artsybàshev, 1, 100
Asèyev, 170, *176–77*
Attila, 19, 22, 119
Avdèyenko, 247, 332
Averbach, 85–6, 227, 229
Axelròd-Orthodòx, Mme, 216

Bàbel, xix, 6, *23–27*, 28, 191, 276, 325, 338, 340, 341

Babœuf, 157
Bagrìtsky, *175–76*
Bakhmètyev, 88
Bàkhterev, 297
Bakùnin, 191
Bàlmont, 1, 3
Balzac, 198, 245, 251
Barea, Arturo, 259
Basìly, N. de, 334
Batu, 296
Bàtyushkov, 320
Bédier, 209
Bèdny, Demyàn, 178
Belìnsky, 154, 209, 241
Bèly, Andrèy, xiv, xviii, 1, *3–5*, 102, 116, 162, 169, 202, 209, 210, 249, 323
Berdyàev, 294
Bergelsòn, 341
Bezymènsky, 173, *177–80*, 229, 240, 330
Bìbìk, 88
Bill-Belotserkòvsky, 191, 193–94, 200
Blake, Ben, 341
Blok, xiv, 1–3, 129, 169
Bogdànov, 80–82, 84
Bolòtnikov, 292
Borkenau, 334
Borodìn, Sergey (Sargidzhiàn), 295
" Bourgeois Formalism," 255, 271

342

Boùtchik, 255
Brik, 212, 221
Brusìlov, General, 298, 299
Bryùsov, xv, 1, 3, 155, 156, 215
Budàntsev, 128, *142-45*
Budberg, 338
Budènny, 24, 25
Bukhàrin, 85, 223, 337
Bulgàkov, S., 294
Bulgàkov, M., 128, *145-52*, 191, 193, 194, 289, 329, 331
Bùnin, 1, 33, 67, 68
Burshtein, 316
Byron, 208, 215

Cervantes, 51
Chamberlin, W. H., 258, 334
Change-of-Landmarks, 8
Chapygin, 157, 261, 290
Chèkov, xiii, 16, 33, 56, 65, 71, 72, 183, 188, 197, 215, 277
Chesterton, Mrs. Cecil, 334
Children's Theatre, 191, 271
Chpilèvsky, 332
Chumàndrin, 338
Commedia dell' Arte, 19
Communism and Communists, *passim*
Communist Academy, 130
Conolly, Violet, 335
Constructivism (in theatre), 197
Constructivism (poetical school), 174-176, 212
Cosmism and Cosmists (poetical group), 81, 173, 178, 181
Cournos, 322, 324, 325, 326, 332
Crimean War, The, 297
Cross, S. H., 335
Cubism, 20, 21, 123

Dana, H. W. L., 335
Dante, 179
Davies, J. E., 335
Decembrists, The, 159, 291
Demìdov, 101, 328
Denìkin, General, 260
Deterding, 41, 266
Dickens, 55
Dickinson, T. H., 335
Dmìtry Donskòy, 291, 295, 296
Dolmatòvsky, 319
Dorònin, 178, 180
Dos Passos, 124, 249, 250
Dostoèvsky, 16, 19, 42, 45, 46, 48, 49, 57, 88, 92, 100, 103, 106, 107, 117, 118, 198, 210, 215, 217, 241, 245, 265, 294, 295

Dumas, 198
Duncan, Isadora, 169
" Dynamic " Prose, xviii, xix, 24, 28, 32, 61, 69
Dzhanàn, 199
Dzhavakhishvìli, 236, 237

Eastman, xx, 256, 321, 329, 330, 331
Efìmov, 213-14, 218
Ehrenbùrg, ix, 2, *11-13*, 128, 157, 193, 259, 261, 273-75, 291, 300, 302, 324, 338, 340
Ehrfurt Programme, The, 138
Eichenbàum, 203, 207-8, 213, 215
Engelhàrdt, 203-4, 211
Engels, 199
Epstein, F., 334
Èrdman, 191, 193
Èrenburg, see Ehrenburg
Ermìlov, 294
Esènin, 129, 165, 166, *167-69*, 330
Expressionism, 104

Fadèyev, 6, *95-97*, 198, 232, 240, 249, 327
Faykò, 191
Fèdin, xix, 6, 32, *33-42*, 43, 50, 55, 56, 61, 83, 88, 91, 103, 115, 191, 226, 227, 240, 265-69, 304, 325, 341
" Fellow-Travellers," 40, 42, 83, 84, 86, 87, 88, 102, 114, 222-27, 229, 231, 234
Fen, Elisaveta, 340
Fìbikh, 264
Fisher, Louis, 290, 293
Five-Year Plan Literature, 10, 27, 41, 49, 69, 86, 87, 99, *114-26*, 175, 180, 190, 195, 229-31, 233, 234
Flaubert, 24, 27, 198
Formalism and Formalists, 55, 159, *201-15*, 216, 218, 236
Forsh, 157, 159, 291
Forster, E. M., x
France, Anatole, 58, 198
Freiermàn, 341
Frìtsche, 85, 216, 217
Fùrmanov, 101, 328
Futurism and Futurists, xv-xvii, 1, 79, 80, 166-70, 172-74, 176, 177, 180, 202, 203, 220, 221, 222, 234

Gabrilòvich, 332
Gaidàr, 338
Gàstev, 80
Geràsimov, 79, 330
Ghenghiz-Khan, 296
Gidàssy, 247

Gide, 250, 324, 335
Gippius, see Hippius
Gladkòv, *88–91*, 97, 115, 117, 118, 123, 191, 227, 249, 258, 327
Glèbov, 192, 331
Glòba, 191
Goebbels, 266
Goethe, 290
Gògol, xviii, 18, 19, 20, 21, 24, 26, 34, 63, 71, 72, 77, 116, 148, 151, 152, 153, 158, 163, 189, 193, 198, 210, 216, 241, 273, 303
Golòdny, 178, 180
Goncharòv, 243
Gorbachèv, 85, 127, 216, 219, 226, 321
Gorbàtov, 301
Gòrbov, 219, 321
Gorèly, 262
Gòrky, 1, 2, *5–8*, 16, 23, 24, 27, 46, 87, 90, 93, 97, 98, 158, 196, 197, 232, 233, 240, 241, 244, 249, 273, 323, 324, 337, 338, 341
Gourfìnkel, 330, 331
Grabàr, 101
Graham, Stephen, 322
Granville-Barker, 189
Gregor, 335
Griboèdov, 160–63, 215
Grierson, Philip, 333, 334
Griffith, H., 336, 338
Grigòryev, Apollon, 153
Grigòryev, Sergey, 78
Grigòryeva, 215
Grindea, 341
Gròssman, L., 215
Gròssman, Vasily, 302, 341
Gul, 157, 160, 329
Gumilèv, xiv, 2, 173

Hamann, 205
Hemingway, Ernest, 258, 259
Henry, O., 198
Hèrman, Yury, 277–81, 301, 338
Hèrzen, 143
Hindus, M., 335
Hìppius, Mme Zinaìda, 1, 3
Hitler, vii, 273
Hoffmann, E. T. A., 32, 42, 49, 108, 250
Hòfmann, M., 322
Holme, C. G., 334
Horizon (review), 255, 259
Houghton, N., 335
Hugo, Victor, 154, 198
Huxley, Aldous, 131, 132, 133, 135, 138, 338
Huxley, J. S., 339

Ibsen, 197, 277
Ilf (and Petròv), *76–77*, 152, 189, 276, 289, 290, 301, 327, 338
Illes, 247
Ilyènkov, 338
Ilyìn, Yàkov, 247
Imaginism, 20, 26, 81, 166, 168, 173
Impressionism, 104
Inber, 236, 332
International Literature (magazine), 319, 341
Ìsbach, 340
Iskùsstvo Kommùny (newspaper), 220, 221
Iswòlsky, H., 335
Ivànov, Alexander, 158
Ivànov, General, 299
Ivànov, Geòrgy, 1
Ivànov, Vsèvolod, xviii, 6, *27–31*, 32, 34, 60, 62, 78, 96, 191, 193, 235, 325, 330, 340, 341
Ivànov, Vyacheslàv, 3, 294
Ivàn the Terrible, 272, 292, 293, 296
Izvèstia (newspaper), 232

James, C. L. R., 335
Jasienski, see Yasensky
Johnson, Hewlett, 335
Joyce, James, 4, 249, 251

Kaledìn, 98, 99
Kamènsky, Anatòly, 100
Kàmerny Theatre, 187
Kàrpov, M., 101
Kassìl, 338
Katàev, Valentìn, 60, *67–69*, 115, *123–125*, 126, 152, 190, 191, 194, 198, 248, 249, 250, 269–71, 301, 326, 338, 341
Kaun, 323, 335
Kavèrin, xix, 6, 32, *49–55*, 61, 91, 114, 128, 195, 249, 250, 271–72, 325, 338, 341
Kàzin, 80, 173, 181
Kèrensky, 156
Khlèbnikov, 166
Khodasèvich, 1
Kipling, 185
Kirìlov, 80
Kìrov, 235, 261, 276, 320
Kirshòn, 192, 194, 199, 330
Klychkòv, *129–30*, 329
Klyùev, 129, 261
Kochergà, 199, 341
Kògan, 85, 212, 216, 217, 219, 321
Kohn, Jonas, 205

Kolchàk, 177
Koltsòv, A., 180
Koltsòv, Mikhail, 259
Komsomól, see Young Communist League
Kornìlov, Admiral, 297
Kornìlov, General, 98, 156
Korniychùk, 199, 261, 303, 304, 315
Kòrobov, 101
Kostylèv, 296
Kozakòv, 157
Kràsnaya Nov (review), 83, 241
Küchelbècker, 159
Kunitz, J., 340
Kuprìn, 1
Kutùzov, Fieldmarshal, 292, 293, 297
Kuzmìn, x, 156
Kùʒnitsa, see Smithy

Lavrènev, 57–58, 191, 194, 326, 331
Lavrin, Yanko, 336, 339
Lazhèchnikov, 154
Lebedènko, 57, 59
Lèbedev-Kumàch, 319
Lèbedev-Polyànsky, 85
Lef (magazine), 177, 212
Lelèvich, 85, 173
Lench, 341
Lènin, 81, 121, 139, 199, 222, 256, 260, 331
Leningrad Dramatic Theatre, 187
Leònov, xix, 6, 15, 42–49, 56, 61, 69, 83, 88, 91, 103, 115, 118–23, 124, 191, 197, 198, 226, 240, 242, 249, 261–264, 305, 314, 315, 316, 325, 328, 338, 339, 341
Lèrmontov, 160, 170, 215, 270, 273
Leskòv, xviii, 5, 18, 19, 20, 34, 42, 72, 191, 210
Lètopis (review), 23
Lèvin, Borìs, 60, 77
Lèzhnev, 219, 321
Libedìnsky, 86, 91, 93–94, 226, 327
Lìdin, 60, 65–66, 326, 340
Lipskerov, 191
Literatùra i Iskùsstvo (newspaper), 294, 300, 301, 316
Literatùrnaya Gaʒèta (newspaper), 232
Literatùrny Sovremènnik (review), 55
Lo Gatto, 253
London, Jack, 158
London, Kurt, 336
Lozìnsky, 254
Lunachàrsky, 81, 82, 85, 93, 187, 191, 192, 216, 221, 223, 330
Lùnin, 131

Lùntz, 192, 222
Lvov-Rogachèvsky, 219
Lyashkò, 88, 340
Lyons, 262, 336

McLeod, Joseph, 255, 277, 336
Makarènko, 284–85, 290, 339
Makhnò, 176
Malàshkin, 100
Malraux, 256
Malyshkin, xviii, 57, 58–59
Màly Theatre, 197, 198, 305
Mandelstàm, xiv, 2, 169, 181–82, 276
Mann, Thomas, 268
Marinètti, xv
Màrkov, 330
Marshall, Herbert, 339, 340, 341
Martiànov, 334
Marx, Karl, 199, 257
Marxism and Marxists, 4, 16, 74, 80, 111, 131, 175, 194, 211, 212, 213, 216, 217, 218, 219, 228
Matvèyev, 339
Maupassant, 24, 65
Maurois, 159, 161
Mayakòvsky, xv, 165–67, 170, 173, 175, 177, 178, 179, 180, 193, 212, 216, 240, 330, 331, 339
Maynard, Sir John, 336
Medvèdev, 218
Mènshikov, General, 297
Merezhkòvsky, 1, 155, 156, 164
Meyerhòld, 186, 189, 194, 196, 198, 255
Michelangelo, 222
Mille, Cecil de, 188, 189
Mìnin, 292
Mìrsky, xii, xiii, 1, 6, 16, 20, 232, 233, 322, 323, 329, 332
Molière, 197, 215
Montagu, I., 340
Morand, 324
Morgan, Charles, x
Moscow Art Theatre, 28, 147, 186, 187, 191, 193, 196, 197, 320
Motchoùlsky, 322
Muggeridge, 336

Nàdson, 180, 182
Napoleon I, 296
Napoleon III, 297
Na Postù, see On Guard
Nazism, 294, 295
Nekràsov, 209
Neo-Classicism, xiv
Neo-Realism, 2, 20

NEP (New Economic Policy), xvii, 10, 12, 45, 65, 90, 94, 95, 117, 118, 177, 212, 278
Nevèrov, 88, 191, 193, 328, 340, 341
New Economic Policy, see NEP
Nicholas I (Emperor), 139, 297
Nicholas II (Emperor), 139, 156, 299
Nietzsche, 209, 294
Nikìforov, 101, 190
Nikìtin, Nikolay, xviii, 60, 78, 327
Novalis, 209
Nòvikov-Pribòy, 58
Nòvy Mir (review), 228, 298
Nùsinov, 245

Obradòvich, 80, 173
October (literary group), 83, 84, 222
Ognèv, 77–78, 327
O.G.P.U., 248, 286
Okhlòpkov, 187, 248
Olèsha, 6, 50, 52, 103–13, 128, 191, 194, 195, 198, 226, 235, 236, 249, 250, 276, 328, 339, 340
Olminsky, 85
On Guard (literary group and review), 83, 84, 91, 93, 212, 222, 224, 226
"Onguardists," 83, 84, 85, 223, 226, 229
On Literary Guard (literary group and review), 85, 91, 226
"Opoyàz," 203
Ostròvsky, A., 44, 163, 188, 189, 197, 277
Ostròvsky, N., 284, 290

Pànferov, 91–93, 124, 232, 233, 241, 327, 339
Pan-Soviet Literary Congress, 195, 234, 251, 254, 285, 335
Pares, Sir Bernard, xix, 254, 290, 336
Pasternàk, 104, 128, 169–72, 181, 182–183, 250, 319, 320, 330
Patrick, 329, 330
Paustòvsky, 340, 341
Pavlènko, 160, 285–88, 293, 339, 341
Pechàt i Revolyùtsiya (review), 228
Perevèrzev, 216, 217, 243
Pèrventsev, 302, 339
Peter the Great, 11, 153, 163, 164, 272, 292, 293
Petlyùra, 146, 147
Petròv (Ilf and), 76–77, 152, 189, 327
Pìkel, 196, 198
Piksànov, 215, 216, 218

Pilnyàk, xviii, 5, 6, 34, 60, 78, 102, 115, 116–18, 123, 124, 128, 138–42, 160, 227, 249, 276, 328, 329, 340, 341
Pirandello, 197
Pirogòv, 297
Pìsemsky, 34, 243
Platònov, 163, 340
Plekhànov, 218
Pletnèv, 85
Podtèlkov, 98
Poe, 49, 250
Pogòdin, 192, 195, 196, 197, 248, 260, 277, 331, 341
Polònsky, Vyacheslàv, 84, 86, 216, 219, 228, 321, 331
Polyànsky, 216
Popòv, 187
Populism, 62, 87, 88, 90, 243
Popùtchiki, see "Fellow-Travellers"
Poshekhònov, 242
Pòstnikov, 334
Potèbnya, 201, 202, 206
Pozhàrsky, 292
Pòzner, 322, 323
Pràvda (newspaper), 232
Pridvòrov, see Bedny
Prìshvin, 2, 15–16, 324, 339, 341
Prokòfyev, 180
Proletarian Culture, The (magazine), 80
Proletkùlt, xvi, 79, 80, 234
Proust, 183, 249, 250
Prussianism, 294
Pugachèv, 138, 168
Pùnin, 221
Pùshkin, ix, 153, 159, 163, 208, 215, 222, 240, 241, 251, 273, 294

Queen Victoria, 297

Ràdek, 85, 223, 251, 337
Radìshchev, 158, 159
RAPP, 86, 222, 229, 234
Ràskin, 297
Ràzin, Stènka, 138, 157, 158, 291
Razumòvsky, 297
Realism and Realists, xiii, xix, 2, 5, 7, 8, 13, 16, 20, 29, 31, 42, 43, 47, 50, 56, 61, 63, 87, 90, 94, 104, 109, 172, 178, 184, 185, 192, 195, 196, 239, 240, 242–45, 247, 249, 250, 251, 259
Realistic Theatre, 187, 248
Reavey, 322, 330
Reformàtsky, 215
Reinhardt, 189
Remarque, 59
Rèmizov, xviii, 1, 5, 16, 18, 34, 210

Reshètnikov, 243
Rice, Elmer, 330
Rilke, 183
Rodker, John, 341
Ròdov, 173
Romains, 250, 324
Romànov, 60, 63–65, 66, 290, 326, 339, 340, 341
Romanticism, 25, 26, 50, 51, 52, 58, 109, 110, 111, 113, 118, 130, 154, 173, 175, 176, 184, 185, 193, 239, 243, 244, 250, 255
Romashòv, 191, 194, 197, 199
Ròzanov, M., see Ognèv
Ròzanov, V., 294
Rùsskoe Bogàtstvo (review), 88
Rykov, 139

St. Sergius of Radonezh, 295
Sakùlin, 216, 217, 218, 322
Saliàs, 155
Saltykòv-Shchedrìn, 18
Sargidzhiàn, see Borodin
Sàvich, 57
Sàvinkov, 157
Schiller, 197
Schmidt, Lieutenant, 171
School Youth Theatre, 55
Scott, H. G., 337
Scott, Sir Walter, 153, 154
Scribe, 198
Segal, Louis, 337
Selvìnsky, 174–75, 227, 320, 330
Semènov, Sergèy, 101, 328
Senkòvsky, 154
Serafimòvich, 1, 87, 93, 328, 339
Seràpion Brothers, 18, 28, 32–33, 49, 55, 69, 78, 192, 222, 235
Sergèyev-Tsènsky, ix, 2, 15, 16–17, 160, 297, 298, 324, 341
Seyfùllina, 60, 61–63, 96, 191, 198, 326, 340
Shaginyàn, 115, 123, 249, 329, 340
Shakespeare, 154, 197
Shchègolev, 163
Shchipachèv, 319
Shelgunòv, 243
Shestòv, Lev, 294
Shiryàev, 339
Shishkòv, 96, 332, 340
Shklòvsky, 203, 206, 208, 213–15, 236
Shkvàrkin, 194
Shmelèv, 1
Shòlokhov, ix, 6, 98–99, 115, 125–26, 157, 246, 248, 261, 275, 300, 327, 332, 339

Shostakòvich, 255
Shpanòv, 288-89
Sìmonov, 198, 259, 261, 303, 318, 319
Skoropàdsky, 146
Slavik, Jan, 334
Slàvin, 196, 197, 198
Slobodskòy, 341
Slònim, 321, 322, 323, 325, 326, 327, 330, 332
Slonìmsky, 55–56
Smidòwicz, see Veresàev
Smithy, 80, 81, 85, 88, 173, 178
Sòbolev, 58
Socialism and Socialists, 13, 51, 72, 74, 120, 130, 194, 199, 238, 243, 245
" Socialist Humanism," 254, 276
" Socialist Idealism," 261
Socialist Realism, 6, 15, 58, 102, 113, 195, 196, 198, 230, 231, 232, 234, 237, 238–51, 253–61, 271, 285, 314, 335
Sociological Method, 215–19
Solodàr, 319
Sologùb, 2, 3
Solovyèv, Nikolày, 197, 200
Solovyèv, Vladimir (playwright), 197, 200, 297
Solovyèv, Vsèvolod, 154
Sophocles, 197, 283
Souvarine, B., 337
Soviet Government, passim
Soviet Literary Encyclopedia, 131
Stàlin, 14, 15, 199, 239, 248, 258, 272, 321, 337
Stanislàvsky, 186, 198
Stàvsky, 301
Steiner, Dr. Rudolf, 3
Stendhal, 162, 210, 245
Stepùn, F., 337
Sterne, Laurence, 215
Stètsky, 337
Strachey, Lytton, 159
Surkòv, 319
Suvòrov, Fieldmarshal, 292, 293, 297
Svetlòv, 178, 180
Symbolism and Symbolists, xiii–xv, xviii, 1, 3, 5, 16, 20, 40, 80, 104, 155, 156, 158, 166, 168, 178, 181, 201, 202, 203

Taìrov, 186, 197, 255
Talmud, 23
Taràsov-Rodiònov, 10, 156, 328, 329
Terrell, 337
Theatre of the Revolution, 187, 197
Tìkhonov, 172–74, 181, 184–85, 261, 301, 320, 330, 341

347

INDEX

Tolstòy, A. K., 296
Tolstòy, A. N., ix, 2, *8-11*, 114, 128, 163, 164, 190, 192, 198, 258, 261, 272-73, 290, 296, 302, 324, 329, 340, 341
Tolstòy, Leo, ix, 19, 49, 59, 74, 92, 96, 97, 98, 99, 100, 103, 154, 155, 162, 198, 207, 210, 213, 214, 215, 240, 241, 243, 245, 251, 273, 297
Tomashèvsky, 208, 215, 331
Toussaint-Louverture, 162
Trades Unions' Theatre, 187
Trenèv, 190, 191, 193
Tretyakòv, 191, 193, 263
Tròtsky, 81, 83, 85, 102, 212, 216, 219, 222, 223, 258, 321, 331, 337
Tsèytlin, 215
Tsvetàeva, 1
Turgènev, Alexander, 162
Turgènev, Ivan, 19, 56, 63, 154, 163, 198, 243
Turgènev, Nikolay, 162
Tveryàk, 101
Tynyànov, *159-63*, 207, 215, 291, 340
Tyùtchev, 171, 172

Unamuno, 324
Unanimisme, 250
Union of Soviet Writers, 229, 231, 234, 238, 239, 248, 299
Ushakòv, 178, 180, 330
Uspènsky, 192, 194

Vakhtàngov Theatre, 187, 196, 197
VAPP, 85
Vàrdin, 223
Veresàev, 2, *13-15*, 163, 324
Veselòvsky, Alexander, 201, 202
Vesèly, *102*, 328
Victoroff-Tòporoff, 322
Vinogràdov, Anatòly, *162-63*, 329
Vinogràdov, Viktor, 215
Virtà, 261, 281-84, 341
Vishnèvsky, 192, 235, 285, 341
Vladìmirov, 198
Vladislàvlev, 215

Voigt, F., 337
Vòinova, 332
Vòlosov, 341
Vorònsky, 83, 85, 86, 216, 219, 241, 242, 321, 331, 340
Voroshìlov, 235, 272, 331
Voznesènsky, 215, 331
Vsevolòdsky-Gèrngross, 215

Walzel, 208
Webb, S. and B., 337
Weisenbèrg, 341
Wells, H. G., 8, 131, 149
Werth, A., 337
Williams, A. R., 337
Wilson, Woodrow, 167
Wòlkenstein, 189, 191, 215
Woolf, Virginia, x

Yakobsòn, R., 206, 208, 209
Yakobsòn, S., 334
Yàkovlev, A., 332
Yàkovlev, N., 215
Yarmolìnsky, A., 338
Yasènsky (Jasienski), 247
Yòffe, 76
Young Communist League, 14, 15, 78, 100, 178
Yudènich, 36, 38

Zabolòtsky, 181
Zagòskin, ix, 153
Zamyàtin, 2, *17-22*, 32, 34, 127, 128, *130-38*, 188, 189, 190, 191, 227, 257, 290, 324, 329
Zayàltsky, 78, 191, 327
Zàytsev, 1
Zelìnsky, Kornèly, 174
Zhàrov, 178, 180
Zhdànov, 235, 337
Zhirmùnsky, 206, 208-10, 214, 215
Zhukòvsky, 160
Zìlberg, see Kavèrin
Znànie (literary group), 87
Zòshchenko, 32, 60, *69-76*, 82, 248, 326, 340, 341
Zozùlya, 332